# GREAT
## Economists
## before Keynes

# GREAT
## Economists
## before Keynes

### AN INTRODUCTION TO THE
### LIVES & WORKS OF ONE HUNDRED
### GREAT ECONOMISTS OF THE PAST

# MARK
# BLAUG

*Professor Emeritus, University of London and Consultant
Professor of Economics, University of Buckingham.*

HUMANITIES PRESS INTERNATIONAL, INC.

ATLANTIC HIGHLANDS, N.J.

First published in 1986 in the United States of America by
Humanities Press International, Inc., Atlantic Highlands, NJ 07716

Library of Congress Cataloging-in-Publication Data

Blaug, Mark.
   Great economists before Keynes.
   1.Economists — Biography.   I. Title.
HB76.B54 1986        330'.092'2 [B]        85-27083
ISBN 0-391-03381-6

Printed in Great Britain

# Contents

# Preface

This book is a companion piece to my *Great Economists since Keynes,* and like it is addressed to those who are studying economics for the first time, who hear their teachers dropping names like Ricardo, Walras and Marshall, and want a quick guide to the lives and ideas of these great economists of the past.

Why 100 entries and not 200 or 300? The number 100 is arbitrary: we have to draw the line somewhere and 100 is a round number. Nevertheless, it is surprising how 100 seems to be just about enough to catch all the first-rank and even the second-rank economists of the past up to and including Keynes. Needless to say, this is my own personal list of the great names in the history of economic thought and another author might have drawn up a somewhat different list. However, I feel sure that a referendum among historians of economic thought would endorse 90 and perhaps even 95 per cent of my list.

The book may be consulted like a reference book; every entry is self-contained and, hopefully, self-explanatory; wherever a portrait of a past economist exists, it is included to lend spice to the entry; these are asterisked in the *List of Entries.* However, the book can also be read from beginning to end in chronological order. In that case, I recommend that the entries be read in the following sequence:

| | | |
|---|---|---|
| Mun | Malthus | Rae |
| Petty | Lauderdale | List |
| Locke | Bentham | Torrens |
| North | Thornton | Tooke |
| Davenant | Ricardo | Babbage |
| Law | Owen | Bastiat |
| Mandeville | Say | Wakefield |
| Bernoulli | Sismondi | Proudhon |
| Galiani | St-Simon | Cournot |
| Hume | McCulloch | Dupuit |
| Quesnay | Bailey | Mill |
| Cantillon | Jones | Thünen |
| Turgot | Carey | Cairnes |
| Steuart | Senior | Marx |
| Smith | Longfield | Mangoldt |

Gossen
Leslie
Bagehot
Juglar
Roscher
Jevons
Menger
Walras
Barone
Sidgwick
George
Wicksteed
Edgeworth
Launhardt
Keynes, J.N.
Marshall
Clark, J.B.
Schmoller
Spiethoff

Aftalion
Pareto
Böhm-Bawerk
Wieser
Wicksell
Bortkiewicz
Weber, M.
Cunningham
Cassel
Newcomb
Ely
Seligman
Bernstein
Sombart
Hilferding
Fisher
Veblen
Fetter
Hobson

Luxemburg
Moore
Slutsky
Mitchell
Commons
Weber, A.
Schumpeter
Bowley
Clapham
Pigou
Robertson
Clark, J.M.
Chamberlin
Kondratieff
Simons
Lange
Keynes, J.M.

Mark Blaug

# List of Entries

# Aftalion, Albert (1874-1956)

Albert Aftalion followed Spiethoff (q.v.) by several years in attempting to provide a theory of the business cycle. After an early work on the economic ideas of Sismondi (q.v.), he published some articles on 'general over-production' in 1908, followed by a massive work in two volumes on *Les crises périodiques de surproduction* (1913). The *leitmotif* of this book was the acceleration principle of derived demand based on Böhm-Bawerk's (q.v.) theory of roundabout, capitalistic production, according to which changes in the demand for consumer goods bring about accelerated changes in the demand for investment goods. (The 'acceleration principle' was independently rediscovered and so-named by J.M. Clark (q.v.) in 1917.)

The roundabout nature of production also explained why the fall in prices after the downturn leads not to an immediate recovery but to a downward spiralling slump: entrepreneurs contract the hiring of factors of production at rates justified by earlier, higher prices and hence suffer losses, which lead to cutbacks in investment. It was not only Böhm-Bawerk's theory of capital which led Aftalion to the acceleration principle but also his continuous appeal to Wieser's

1

(q.v.) theory of imputation by which the values of consumer goods are reflected back or imputed to the investment goods which produce them; all Aftalion added was that changes in the prices of consumer goods produce magnified effects on the prices of capital goods because of the long duration of production processes. Thus, the whole of Aftalion's theory is woven together with 'Austrian' strands and yet is quite different from the so-called Austrian theory of business cycles in the later works of Mises and Hayek. (In Mises and Hayek, it is the over-issue of bank credit working through the rate of interest that causes a downturn by encouraging the undue lengthening of the period of production.)

Aftalion was born in 1874 in Bulgaria and educated in France. He was a professor at the University of Lille from 1904-20 and then at the University of Paris from 1920-40. Apart from his work on business cycles, he published several books on monetary economics in which he criticised the quantity theory of money and the Hume–Ricardo specie-flow mechanism.

*Secondary Literature*
D. Villey, 'Aftalion, Albert', *International Encyclopedia of the Social Sciences,* vol. 1, ed. D.L. Sills (Macmillan Free Press, 1968).

# Babbage, Charles (1792-1871)

Charles Babbage, Lucasian Professor of Mathematics at the University of Cambridge 1828-39, invented the 'difference engine', a machine for integrating difference equations and setting the results directly into type. While it was being built with the aid of a Parliamentary grant he dropped it in favour of the 'analytical engine', another machine which in addition incorporated a memory that was capable of programming further calculations. Although he never succeeded in building a complete version of this machine, he did write down fairly detailed specifications for its construction. He may legitimately be regarded therefore as the 'father' of the modern computer. It is not this, however, which earns him a place in this book. As he laboured to translate his designs into a workable machine, he undertook a tour of factories throughout England and the Continent in order to learn more about the practical problems of manufacturing mechanical parts. This resulted in his most popular book, *On the Economy of Machinery and Manufacturers* (1832), an unprecedented study of what we would now call operation research, being a cross between a work on production engineering and management science.

The book had a profound influence on John Stuart Mill (q.v.) and later on Karl Marx (q.v.), both of whom cited it repeatedly and drew many examples from it. It was responsible for Mill's increasing recognition of the problems thrown up under a regime of competition by economies of scale and the resulting growth in the size of firms. It was likewise responsible, along with Rae's (q.v.) *Some New Principles on the Subject of Political Economy* (1834), for his sophisticated treatment of the division of labour, which marked a considerable advance over Adam Smith's (q.v.) treatment of the theme, constituting the beginning of an analysis of the conditions required for rapid technical progress. Babbage caused Mill to take a more positive attitude to the concept of joint stock companies based on the principle of limited liability in contrast to Smith and most classical economists. The effect of Babbage's book is also clearly evident in Volume III of Marx's *Capital*, where he investigates the details of the technology that he thought would increasingly characterise the capitalist system.

Babbage was born in 1792, the son of a prosperous Devonshire banker, and educated at Cambridge University where he struck up a life-long friendship with John Herschel, later the Astronomer Royal. Even as an under-graduate, he and Herschel began to translate a French work on calculus and, after graduating from Cambridge in 1817, Babbage continued to write papers on a variety of mathematical topics. He also wrote widely in the field of natural science. In another influential book, *Reflections on the Decline of Science in England* (1830), he attacked the neglect of science in British universities and urged government support of scientists. His book was directly responsible for the founding of the British Association for the Advancement of Science in the following year.

*Secondary Literature.*
P. Morrison and E. Morrison, 'Babbage, Charles', *International Encyclopedia of the Social Sciences,* vol. 1, ed. D.L. Sills (Macmillan Free Press, 1968).

# Bagehot, Walter (1826-1877)

Walter Bagehot is a name known to all monetary economists and to all historians of economic thought: *Lombard Street: A Description of the Money Market* (1873) must be the most frequently quoted book in the entire banking literature, and his two essays on 'The Postulates of English Political Economy' (1876) were considered sufficiently important by Marshall to warrant re-publication in 1885 with a preface by himself. Reading *Lombard Street* nowadays is bound to be a somewhat disillusioning experience: Bagehot's theory of central banking, with its fundamental distinction between the contrasting policies required to meet internal and external drains — lend freely on good commercial paper to meet internal drains, but do so at high interest rates so as to counter external drains — is too familiar to sustain our interest. Even his much-admired ironic style soon begins to pall as one becomes aware that he fails to maintain any abstract argument for more that a few sentences at a time. The one chapter that can still make the modern reader sit up is Chapter 6, 'Why Lombard Street is Often Very Dull and Sometimes Extremely Excited', with its hint of a multiplier process, a psychological theory

5

of the trade cycle resting on the mainspring of agricultural harvests, and abounding in such phrases as 'the excess of savings over investment'. As a matter of fact, Bagehot distinguishes consistently between intended saving and intended investment and seems perfectly aware of their partial independence. But perhaps it is unfair to judge *Lombard Street* as a professional monograph on money and banking. Bagehot addressed the book to Victorian businessmen and for them it married what were at the time regarded as two irreconcilable ideas: the concept of central bank statesmanship and the philosophy of *laissez-faire.*

Bagehot's fragmentary and incomplete writings on the history of economic thought (he drafted a treatise that he never lived to complete) must be judged on different grounds. They *were* directed at professional economists. His work is not easy to classify but he might be fairly described as an English historical economist — together with Cliffe Leslie (q.v.), John Ingram (1823-1907), Arnold Toynbee (1852-83) and Thorold Rogers (1823-90) — with an unusual interest in questions of social psychology. His 'Postulates of English Political Economy' started the hunt that has now gone on for 100 years for the explicit list of all the assumptions upon which the deductive structure of Ricardian economics was based. Bagehot's unequivocal description of English classical economics as a valid but historically time-bound analysis of the heyday of capitalism — a bourgeois piece of analysis that Marx may have read but never acknowledged — still carries conviction but, that apart, many of his judgements on the 'four great men' of the subject (Adam Smith, Malthus, Ricardo and John Stuart Mill) were little short of banal. What is striking in these and other economic essays is the frequency with which he expresses dismay at the passing away of public interest in economics: 'It lies rather dead in the public mind. Not only does it not excite the same interest as formerly, but there is not exactly the same confidence in it'. Remarks such as these perfectly convey the flavour of British economic debates in the 1870s — that crucial decade, in which Jevons (q.v.) was attempting to overturn 'the authority of Mr. Mill'.

Bagehot's published economic writings were only a part of his prodigious literary output, which included two books on political philosophy, *The English Constitution* (1867) and *Physics and Politics* (1872), and dozens of historical and literary essays. As editor of *The Economist* from 1861 until his death in 1877, he wrote as many as

106 unsigned articles on a bewildering variety of monetary and financial problems both at home and abroad. He was born in 1826 in Somerset, the son of a prominent Unitarian banker. He entered University College, London at the age of 16 and received his BA in 1846, followed by an MA in 1848. He subsequently studied law but never practised it, entered his father's business, and married the daughter of James Wilson, the founder and editor of the influential financial weekly, *The Economist,* established in 1838 to lend support to the free trade movement; on Wilson's death, Bagehot assumed the editorship. He sought political office but failed on four successive occasions to be nominated for or elected to a Parliamentary seat. He frequently advised ministers, however, and Gladstone once referred to him as 'a kind of spare Chancellor of Exchequer'.

*Secondary Literature*
H.S.Gordon, 'Bagehot, Walter', *International Encyclopedia of the Social Sciences,* vol.1, ed. D.L. Sills (Macmillan Free Press, 1968); R.S. Sayers, 'Bagehot as an Economist', *The Collected Works of Walter Bagehot,* vol. 9, ed. N. St John-Stevas *(The Economist,* 1978).

# Bailey, Samuel (1791-1870)

Samuel Bailey was born in Sheffield in 1791 and entered his family's cutlery firm at the age of 15, taking it over on his father's death 18 years later. Despite managing a thriving business, he found time to publish voluminously on a wide variety of topics, ranging from political economy to politics, psychology, ethics, logic and literary criticism. He took an active part in the political agitation that led up to the passage of the Reform Bill of 1832, and was narrowly defeated as a Parliamentary candidate in the election of 1835. Even at the age of 75 he was still publishing on such topics as the order in which Shakespeare's plays were written.

In 1825, two years after the death of Ricardo, he published *A Critical Dissertation on the Nature, Measures, and Causes of Value; Chiefly in Reference to the Writings of Mr. Ricardo and his Followers*, the most trenchant and devastating of all contemporary attacks on Ricardian economics. Much of Bailey's *exposé* took the form of a semantic analysis of Ricardo's linguistic style, noting carefully the inconsistent employment of terms and the unconscious transition from one meaning of a particular term to another. Bailey traced all of the confusions in Ricardo to the latter's belief in the concept of absolute value — the failure to recognise that value is always a relation between two commodities in exchange — and the associated quest for an invariable standard of value that would somehow tell us that when the exchange ratio between two commodities has changed in which of them the change has originated. Bailey shrewdly perceived what no one had noticed before — namely, that Ricardo's value theory is not of the common run; it is concerned with the measurement of the value of commodities over time instead of over space; in short, with intertemporal rather than intratemporal comparisons of value. Bailey rejected the very possibility of finding any satisfactory measure of value either in Ricardo's sense or in the ordinary sense of the term. As for the 'cause' as distinct from the 'measure' of value, he denied that it was labour, arguing instead that it was the esteem in which commodities were held: 'Value ... denotes, strictly speaking, an effect produced on the mind'. His fundamental criticism of the labour theory of value — made many times since — is that the very idea of labour costs as the source of value leads to a vicious circle: value is said to be determined by labour-time and the value of labour-time is itself in turn made dependent on the amount of labour required to produce wage goods, whose value in turn..., and so forth.

It is only in the closing chapter of his book that Bailey branched out from an exegesis of Ricardo to something like a critique of the whole superstructure of the Ricardian system. His method was to advocate a threefold classification of commodities according to the 'degree of competition'. First, there are 'monopolised commodities', which category is in turn divided into pure monopoly and imperfect competition, depending on whether the elasticity of supply is zero or between zero and one. Secondly, there are commodities which can only be produced at rising costs, such as wheat, coal, metals, and other primary products. Rising costs are always due to specialised factors of production in limited supply and the owners of these specialised factors command a 'monopoly rent'; thus, what is ordinarily called rent is perfectly analogous to the superior wages of a skilled artisan. The third and last category comprises those commodities produced at constant costs under conditions of perfect competition which Ricardo's theory of value is specifically designed to explain. But even here labour alone does not determine prices. Not only is labour non-homogeneous in quality but the risks involved in employing capital and the premium that must be paid to overcome what was later to be called time preference ('we generally prefer', Bailey declared, 'a present pleasure or enjoyment to a distant one, not superior to it in other respects') all tend to enhance the value of the product above its costs in labour time. Moreover, the raw materials which go to produce this third range of articles frequently fall into the first two categories. Therefore, instead of 'protection from competition' affecting only a small part of the total volume of commodities exchanged, as Ricardo had claimed, the value of most commodities in fact depends on a low 'degree of competition'.

The impact of Bailey's *Critical Dissertation* was profound, judging by the number of references to it in an age not given to crediting sources. *The Westminster Review* published a bitter anonymous attack on the book, which was almost certainly written by James Mill, the father of John Stuart Mill. McCulloch (q.v.), Torrens (q.v.) and Tooke (q.v.) all cited it if only to refute it, and Senior (q.v.) not only cited it but adopted Bailey's generalisation of the concept of ground rent as only a 'species of an extensive genus' as well as his theory of profits as a payment for forgoing the preference for present over future goods. It is only because John Stuart Mill deliberately failed to mention Bailey in his influential *Principles of Political Economy* (1848) that later generations had to discover Bailey for themselves as a neglected writer.

*Secondary Literature*
R.M. Rauner, *Samuel Bailey and the Classical Theory of Value* (G. Bell, 1961).

# Barone, Enrico (1859-1924)

Enrico Barone was an outstanding early Italian mathematical economist who spent almost as many years as an army officer and professor of military science at the War College in Turin (1894-1907) as he did as a professor of economics at the Instituto di Scienze Economiche in Rome (1907-24), writing as much on military strategy as he did on economics. As a disciple and friend of Walras (q.v.), he played a significant role in developing marginal productivity theory and convincing Walras that it could be incorporated into general equilibrium theory. Walras had taught that perfect competition drives prices into equality with average costs of production so that the attempts of entrepreneurs to maximise profits paradoxically results eventually in zero profits. On the other hand, when factors of production are freely variable and not fixed by technical conditions, the desire to minimise costs ensures that they will be employed until their marginal value products equal their prices. Will factor payments in accordance with the principle of marginal productivity exactly 'exhaust the product' so as to leave zero profits? Walras at first thought that zero profits were incompatible with marginal productivity factor payments and so refused to accept the idea of factor substitutability. In an unpublished review of Wicksteed's (q.v.) *Essay on the Coordination of the Laws of Distribution* (1894), and even better in a letter to Walras, Barone showed him that profit-maximisation also implies cost-minimisation and that it is precisely when factor proportions are variable that marginal productivity factor payments generate input-demand functions for firms and, in turn, cost functions for determining the equilibrium level of output of firms. Walras was convinced, and in the third edition of the *Elements* (1896) he frankly espoused a marginal productivity theory of distribution without qualification.

Barone's most widely-known contribution, however, was his demonstration that 'The Ministry of Production in a Collectivist State' (1908) would be able to establish a perfectly competitive equilibrium by the use of 'shadow prices'. The article grew out of Walras's unsuccessful attempt to show that a perfect competitive equilibrium would also maximise economic welfare. Barone's idea was to test this conclusion to see if it really depended on a regime of private property. He argued that perfectly competitive equilibrium implied at least two conditions; namely, minimum costs of production and prices equal to costs of production. These two conditions in turn, he thought, implied a welfare maximum simply in the sense that a departure from them would reduce output and hence leave at least one person worse-off. The ministry is supposed to start with a distribution of income inherited from the past and with free choice of consumption and employment, all other resources of the community apart from labour being collectively owned. It proceeds by trial and error raising or lowering wages and prices until the two essential conditions for a welfare optimum are everywhere fulfilled. The upshot of the essay was to show that, despite all the practical difficulties, a socialist economy could — at least in principle — obtain the same results as that of an idealised capitalist economy. This was not meant to be an argument for socialism — Barone was an anti-socialist — but simply an exercise in theorising of the general equilibrium kind.

The essay attracted little attention when it was first published and never figured in the socialist debates of the 1910s. But during the 1930s, when the experiences of the Soviet Union caused a revival in socialist planning, economists in English-speaking countries were amazed to discover that Barone had more or less laid the outlines of a 'theory of socialism' that Lange (q.v.) was soon to make his own.

*Secondary Literature*
R.E. Kuenne, 'Barone, Enrico', *International Encyclopedia of the Social Sciences,* vol. 2, ed. D.L. Sills (Macmillan Free Press, 1968).

# Bastiat,
# Frédéric
# (1801-1850)

The idea that the classical economists believed in *laissez-faire* — 'anarchy plus a constable', as Carlyle once said — is part of the folklore of political and social history of the nineteenth century. But although Adam Smith (q.v.), Ricardo (q.v.), McCulloch (q.v.), Senior (q.v.) and John Stuart Mill (q.v.) certainly believed that least government is best government, it is false to think that their attitude to government intervention was wholly negative and that they closed their minds and hearts totally to the costs that the untrammelled operation of the market economy imposes on some sections of the community. A dogmatic and doctrinaire belief in *laissez-faire* certainly was common among nineteenth-century journalists and statesmen but it is difficult to find any respected economist of the period who espoused the credo of *laissez-faire* without exception. Nevertheless, Bastiat in France comes pretty close to the strawman 'classical economist' of the history books, complete with a quasi-religious conviction of the natural harmony of economic interests if only the government would keep its hands off the spontaneous action of individuals. The three great enemies which he never tired of attacking were protectionism, socialism and, of course, Ricardian economics, whose pessimistic predictions tended to undermine the faith of universal harmony. He even sought to provide his liberalism with a theoretical pedigree, including a theory of value based on the notion that exchange-value reflects an exchange of 'services'.

As an economic theorist, he was third-rate, but as a popularist of economic ideas, employing satire and irony with the skills of Daniel Defoe or George Bernard Shaw, he has no equal in the history of economic thought. The best example of his art is the famous 'Petition of the Candlemakers' (1845), in which the manufacturers of candles urge Parliament to pass a law ordering the shutting-up of all windows, skylights, openings, holes, chinks, clefts and fissures through which the intolerable competition of the sun is bringing light inside houses free of charge, thus threatening to destroy a native industry affording employment directly and indirectly to thousands of people. These and other satires and parables, bound together in his *Sophisms of Protection* (1877), have been endlessly reprinted by free-traders and anti-socialists down to the present time.

Bastiat was born in Bayonne, in 1801, the son of a small merchant. At the age of 17 he entered the business firm of an uncle. In 1825, an inheritance brought him back to his birthplace to manage his small estate. Sometime in the early 1840s he started to read the speeches of Richard Cobden and John Bright, leaders of the British Anti-Corn Law League, who had launched a great campaign to repeal Britain's agricultural protective duties. Bastiat decided to become a 'French Cobden' and began to contribute furiously to newspapers and magazines, founding in 1846 a weekly newspaper of his own.

At the time of the revolution of 1848, he was elected to the Constituent Assembly and later to the Legislative Assembly. In the meanwhile, he had started writing the *Harmonies Economiques,* a work designed to provide a systematic exposition of his economic ideas. In the event, he only lived to finish the first volume, dying in 1850 at the age of 49.

*Secondary Literature*
H. Durand, 'Bastiat, Frédéric', *International Encyclopedia of the Social Sciences,* vol. 2, ed. D.L. Sills (Macmillan Free Press, 1968).

# Bentham, Jeremy (1748-1832)

Jeremy Bentham is one of those extraordinary eccentrics that the English intellectual scene is forever throwing up. To most students of social science he is a philosopher, the inventor of 'utilitarianism' — namely, the belief that every individual action can be submitted to a 'felicific calculus', a quantitative comparison of pleasures and pains; moreover, such comparisons can be summed over individuals for purposes of appraising social action and every social action should be judged in terms of 'the greatest happiness of the greatest number'. Unfortunately, no one can ever explain how this sort of crude cost-benefit analysis is to be applied in an individual case, with the result that the 'felicific calculus' is no sooner mentioned than it is dismissed with laughter and ridicule. But Bentham's notorious calculus of pleasures and pains was never meant to be more than a working hypothesis for judges and legislators; an appeal to pragmatism to take the place of the doctrine of 'natural rights' which ruled the roost in Bentham's own day.

Furthermore, it was only one element in Bentham's programme for legislative and legal reform; the other and much more important element was his unbelievably detailed schemes for the improved administration of law courts, prisons, hospitals and schools, right down to the design of the buildings, a timetable for the judges, wardens, doctors and teachers, and a concrete scheme for paying them. When he set about reforming the Poor Laws or the Factory Acts or the Metropolitan Police, he provided an exact plan for organising the new service and a precise specification of the administrative steps to be taken to implement the reform proposals. In other words, he was the 'father' of what is now called public law, and sometimes administrative science. Most of his ideas were set out in thousands of unpublished pages for purposes of distribution to his small army of followers and to key individuals with political influence. In his own lifetime he actually published very little, principally *A Fragment on Government* (1776), *An Introduction to the Principles of Morals and Legislation* (1780) and *Rationale of Judicial Evidence* (1827), edited by the young John Stuart Mill (q.v.). An 11-volume edition of his *Works* was published shortly after his death but even this was less than a quarter of his total written output. (The current Oxford University Press edition of the *Works and Correspondence of Jeremy Bentham* is projected in 36 volumes and may well run to more). In short, he was one of those thinkers whose influence did not depend on publication but on personal contacts. And his influence was immense: nearly all the great British administrative reforms in civil and criminal law in the first half of the nineteenth century were due to the work of Bentham's enthusiastic disciples.

Among his disciples were such well-known economists as Ricardo (q.v.), James Mill and John Stuart Mill. Nevertheless, Bentham's influence on economic ideas is difficult to assess. In his lifetime, he published a few highly effective economic pamphlets, such as *Defence of Usury* (1790) and *Supply Without Burthen* (1795), and a number of his incomplete economic manuscripts circulated among friends and admirers. Nevertheless, his ideas on economics, as on so much else, were so far ahead of his times or at least so out of tune with his times that it is doubtful that they had much impact on his contemporaries. For example, he showed an extraordinary awareness of the problem of unemployed resources, and in advocating monetary expansion to secure full employment, he employed a number of concepts that bear a family resemblance to those of J.M. Keynes (q.v.), such as hoarding, forced saving and the equality of saving and investment. Moreover, he gradually shifted from an early phase of extreme Toryism — denying that even the money market should be regulated by government; to an equally extreme Whiggism — advocating guaranteed employment, minimum wages and a variety of social benefits. Lastly, his deliberations on the measurement of utility, interpersonal comparisons of utility and the principle of diminishing marginal utility, while virtually unknown to his contemporaries, proved stimulating to later generations, and in the case of Jevons (q.v.) inspired him to develop the utility theory of value.

Bentham was educated at Westminster School, London and Queen's College, Oxford. After graduating at the age of 18, he read law at Lincoln's Inn, London. He never practised as a lawyer, however, but took advantage of an inherited income to devote his life to the reform of English Common Law. His economic writings were entirely confined to the 18 years between 1786 and 1804, after which he turned increasingly to the general issue of parliamentary reform, while still pursuing specific legislative questions, including the writing of entire constitutions for new nations in the Spanish-speaking world. He died at the age of 84, living just long enough to see some of his political ideas reach fruition in the Reform Bill of 1832. Had he lived another two years, he might have added the Education Act 1833, the Factory Act 1833 and the new Poor Law 1834 to the sum of his achievements.

His will included a large bequest to University College, London, an institution which he had helped to found, subject to the condition that his waxed remains would be permanently displayed in a conspicuous place. University College met this condition for over a century. Nowadays, however, the waxed effigy of Bentham is only brought out once a year.

*Secondary Literature*
W. Stark (ed.), *Jeremy Bentham's Economic Writings,* 3 vols. (Allen & Unwin, 1952); M.P. Mack, 'Bentham, Jeremy', *International Encyclopedia of the Social Sciences,* vol. 2, ed. D.L. Sills (Macmillan Free Press, 1968).

# Bernoulli, Daniel (1700-1782)

Daniel Bernoulli was one of the last of nine Bernoullis who made fundamental contributions to calculus, the theory of probability and mathematical statistics in the seventeenth and eighteenth centuries. In one of his many papers published in Latin, *'Specimen theoriae novae de mensura sortis' (Specimen of a New Theory for Measuring Risk)* (1738), he solved the so-called 'St Petersburg Paradox', according to which the actuarial value of winning a certain carefully constructed but 'fair' game of change is infinite. A 'fair' game is one in which the player is never asked to pay more than the actuarial value of the gamble, that is, the amount of the pay-off multiplied by the probability of winning. Since no one will pay an infinite sum of money for the privilege of playing the St Petersburg game, something is wrong; hence, the 'paradox'. Bernoulli solved the paradox by denying that gamblers act to maximise the actuarial value of a gamble, asserting instead that they act to maximise the actuarial value of the *utilities* of a gamble. Moreover, by assuming that the marginal utility of income declines with every increment of income, he showed that the expected utility of a 'fair' gamble is actually negative: no one will pay as much as £1 for the 50-50 chance of winning £2 because they will always insist on a larger gain to compensate them for the risk of a given loss.

Bernoulli was writing on probability and was totally unaware that his argument had any implications for economics. And indeed it was almost 140 years before Jevons (q.v.) drew attention to Bernoulli's paper as relevant to the law of the diminishing marginal utility of income, which he had independently discovered. It took another 10 years for the paper to be translated into German and another 60 years for it to be translated into English, by which time it had become another famous but long-neglected classic. It is therefore only in a special sense that one can claim Bernoulli as a great economist. His 1738 paper, however, provides a paradigm example of an important principle in intellectual history: it is not enough to have a good idea, there must be an intellectual context into which the idea can be fitted; lacking that, the idea is bound to be ignored.

Bernoulli's paper has additional significance: it marks the first use of a geometrical diagram in an argument that was later construed as falling within the scope of economics. It is typical of the utility diagrams of the marginalists of the 1870s. It looks as follows:

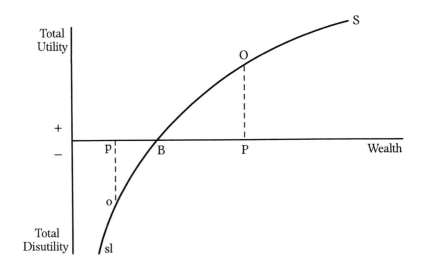

A man possessing AB amounts of wealth or income is given the opportunity in a 'fair' gamble of winning an additional slice of income, BP; the gain in utility of this expected increment in income is PO; he is willing to pay a fee, pB, to play the gamble whose disutility, po, equals the utility of the expected gain, PO; but this fee pB, turns out to be smaller than the expected gain, BP, because the curve sS expressing the relationship between the change in income and the change in utility is not a straight line but a curve which is convex from below: the *marginal* utility of income declines with every increment of income. Bernoulli went on to assume that the curve is of a particular shape such that the marginal utility of income declines at the same percentage rate at which income increases no matter what the level of income.

The early marginalists, and particularly Marshall (q.v.), realised that Bernoulli's hypothesis of the diminishing marginal utility of income implied that a rational individual will never gamble at 'fair' odds; the widespread phenomenon of buying lottery tickets at even less than fair odds must therefore be explained by the 'love of gambling'; in short, in games of chance people do not behave as if they are maximising the expected utility of income. Another implication of Bernoulli's hypothesis is to justify the equalisation of incomes by, say, progressive taxation on the grounds that a pound taken from a rich man results in a loss of utility to him which is smaller than the gain in utility that results from giving that sum to a poor man; in other words, the law of the diminishing marginal utility of income justifies income-equalisation without limits, at least if one assumes that the marginal utility of income declines at the same rate for everyone. The followers of Marshall, such as Edgeworth (q.v.) and Pigou (q.v.) spent years sorting out the theory of progressive taxation based on Bernoulli's hypothesis. Suffice it to say that diminishing marginal utility of income is not enough to rationalise tax progression, that is, a system in which a larger *percentage* of tax is imposed on those with larger incomes; what is needed is a particular shape of the income utility curve, sS; in addition, the argument must address the expenditure and not just the tax side of government and, of course, there is nothing in Bernoulli that will guarantee that the pound levied on the rich man will actually end up in the pocket of the poor man.

*Secondary Literature*
O. Ore, 'Bernoulli Family'. *International Encyclopedia of the Social Sciences,* vol. 2, ed. D.L. Sills (Macmillan Free Press, 1968).

# Bernstein, Eduard (1850-1932)

Eduard Bernstein dealt Marxism a blow from which it perhaps never fully recovered: a personal friend of Friedrich Engels, Marx's *alter ego,* and a leading theoretician of the German Social Democratic Party (SPD), the first mass political party based on Marxist docrine, Bernstein's *Evolutionary Socialism: A Criticism and Affirmation* (1899) called into question the very foundations of Marx's vision of socialism. Struck by the increasing discrepancies between Marxist doctrine and the economic development of Western Europe, he used statistical data to show how capitalism was differentiating rather than polarising social classes, and then moved from this exposure of specific Marxist predictions to an attack on the entire theory of economic determinism enshrined in Marx's philosophy of history. Bernstein's apostasy was quickly condemned by Karl Kautsky (1854-1938), the editor of the SPD's theoretical journal, *Die Neue Zeit;* Bernstein replied, Kautsky counter-replied, and the war of revisionism was on. The SPD officially condemned Bernstein's views at their annual party conference in 1903 but the rot had set in: thereafter, the SPD was continuously to be torn apart by the dreadful 'cancer' of revisionism.

Bernstein was born in Berlin in 1850 and left school at the age of 16 to work as an apprentice and then a bank employee. He joined the SPD in his early twenties and launched himself on a career in party journalism. When Bismarck outlawed socialist publications in 1878, Bernstein was forced to flee abroad, first to Switzerland and then to England. In London, he met Engels and all the prominent figures of the new Fabian Society (founded in 1883), while continuing to write for German journals and newspapers. The anti-socialist laws of Germany were repealed in 1890 but Bernstein was not given permission to return to Germany until 1901, two years after the publication of his *Evolutionary Socialism.* Upon his arrival in Germany, he followed up his earlier book with another, *Wie ist wissenschaftlicher Socialismus möglich?* (1901) *(How is Scientific Socialism Possible?),* which proved to be even more popular in German-speaking countries than *Evolutionary Socialism.* In it, he broke totally with the Marxist dogma of the inevitable coming of socialism and argued the case entirely on ethical grounds: socialism is not predestined but nevertheless ought to succeed capitalism as a higher stage of human society.

The SPD survived the Nazi era and surfaced once again as a major German political party after the Second World War. In 1959, it adopted the so-called Bad Gödesberg manifesto of principles, repudiating its long-standing advocacy of Marxism but declaring itself nevertheless in favour of socialism via the ballot box. In other words, after 60 years the SPD finally vindicated the ideas of Eduard Bernstein.

*Secondary Literature*
P. Gay, *The Dilemma of Democratic Socialism: Eduard Bernstein's Challenge to Marx* (Collier Books, 1962); C. Gueuss, 'Bernstein, Eduard', *International Encyclopedia of the Social Sciences,* vol. 2, ed. D.L. Sills (Macmillan Free Press, 1968).

# Böhm-Bawerk, Eugen von (1851-1914)

If Menger (q.v.) was the founding-father of the Austrian School of Economics, Böhm-Bawerk was his St. Paul: he did more than anyone to popularise and to publicise the distinctively Austrian approach to economic problems. He had his own axe to grind, however, namely a theory of capital and interest based on the 'roundaboutness' of capital intensive production, and it was this theory which soon came to typify Austrian economics to foreign readers.

It aroused furious controversy (even with Menger himself) which Böhm-Bawerk relished to the hilt, writing more pages in defence of the theory than he had devoted to its original formulation. His remarkable polemical powers were further demonstrated by *The Close of the Marxian System* (1896), which remains — despite its mistaken belief that Marx wrote the three volumes of *Capital* in an orderly sequence — one of the most powerful attacks on Marxist economics ever penned. Böhm-Bawerk's reputation in his own lifetime was such as to place him alongside Ricardo and Jevons over even such contemporaries as Marshall but his appeal declined as the years went by and his theory of capital and interest, for better or for worse, commands little attention today.

Böhm-Bawerk was born in 1851 in Vienna, the capital of the Austro-Hungarian Empire. He graduated in law from the University of Vienna and took his first teaching post at the University of Innsbruck in 1881. He joined the civil service in 1889 and served as Minister of Finance on three separate occasions in 1895, 1897 and 1900. He finally resigned from the Ministry in 1904 and returned to academic life as a professor of economics at the University of Vienna, where he remained for the rest of his life. He died in 1914 at the age of 63.

After a number of early essays, his first major work was *Capital and Interest* (1884), a painstaking classification of over 100 authors into five types of interest theories, demonstrating that the true nature of interest had eluded all of them. With surprising regularity, those authors who came closest to Böhm-Bawerk's own eventual approach, Ricardo (q.v.), Senior (q.v.), Jevons (q.v.) and Menger (q.v.), received his harshest criticisms. Five years later, he published his own *Positive Theory of Capital* (1889), written in great haste and published without a final revision. When he came back to academic work in 1904 the great debate over his theory of interest was in full swing, with most of the criticism coming from America. Rather than thoroughly revising the first edition of *The Positive Theory,* Böhm-Bawerk sat down to answer each of his major critics, simply adding these 14 'Critical Excursions' as appendices to the second (1909) and third editions (1912) of *The Positive Theory.*

Böhm-Bawerk's theory of interest draws a sharp distinction between the origin of interest payments and the actual determination of the interest rate, between, so to speak, the why? and how? of interest. Interest arises out of the process of lending present income against the promise of future income — that is, some individuals in the community are apparently willing to pay a premium on present income for the privilege of disposing of it as they see fit in the future. The question 'Why is the rate of interest positive?' may be expressed in Böhm-Bawerk's language as, 'Why are people willing to deliver a certain quantity of goods in the present only if they can be sure of being repaid with a greater quantity of goods of the same kind and quality in the future?' His answer was that there are three 'grounds' or reasons why people on average prefer present to future goods. The first two reasons are psychological and may be summed up together in the famous phrase 'positive time-preference': people tend for all sorts of good reasons to overestimate future resources and to underestimate future wants. The third reason is more difficult to grasp: it is the 'technical superiority of present over future goods'. By this he meant not simply that capital goods are physically productive but also that they are productive of value. The investment of capital always implies an increase in the length of the production period, which normally yields a positive return net of the cost of constructing and maintaining the capital goods. But these net returns from indirect, 'roundabout' production are themselves subject to diminishing results. Thus, the later the date of any investment, the smaller its value to investors. In short, Böhm-Bawerk insisted, the net physical productivity of capital by itself creates a premium on present goods independently of the first two reasons for positive time-preference.

This last point was responsible for much of the disagreement over the Austrian theory of capital. Most critics were content to argue that the first two reasons for interest operate to create an excess demand for consumption loans, while the third reason operates to create an excess demand for production loans, the three acting cumulatively to create a positive rate of interest. Moreover, they objected to Böhm-Bawerk's strenuous denial that his theory of interest was simply the old productivity theory of interest of Turgot (q.v.) in disguise, supplemented by the time-preference theory of interest of Senior (q.v.). Böhm-Bawerk always insisted that land and labour are the only 'original', non-reproducible factors of production and that capital is a 'produced' or intermediate factor whose supply is utterly dependent on the land and labour expended on its production in the past. In other words, it is not capital but rather the investment of land and labour in capitalistic 'roundabout' production that is productive.

Moreover, when Böhm-Bawerk finally moved in the last part of *The Positive Theory* beyond the question of why the rate of interest is normally positive to ask how interest is actually determined, the argument turned suddenly into the old classical wages fund doctrine. The economy consists of capitalists and workers and the only capital is circulating capital, that is, wage goods advanced to work to tie them over during the period of production. This wages fund is said to be fixed in size by technical conditions. At a zero rate of interest, capitalists would have an infinite demand for present wage goods to advance to their workers. Thus, the rate of interest rises until the entire wages fund is used in lengthening the average period of production. Therefore, the equilibrium rate of interest is determined by the marginal product of the longest period of production that is adopted.

The contrast between Böhm-Bawerk's fierce criticisms of everybody else's theories of interest, the careful setting-up of the problem of why interest should ever be positive, and the final deliverance of a rather feeble theory of how the rate of interest is actually determined was enough to discourage even those who were originally favourably disposed to his argument. Wicksell (q.v.) did his best to reformulate Böhm-Bawerk's theory of interest and to free it from certain technical errors, but most economists lost interest in it, particularly after Fisher's (q.v.) *Theory of Interest* (1907) succeeded in restating the entire problem in general equilibrium terms as an interaction between 'willingness' and 'opportunity', thus discarding Böhm-Bawerk's reliance on the dubious concept of a measurable 'period of production'.

*Secondary Literature*
J. Schumpeter, *Ten Great Economists from Marx to Keynes* (Oxford University Press, 1951); E. Kauder, 'Böhm-Bawerk, Eugen von', *International Encyclopedia of the Social Sciences,* vol. 2, ed. D.L. Sills (Macmillan Free Press, 1968).

# Bortkiewicz, Ladislaus von (1868-1931)

Ladislaus von Bortkiewicz was a mathematical statistician who made a number of contributions to probability theory, small sample theory and the statistical interpretation of radioactivity. He was also a mathematical economist who published a number of critical articles in the first decade of this century, all of which left a mark on their subject-matter: for example, a paper on 'The Marginal Utility Doctrine as the Basis of an Ultra-Liberal Economic Policy' (1902), ostensibly a review of Pareto's *Cours d'économie politique* (1896-97), but in fact a cutting criticism of the way Walras (q.v.) and the young Pareto (q.v.) had employed general equilibrium theory to support the 'doctrine of maximum satisfactions', (the view that free competition maximises the sum of satisfactions of individuals); and an equally critical review of Alfred Weber's *Theory of the Location of Industries* (1909), which sorted out many of Weber's (q.v.) mistakes in the graphical representation of spatial location. But these and other articles are as nothing to two papers that Bortkiewicz published on Marxian economics, the only two of his numerous contributions to have been translated into English: 'Value and Price in the Marxian

System' (1906-7), and 'On the Correction in Marx's Fundamental Theoretical Construction in the Third Volume of Capital' (1907).

The contrast between the tone of these papers and, say, a book like Böhm-Bawerk's (q.v.) *The Close of the Marxian System* (1896) could not be greater. Böhm-Bawerk's intention was to assess the whole of Marx's economic ideas and to show that they were untenable. The purpose of Bortkiewicz's papers, however, was to seize on an interesting problem in Marx that Marx had failed to solve but that he, Bortkiewicz, thought was in fact solvable. What this implied for the Marxist system as a whole, he left it to others to decide. The only note of passion in the essays came when he found Marx being unfair to Ricardo because Ricardo was Bortkiewicz's idol (if he had any idols).

Böhm-Bawerk had found a 'great contradiction' between Volumes I and III of Marx's *Capital:* in Volume I, the value of commodities is determined by the labour time required to produce them, but in Volume III actual prices are determined by their costs of production plus the average rate of profit on capital invested. Marx argued that it was possible to 'transform' value into prices so as to preserve the labour theory of value and with it the labour theory of profits as 'surplus value created only by labour'. Böhm-Bawerk denied Marx's argument as a retreat from the pure labour theory of value but without entering into the technical difficulties of Marx's 'transformation problem'. Bortkiewicz, however, noted that Marx had committed a serious error in transforming values into prices: he had expressed outputs in prices but had continued to treat inputs in labour value terms. Bortkiewicz then went on to show that if the entire economy is divided into three sectors, it is in fact possible to transform the value of both inputs and outputs into prices, thus vindicating Marx on purely logical grounds.

Marx died in 1883. Bortkiewicz's paper appeared in 1906-7. Thus, for 24 years Marxists had failed to notice a fundamental inconsistency in Marx's own schema which gives one a pretty good idea of the state of Marxian economics around the turn of the century. Even after the publication of Bortkiewicz's two papers, the point Bortkiewicz was making was largely ignored in Marxist circles and even knowledge of the papers disappeared until they were rediscovered by Paul Sweezy (1910-) in his *Theory of Capitalist Development* (1942). Since then Bortkiewicz's proof of the logical consistency of Marx's transformation problem has been extended from three to *n* sectors; in short, it is possible mathematically to transform labour values into ordinary prices. What this proves about the validity of the Marxian system is of course another question.

Bortkiewicz was born in St Petersburg in 1868 and studied at the University of St Petersburg, graduating in 1890. His first paper on demography was published in Russian but after moving to Germany to take a doctor's degree at the University of Göttingen under Wilhelm Lexis (1837-1914), from whom he probably derived his interest in Marx, all his later writings were in German. After a brief spell back in St Petersburg, he joined the University of Berlin in 1901, where he remained for 30 years, becoming full professor of economics and statistics in 1920. He wrote little on economics after 1910, but remained active in statistics until his death in 1931.

*Secondary Literature*
J.A. Schumpeter, 'Ladislaus von Bortkiewicz: 1868–1931', *Ten Great Economists from Marx to Keynes* (Oxford University Press, 1951); E.J. Gumbel, 'Bortkiewicz, Ladislaus von', *International Encyclopedia of the Social Sciences,* vol. 2, ed. D.L. Sills (Macmillan Free Press, 1968).

# Bowley,
# Arthur Lyon
# (1869-1957)

Arthur Bowley began his career as a mathematician but turned to economics because of its relevance to problems of social reform with which he was passionately concerned. His early work on the history of wages and prices in Britain led him from applied statistics to theoretical statistics and in particular to the problem of sampling procedures in conducting social surveys. He published the first English textbook on statistics, the first English textbook on mathematical economics and co-authored the first attempt in modern times to estimate the national income of Britain. He has come down in history as the discoverer of Bowley's Law referring to an alleged constancy of the share of wages in national income. As is so frequently the case with such labels, there is no warrant in any of his writings for the notion that labour's relative share tends to be constant over long periods of time; his only connection with this idea is that he was one of the first to attempt to measure the share of wages in national income.

Bowley was born in Bristol in 1869, the son of a vicar and schoolmaster. His father died when Bowley was still in his teens and he was educated in a strictly religious boarding school. He attended Trinity College, Cambridge, to study mathematics and received his BA in 1891. On Marshall's urging, he entered and won the Cobden Essay Prize in 1892 on *England's Foreign Trade in the Nineteenth Century* (1893), his first publication. This was followed by the Adam Smith Prize in 1894 with an essay on 'Changes in Average Wages in the United Kingdom Between 1860 and 1891', which laid the basis for a long series of articles, some written jointly with G.H. Wood, which pieced together in painstaking detail a large number of isolated time series on wage rates and earnings in British industries going back to the turn of the eighteenth century. Some of these essays were eventually brought together in Bowley's *Wages and Income in the United Kingdom Since 1860* (1900) and supplemented by additional articles on the history of wages in France and the USA. It was this data bank which A.W. Phillips (1914-75) exploited years later in 1958 when he estimated the so-called Phillips curve relating the percentage change of money wages to the rate of unemployment.

Throughout the 1890s, Bowley taught mathematics at various schools in the south of England and after 1895 he also taught statistics in the evening at the new London School of Economics. In 1900 he was appointed as lecturer in mathematics at the University Extension College, Reading, becoming professor of mathematics and economics there in 1907, while still retaining his part-time post at the LSE. It was only in 1919 that he was appointed to the first Chair in Statistics in the Social Sciences at LSE and so became a full-time member of the faculty there. He remained at LSE until 1936, the year of his retirement.

His *Elements of Statistics* appeared in 1901 and was constantly revised through six editions, the last of which was published in 1937. No less successful was *An Elementary Manual of Statistics* (1910), which went through seven editions in the next 40 years. In 1915, he and A.R. Burnett-Hurst published the results of sample surveys in five English towns, *Livelihood and Poverty: A Study in the Economic Conditions of Working-class Households,* which used and defended the method of 'cluster sampling'. He surveyed the five towns again ten years later in *Has Poverty Diminished?* (1925) and this time gave due attention to the measurement of sampling errors to which he had only alluded in the first book.

His *Mathematical Groundwork of Economics* (1924) was a landmark in attempting to 'reduce to a uniform notation, and to present as a properly related whole, the main part of the mathematical methods used by Cournot, Jevons, Pareto, Edgeworth, Marshall, Pigou and Johnson'. It was also a landmark in attempting to exemplify the use of mathematics in the analysis of the entire range of market structures, from perfect competition at one extreme to monopoly at the other. It was widely reviewed by such figures as Edgeworth (q.v.) and Wicksell (q.v.). Wicksell discovered a long list of typographical errors in the book, which he hoped would be eliminated in the second edition. The book sold so badly, however, that no second edition was ever published. The book as it stands, therefore, remains riddled with errors but for all that it represents a splendid testament to the achievements of two generations of mathematical economists and was not itself superseded until the publication of R.G.D. Allen's classic text, *Mathematical Analysis for Economists* (1938). One of the great fascinations of Bowley's book is to see what is included and what is left out: so, for example, there is no mention of Slutsky (q.v.) and hence the distinction between income and substitution effects and there is only a disguised reference to Pareto optimality and the theorem that a perfectly competitive equilibrium is Pareto-optimal.

Another pioneering task taken up by Bowley was the estimation of national income. After some early papers on the subject, he joined with Josiah Stamp (1880-1941) in publishing *The National Income 1924* (1927). This book — apart from introducing the term if not the concept of 'transfer payments' — contained a surprisingly modern discussion of the fundamental distinction between factor cost and market price valuations of national income. The book was influential in inspiring the first official estimates of British national income during the Second World War. Bowley's continued interest in the problem of national income accounting is reflected in *Three Studies on the National Income* (1938) and a series which he edited, *Studies in the National Income: 1924-1938* (1942). In 1935, he collaborated with R.G.D. Allen in the writing of another path-breaking book on *Family Expenditure,* which examined various expenditure–income relationships or Engel curves, devised 'adult equivalent scales', and generally laid the foundation for all later econometric studies of household consumption behaviour.

With the exception of this last book, most of Bowley's other work in statistics throughout a long and fruitful career did not involve the testing of economic hypotheses by use of available statistics but rather the collection and processing of statistics for their own sake or else to verify the deduced implications of economic theory. In other words, the task of the statistician as Bowley saw it was to assist economic theory, not to challenge it. His attitude is to be contrasted with that of Henry Moore (q.v.) and Wesley Mitchell (q.v.) working in the United States at exactly the same time: Moore and Mitchell were already doing econometrics, that is, testing economic theories, years before the term had become fashionable.

Bowley remained active in statistics right up to his seventies. In 1940 he was invited out of retirement to become acting director of the Oxford Institute of Statistics, retiring a second time in 1944. He died in 1957 at the age of 88.

*Secondary Literature*
R.G.D. Allen, 'Bowley, Arthur Lyon' *International Encyclopedia of the Social Sciences,* vol. 2, ed. D.L. Sills (Macmillan Free Press, 1968); A Darnell 'A.L. Bowley', *Pioneers of Modern Economics in Britain,* D.P. O'Brien and J.R. Presley (eds.) (Macmillan, 1981).

# Cairnes, John Elliott (1823-1875)

What McCulloch (q.v.) was to Ricardo (q.v.), John Elliott Cairnes was to John Stuart Mill (q.v.), a faithful disciple who nevertheless did not always see eye to eye with his master. In *Some Leading Principles of Political Economy Newly Expounded* (1874), he defended the Ricardian system as expounded by Mill but disagreed with Mill's 'recantation' in respect of the wages fund theory. In addition, he took up Mill's concept of non-competing skills in labour markets and generalised it to both domestic and international trade, arguing that both reciprocal demand and costs of production are involved in the determination of value whenever there is less than perfect mobility of factors between alternative uses. This might have caused him to look with favour at Jevons' (q.v.) radical introduction of a subjective theory of value in *The Theory of Political Economy* (1871). But Cairnes was too steeped in the Ricardian tradition to tolerate Jevons' iconoclasm. His totally uncomprehending review (1892) of Jevons' book is one of the best examples in the history of economic thought of the difficulties of communication between a new and an old 'paradigm'. Cairnes has been called the last of the classical economists, and the title is well deserved.

Just as McCulloch excelled more in applied than in theoretical work, so Cairnes was at his best when tackling practical problems. In a number of papers on the effects of the Australian gold discoveries on the level of prices published between 1858 and 1860, he sought to vindicate the old quantity theory of money. A major book on *The Slave Power* (1862) was intended to demonstrate that Adam Smith had been correct in condemning a slave economy as inherently inefficient. The book was something of a best-seller in Britain and had a decided influence on public opinion in favour of the Northern cause in the American civil war. An earlier work, *The Character and Logical Method of Political Economy* (1857), stands out as the first full-scale statement of the methodology of the English classical economists, building on the essays of Senior (q.v.) and John Stuart Mill, but going beyond them in the uncompromising insistence on the abstract-deductive method, grounded in a few industrial facts (such as diminishing returns) and the principles of human nature (such as the desire to maximise returns at least cost), and achieving universal truths independent of any particular political or social system.

Cairnes was born in County Louth, Ireland in 1823. He graduated from Trinity College, Dublin in 1848 and went on to do an MA in 1854. In 1856 he was appointed to the Whately Chair of Political Economy at Trinity College, Dublin. A year later he was admitted to the Irish bar but never in fact practised law. In 1859 he became professor of political economy and jurisprudence at Queen's College, Galway. He retained this post until 1870 although he lived in London from 1865 onwards. In 1866, he combined this post with a professorship at University College, London (here too there is a parallel with McCulloch) from which he resigned in 1872 because of ill-health. He died in 1875 at the relatively early age of 52.

*Secondary Literature*
R.D.C. Black, 'Cairnes, John Elliott', *International Encyclopedia of the Social Sciences,* vol. 2, ed. D.L. Sills (Macmillan Free Press, 1968).

# Cantillon, Richard (1680-1734)

Richard Cantillon is the great 'mystery man' of economics: we are not sure when or where he was born, although there are good reasons to think that he was Irish, and we know almost nothing about his career except that he was a merchant banker who spent most of his life in Paris. He seems to have made a great fortune from speculating in land bonds and spend the last years of his life travelling extensively through Europe. Even his death is surrounded by mystery: he was murdered in London in 1734 by an irate servant. We do not know just when he wrote his one great book, *Essay on the Nature of Commerce in General,* but it was published posthumously in 1755, 21 years after his murder. Long before that it circulated in manuscript among French and English economic writers and was widely quoted and even plagiarised without acknowledgement. Hume (q.v.), Turgot (q.v.), Steuart (q.v.) and Adam Smith(q.v.) cited it and were clearly influenced by it. Nevertheless, the *Essay,* remarkable as it is as virtually the first explicit study of the workings of an automatic market mechanism, went into total eclipse and came to be so forgotten that Jevons (q.v.) made a great stir in 1881 when he once again drew attention to this long-neglected masterpiece.

Cantillon was a physiocrat in his emphasis on the spending patterns of landlords and a mercantilist in his belief that there was merit in an export surplus. But apart from such reminders that he wrote 30 and perhaps 40 years before Adam Smith, his treatment is amazingly post-Smithian, operating with a tripartite division of wages, profits and interests as the income of three distinct social classes, distinguishing between the 'intrinsic value' of goods and their 'market price', constantly dividing the analysis in terms of the forces of demand and supply, focusing attention on equilibrium outcomes, and dismissing moral considerations as foreign to his discussion.

Among the many marvellous strokes of genius in the *Essay* at least two stand out as superior to anything to be found in economics until the twentieth century. There is, first, his analysis of the entrepreneur as a person who 'buys at a certain price to sell at an uncertain price' — arbitrage through time and across space. The entrepreneur may be a merchant or a landowner but he may equally be a capitalist employing labour; in all cases, however, the entrepreneurial role remains distinctly that of someone making decisions under uncertainty. Adam Smith read Cantillon, but totally ignored his discussion of entrepreneurship; in consequence, entrepreneurship simply disappeared from economics for over a century. Secondly, there is Cantillon's detailed analysis of the effects of an increase in the money supply on prices, distinguishing between the cases in which the money supply increases because more gold is mined domestically and those in which there is a favourable balance of trade even though there are no domestic gold mines. His main conclusion was that in all cases not just the level of prices but also the structure of prices would alter via the direct impact of the extra money on the pattern of spending of different social groups.

*Secondary Literature*
J.J. Spengler, 'Cantillon, Richard', *International Encyclopedia of the Social Sciences,* vol. 2, ed. D.L. Sills (Macmillan Free Press, 1968).

# Carey, Henry (1793-1879)

Of all the many American economists in the first half of the nineteenth century, the best-known, particularly outside America, was Henry Carey. His views are in many respects typically American: a deep antipathy to the theory of Malthus (q.v.) and Ricardo (q.v.), who he thought had perverted the teachings of Adam Smith (q.v.); a belief that all of classical economics needed revision in the light of the American context of abundant land and scarce labour; an optimistic faith in the essential harmony of economic interests, particularly in respect to the interest of labour and capital on the one hand and landowners on the other; and support for protectionism. (Which only emerged gradually in the course of his publications.) In his major work, *Principles of Political Economy* (1837-40), he developed a reproduction theory of labour value — value is determined not by past but by prospective labour costs — which impressed even Marx. In *The Past, The Present, and the Future* (1848) he elaborated his theory of rent and argued that the historical sequence of cultivation at least in the United States was the exact reverse of the one proposed by Ricardo, namely, from inferior to superior land, apparently because returns from the application of capital to land yield increasing rather than diminishing returns. Carey failed to realise that this applies only to what has been called the 'extensive margin' (applying the same capital and labour to more land) and not to the 'intensive margin' (applying more capital and labour to the same land). Nevertheless, his objection troubled many of the classical economists, and even John Stuart Mill (q.v.) thought it necessary to refute Carey in his *Principles of Political Economy* (1848).

Henry Carey was born in Philadephia in 1793, the son of Mathew Carey, a self-made Irish immigrant, a prominent publisher and leading publicist for protectionism. Henry Carey was also self-taught and eventually took over his father's publishing firm, combining journalism with widespread business interests in and around Philadelphia. He nevertheless found time to publish more than a dozen books and thousands of newspaper articles and pamphlets. In the late 1850s he moved increasingly away from economic to sociological writings, responding to the rising influence of Auguste Comte and Herbert Spencer. In books like *Principles of Social Science* (1858-60) and *The Unity of Law: As Exhibited in the Relations of Physical, Social, Mental and Moral Science* (1872) he bit off more than he could chew, but they were again characteristically American, expressing a commonly-held belief among American social scientists of the period that the days of a specialised economic science were over.

*Secondary Literature*
A.D.H. Kaplan, *Henry Charles Carey: A Study in American Economic Thought* (Johns Hopkins University Press, 1931); H.W. Spiegel, 'Carey, Henry C.', *International Encyclopedia of the Social Sciences*, vol. 2, ed. D.L. Sills (Macmillan Free Press, 1968).

# Cassel, Carl Gustav (1866-1945)

At the time of his death in 1910, Walras (q.v.) had a number of followers in Italy and America but in the great centres of academic economics of the day, England, Germany and Austria, the reaction to general equilibrium theory was at best lukewarm and at worst hostile; the mathematical form in which Walras expressed his ideas was itself enough to guarantee continued neglect of his writings. What kept general equilibrium economics alive was Cassel's *Theory of Social Economy* (1918), which presented the Walrasian system in a highly simplified form, stripped of all its mathematical detail. Indeed, simplification was the watchword of Cassel's entire presentation: utility theory was rejected on the grounds that no one had ever devised a method of measuring utility, and a negatively-inclined demand curve for commodities was postulated in the manner of Cournot (q.v.) as an empirically ascertainable fact. The whole of the marginal productivity of distribution was similarly rejected and the pricing of factors of production was instead explained, somewhat arcanely, on the basis of an assumption of fixed coefficients of production. In general, relative prices were explained simply by the relationship between 'scarcity' and 'wants'. The simplicity of argument and great accessibility of Cassel's book ensured its success. It was translated into many languages and was probably the most widely-read textbook on economics in the interwar years.

An earlier work, *The Nature and Necessity of Interest* (1903), also received widespread distribution. Cassel dismissed all the intricate arguments of Böhm-Bawerk's (q.v.) theory of capital and interest, and instead went back to Walras's distinction between single-use consumption goods and multi-use durable capital goods, the services of the latter only being obtainable after an unspecified period of 'waiting. 'Waiting' as a two-dimensional quantity — a sum of money and a period of time — was regarded as a separate factor of production; interest was due simply to the inherent scarcity of this factor. Turning to the causes governing the supply of waiting, Cassel denied that the supply curve of saving is necessarily positive throughout its entire range. Nevertheless — and this was one of the most striking arguments of the book — there is a floor of about 2 to 3 per cent below which the rate of interest is unlikely to fall due to the limited length of the human lifespan. At a rate of interest below, say, 2 per cent, the length of a working life is too short to make it possible for most people to save a sufficient sum to provide for their old age, thus killing off the incentive to save. In short, as the rate of interest falls to 2 or 3 per cent, the acute scarcity of waiting guarantees its subsequent rise.

Cassel's international reputation was enhanced after the First World War by his participation in the discussions about Germany's reparation payments and the restoration of the gold standard. In *The World's Monetary Problems* (1921), containing two memoranda written for the League of Nations, Cassel expounded a simple rule for determining whether a country's rate of foreign exchange is in equilibrium; namely, that it is in the same relation as the price levels between that country and every other; in short, equilibrium rates of exchange are found as quotients between the price levels of different countries. This is the famous 'purchasing power parity theory', which stands forever connected with Cassel's name. It is, strictly speaking, an incorrect theory because the rates of exchange between two currencies can at best depend on their relative purchasing power over identical exportable goods; but the prices of non-exportable goods usually differ between countries. In other words, the purchasing power parity theory ignores a great many things that create discrepancies in the average prices of all goods between two countries. Nevertheless, in periods of flux when international prices are changing rapidly, the theory provides a useful dynamic rule for approximating the equilibrium rates of exchange and, in general, it is true to say that no country can escape a fall in the exchange rate if its domestic prices are inflating at a rate that exceeds the average rate of inflation in the rest of the world.

With the rise of unemployment in the 1930s, Cassel emerged as one of the leading critics of all quasi-Keynesian remedies for the Great Depression, such as public works, unemployment relief and indeed all forms of deficit finance. When Keynes' *General Theory* (1936) was published, he reviewed it with total lack of sympathy and took pains to refute Keynes' policy proposals for curing unemployment.

Cassel was born in Stockholm in 1866 and received his PhD in mathematics from the University of Uppsåla in 1895. After working as a schoolmaster in Stockholm for several years, he became interested in economics and went to Germany for a training in the subject. His first article in 1899 and his first book in 1900 were both published in German. He returned to Sweden in 1901 and was appointed professor of economics at the University of Stockholm in 1903, a post which he held until 1936. For some years, his Chair at Stockholm overlapped with Wicksell's Chair at the University of Lund, but the two men never saw eye to eye. Wicksell (q.v.) published a bitter but effective critique of Cassel's *Theory of Social Economy* and of course, in terms of social and political outlook, it is difficult to imagine any two men further apart. Cassel ceased publishing in economics in 1938 and died in 1945 at the age of 78.

*Secondary Literature*
K.G. Landgren, 'Cassel, Karl Gustav', *International Encyclopedia of the Social Sciences,* vol. 2, ed. D.L. Sills (Macmillan Free Press, 1968).

# Chamberlin, Edward H (1899-1967)

Chamberlin's *Theory of Monopolistic Competition* (1933) was published a few months before Joan Robinson's *Economics of Perfect Competition,* and Chamberlin spent the rest of his life refining this one great work and fighting against the tendency to lump the two books together as simply alternative statements of the same new microeconomics. For years his tenacious insistence on the fundamental difference between his approach and that of Robinson was a favourite butt of humour among economists, particularly as the rising tide of Keynesian economics appeared to relegate all problems of microeconomics to a lower order of importance. But in time, Chamberlin's obstinacy won the day. His more penetrating analysis of advertising, product differentiation and locational advantages — those features of modern business firms that cannot be explained either by the theory of perfect competition or the theory of monopoly — gradually persuaded his fellow economists that monopolistic competition is indeed different from imperfect competition. When he died in 1967 a large number of distinguished economists contributed a volume of essays in his honour, *Monopolistic Competition Theory:*

*Studies in Impact,* R.E. Kuenne (ed.) (1967), which agreed that *The Theory of Monopolistic Competition* ranked with Keynes' *General Theory* as one of the most influential economic books of the twentieth century.

Chamberlin's case of monopolistic competition denotes a market structure that combines elements of competition — a large number of sellers, so that each firm can act independently of the others, free entry into the industry, etc. — with elements of monopoly — buyers have definite preferences for the branded, differentiated products of particular sellers for which they are willing to pay a higher price. (Think of the market for toothpaste or any retailing industry.) His analysis demonstrated that the element of monopoly conferred no long-run advantage to the sellers in the industry. In the long run, only normal profits are earned but, nevertheless, the industry achieves equilibrium at less than minimum average costs: there are too many firms in the industry compared with the situation under perfect competition, and each charges a higher price because it is too small for maximum efficiency. This so-called tangency solution was the major empirical implication of monopolistic competition theory, which seemed to shed light on a whole host of observable features of the real world. Chamberlin himself was always insistent that the tangency solution did not provide a blueprint for interfering with monopolistically competitive industries: under-utilisation in monopolistic competition is simply the price we must pay for consumers' preferences for variety in styles and brands.

Chamberlin's tangency solution has been hotly debated ever since. Many economists now argue that monopolistic competition is only trivially different from perfect competition and that both ignore the really important market structure in modern economies, namely, oligopoly or competition among producers so few in number that their actions are interdependent. While it is perfectly true that the *Theory of Monopolistic Competition* contains a brief treatment of mutual interdependence in oligopoly, this is not the core of his book. In short, there appears to be a misplaced emphasis in Chamberlin's treatise: monopolistic competition, as Chamberlin defined it, may be as rare as perfect competition.

Chamberlin was born in La Couner, Washington in 1899, the son of a Methodist minister. He went to high school in Iowa City and graduated from the University of Iowa in 1921. After gaining a master's degree from the University of Michigan, he entered Harvard

University in 1922 as a doctoral student. His thesis, which was completed in 1927, contained all the principal elements of his subsequent book and owed nothing to the Marshallian debates at the University of Cambridge, which were to lead Robinson along a similar path. He began teaching at Harvard in the same year and, except for wartime service with the US Office of Strategic Services and a post-war year as visiting professor at the University of Paris, he spent the rest of his life at Harvard. He was chairman of the department of economics at Harvard during its 'Golden Age' (1939-43) when the department included such renowned figures as Alvin Hansen, Wassily Leontief, Edward Mason, Summer Schlichter, Joseph Schumpeter and Frank Taussig; and he edited Harvard's house journal, the *Quarterly Journal of Economics,* from 1948 to 1958. He received honorary degrees from a number of universities in the 1950s and was elected as Distinguished Fellow of the American Economic Association in 1965.

Chamberlin published a fair number of articles through the 1930s and 1940s on special aspects of the theory of monopolistic competition, many of which he embodied in successive editions of his central masterpiece: the eighth and final edition of *The Theory of Monopolistic Competition* appeared in 1962. *Towards a More General Theory of Value* (1957) collected together 16 of his most important papers.

*Secondary Literature*
R.E. Kuenne (ed.), *Monopolistic Competition Theory: Studies in Impact* (Wiley, 1967); J.W. Markham, 'Chamberlin, E.H.', *International Encyclopedia of the Social Sciences,* vol. 18, ed. D.L. Sills (Macmillan Free Press, 1968).

# Clapham, John Harold (1873-1946)

Originally a European historian, John Clapham turned to the study of British economic history and particularly nineteenth-century British economic history as a result of urging by Marshall (q.v.). He was born in Salford, Lancashire in 1873, the son of a jeweller and silversmith. After receiving his BA in history from the University of Cambridge, Clapham joined Marshall as fellow of King's College, Cambridge from 1898 to 1902. In 1902, he went to Leeds as professor of economics and wrote his first monograph on the nineteenth century, *The Woollen and Worsted Industries* (1907). In 1908, he returned to King's College as Dean, assistant tutor in history and, of course, colleague of Marshall. His next book, *The Economic Development of France and Germany, 1815-1914* (1921) clearly revealed Marshall's influence in its attention to such factors as the role of economies and diseconomies of scale in the structural evolution of French and German industry. But in the following year came the great heresy: an article entitled 'Of Empty Economic Boxes', published in Cambridge's own *Economic Journal* (1922).

The economic boxes which Clapham claimed to be empty were no less than the building-blocks of the Marshallian system, namely, those increasing-cost and decreasing-cost industries that Marshall had told his readers ought to be taxed and subsidised so as to maximise economic welfare. But how are we to tell which industries conform to the one category rather than the other?, Clapham asked. The problem of separating the effects of returns to scale from those of technical progress make it impossible to tell whether any industry conforms to the law of increasing, decreasing or constant costs. There is, he concluded, 'great danger to an essentially practical science such as Economics in the elaboration of hypothetical conclusions about, say, human welfare and taxes in relation to industries which cannot be specified'. This criticism was in fact a crushing blow to the applicability of Marshall's tax-subsidy proposals. Marshall himself did not reply, being by now an old man who never liked controversy even when he was young. But some of his pupils did. The result was a debate that raged on in the pages of the *Economic Journal* for the rest of the decade, culminating 10 years later in Joan Robinson's (q.v.) *Economics of Imperfect Competition* (1933).

Clapham did not participate further in the empty economic boxes debate, but the experience seems to have left him with a life-long scepticism about economic theory, at least in its details. Nevertheless, he never lost sight of the sorts of issue that worry economists and for that reason his books have the unique quality of constantly connecting with the interests of economists. This is particularly true of his one great masterpiece, *An Economic History of Modern Britain* (1926-38), which covers in three volumes an entire century from 1820 to 1929. One of the aims of this book was 'to make the story more nearly quantitative than it has yet been made'. There have of course been great advances in quantitative economic history since it was written and the entire period has been surveyed again at least four or five times. However, Clapham's book has never been totally superseded and it retains its value even after the passage of almost 50 years.

The first Chair of Economic History at Cambridge University was especially created for Clapham in 1928. The 1930s was largely taken up with the second and third volumes of his *Economic History of Modern Britain* and with editing two ambitious series of *Cambridge Studies in Economic History* and the *Cambridge Economic History of Europe.* He combined these duties with that of Dean and later Vice-Provost of King's College, Cambridge, not to mention the presidencies of the Economic History Society and the British Academy. Nevertheless, he managed to complete at least one more major study, the history of *The Bank of England* (1944), and had virtually finished *A Concise Economic History of Britain from the Earliest Time to 1750,* which was published posthumously in 1949 and has been frequently reprinted. He was knighted in 1943 and died in 1946 at the age of 73.

*Secondary Literature*
P. Mathias, 'Clapham, John Harold', *International Encyclopedia of the Social Sciences,* vol. 2, ed. D.L. Sills (Macmillan Free Press, 1968).

# Clark,
# John Bates
# (1847-1938)

The name John Bates Clark stands forever associated with one of the worst fallacies in modern economics: the use of marginal productivity theory to provide an ethical justification for the functional distribution of income, according to which the owners of all factors of production receive exactly what they 'deserve', namely, their marginal products. Despite this awful slip, which absolutely everybody else immediately repudiated, Clark was a leading American pioneer of the marginal productivity theory of distribution, which he developed in a series of path-breaking articles in 1889 and 1891, more or less concurrently with the independent attempts of Stuart Wood (1853–1914), Wicksteed (q.v.), Walras (q.v.) and Barone (q.v.). It is noteworthy that it was Henry George's (q.v.) *Progress and Poverty* (1879) that appears to have stimulated Clark to generalise the Ricardian theory of rent, applying the principle of diminishing returns not only to land but to any factor held constant and combined with variable doses of another factor; thus, every type of income could be interpreted as a differential surplus akin to ground rent, which neatly disposed of George's assault on landlords. In short, George's diatribes not only inspired Clark to develop the marginal productivity theory of distribution but also coloured his presentation of it from the start.

Clark moved steadily throughout his life from the left of the political spectrum to the right. He was born in 1847 in Providence, Rhode Island. His family moved to Minnesota when Clark was in his teens where his father ran a small agricultural implements business. His education at Amherst College was constantly interrupted by financial difficulties and he did not graduate until 1872 at the age of 25. He left to study in Europe for three years, spending some time at the University of Heidelberg working under the supervision of Karl Knies (1821-98), one of the members of the 'older' German Historical School. Returning to Carleton College in 1875, he set to work on what was to become his first book, *The Philosophy of Wealth* (1886). It showed the influence of his German teachers, being critical of the capitalist system, but also hinted at the marginal utility theory of value of Jevons (q.v.) and Menger (q.v.). After 12 years at Smith College (1881-93) and two years at Johns Hopkins University (1893-95), he joined the recently established Faculty of Political Science at Columbia University, where he remained until his retirement in 1923.

His major statement of marginal productivity theory first appeared in book form in *The Distribution of Wealth* (1899). This was superseded by *Essentials of Economic Theory* (1907) in which he attempted to move away from what he considered to be the static analysis of his earlier work towards a more dynamic point of view; the outcome, however, was not dynamic analysis as it is now understood — economic theorising in which the variables are dated — but comparative statics relating one equilibrium position to another. He also published two small but widely-read books on 'unfair competition', *The Control of Trusts* (1901) and *The Problem of Monopoly* (1904), and a book on the preservation of peace, *A Tender Peace* (1935), a subject which had long preoccupied him. He died in 1938 at the age of 91.

*The Distribution of Wealth* not only contained Clark's theory of distribution in accordance with marginal productivity principles but also his theory of capital, developed in stark opposition to the theories of Böhm-Bawerk (q.v.). Clark insisted on a sharp distinction between concrete 'capital goods' and the abstract fund of 'social capital' of which the individual capital goods are a temporary embodiment. Instead of capital being conceived as a series of 'advances' to workers by capitalists during a 'period of production', Clark regarded capital as a permanent fund, a perpetual income stream. If we confine ourselves to stationary conditions as Böhm-Bawerk always does, he argued, the number of production periods that are coming to a close at any moment of time must be just equal to the number of production periods just beginning. A stationary state in which net investment is zero therefore involves the automatic synchronisation of production and consumption; capital is necessarily maintained intact and the only demand for capital in a stationary state is for replacement purposes; there is no Austrian 'waiting' for output because every application of inputs that bears its fruit some time hence is matched by the simultaneous emergence of output from past outlays of productive effort.

Böhm-Bawerk attacked Clark's theory as the 'mythology of capital' and the two of them, joined by Fetter (q.v.), Fisher (q.v.) and a number of lesser-known American and British economists, entered into an acrimonious dispute on capital theory that went on for years even after the turn of the century. It was one of those wonderfully obscure and confusing debates that seems forever to characterise the history of capital theory (Frank Knight and Friedrich Hayek engaged in a similar debate in the 1930s). Posterity gave Clark the best of this battle in the sense that academic interest in the Austrian theory of capital died out very quickly after about 1905 or 1910. Posterity for once was wrong because Clark's theory of the perfect synchronisation of production and consumption now seems to be untenable: even under stationary conditions, the time structure of the capital stock is not a matter of indifference to economic agents since they can in fact increase present income by failing to replace worn-out capital goods.

*Secondary Literature*
J.M. Clark, 'Clark, John Bates', *International Encyclopedia of the Social Sciences,* vol. 2, ed. D.L. Sills (Macmillan Free Press, 1968).

# Clark, John Maurice (1884-1963)

John Maurice Clark, son of the more famous John Bates Clark, regarded himself as a follower of Veblen (q.v.), Mitchell (q.v.) and Commons (q.v.) in short, an institutionalist, but he had no ambition to develop a new economics to take the place of orthodox price theory. On the contrary, he was convinced that there was nothing very much wrong with orthodox economics so far as it went. The trouble was that its preoccupation with static equilibrium deprived it of any value in dealing with practical problems. He thus saw his life-work as that of developing the dynamic implications of economic theory. In that sense, he built upon his father's fundamental distinction between statics and dynamics, agreeing with him (and for that matter with Marshall (q.v.)) that the analysis of static equilibrium is not the end but only the beginning of a thorough investigation of economic phenomena. This point of view is perfectly summed up in his most famous article, 'Toward a Concept of Workable Competition' (1940), which has been aptly described as having had more influence on the development of industrial organisation as a specialised field of economics than any other publication since Chamberlin's (q.v.)

*Theory of Monopolistic Competition* (1934). The concept of perfect competition with its Pareto-optimal properties is, as everyone knows, inapplicable as it stands to any actual market economy. In order to assess the performance of industries and to design effective anti-trust laws to maintain competition, what is needed is some definition of 'workable' in contrast to 'perfect' competition. Clark's effort in this article is to provide not a set of mechanical rules but some rules of thumb relating to freedom of entry and alternative options available to consumers to aid courts in judging whether an industry is workably competitive or not. Clark's article produced an explosion of work in the 1940s and 1950s on what has been called the structure-conduct-performance model of industrial organisation. More recently, the development of the theory of 'contestable markets' represents yet another echo of Clark's seminal article.

Only Clark's article 'Business Acceleration and the Law of Demand' (1917) and his book, *Studies in the Economics of Overhead Costs* (1926), achieved the fame of his essay on workable competition. The article revived Aftalion's (q.v.) principle of acceleration (any change in consumption demand results in an accelerated change in investment demand) and related it to the generation of business cycles. The book on overhead costs investigated the role of internal economies of scale in accounting for the growth of monopolies, distinguishing between internal and external economies and between economies in production and in marketing. It is a dated book in the sense that all of its elements have been incorporated in the works of later writers, but it is full of remarkable anticipations and is essential reading in showing how Chamberlin (q.v.) and Robinson (q.v.) were soon to arrive at their theories of monopolistic and imperfect competition.

John Maurice Clark was born in Northampton, Massachusetts in 1884 and attended Amherst College, receiving his BA in 1905. He pursued graduate studies in economics at Columbia University, where his father was then teaching, receiving his PhD in 1910 with a thesis on railway pricing, strangely entitled *Standards of Reasonableness in Local Freight Discriminations* (1910). He had already started teaching at Colorado College but now he moved to Amherst, followed five years later by a move to the University of Chicago. In 1926 he left Chicago to become professor of economics at Columbia University, where he remained for over 30 years until his retirement in 1957. He served as president of the American

Economic Association in 1922 and was awarded the Francis A Walker Medal by the Association in 1952 for distinguished service to the field of economics. He died in 1963 at the age of 79.

He published prodigiously throughout his life on anti-trust legislation, the business cycle, the economic costs of war, the problems of post-war demobilisation, the macroeconomics of demand management, inflation theory, the workings of the labour market, and the future prospects of capitalism. Few of his books linger in the mind, however, because he tends, in the manner of John Stuart Mill, to assert ideas in the round with all suitable qualifications and modifications. Thus, it takes a careful reading of *Strategic Factors in Business Cycles* (1934) to notice how many of Keynes' ideas it anticipates. Similarly, his *Alternative to Serfdom* (1948), a reply to Friedrich Hayek's *Road to Serfdom* (1944), is seldom credited as an extremely effective answer to Hayek's worries about 'creeping inflation'. Finally, his last book on *Competition as a Dynamic Process* (1961) contains much of what was later hailed as one of the great insights of modern Austrian economics, namely, that orthodox economics consists of a theory of equilibrium states but practically no theory of the process by which competition is achieved. Once again, it appears that there is nothing new in the history of economic thought, or rather that for anything to appear as new, it must be asserted in such a way as to arrest attention

*Secondary Literature*
J.W. Markham, 'Clark, John Maurice', *International Encyclopedia of the Social Sciences,* vol. 2, ed. D.L. Sills (Macmillan Free Press, 1968).

# Commons, John Roger (1862-1945)

John Commons was one of the three founders of American institutionalism — the other two being Veblen (q.v.) and Mitchell (q.v.) — but Commons was as unique a thinker in his own way as were Veblen and Mitchell. For one thing, he was a major historian of American labour and his *History of Labor in the United States,* published in four volumes over a 17-year period (1918-35), would have given him a place in American economic thought even if he had written nothing else. For another, he was an active policy-maker who helped to draft a whole series of Bills for the state of Wisconsin, dealing with the legal position of unions, unemployment insurance, workmen's accident compensation, and the regulation of public utilities, which made Wisconsin famous as the legislative 'laboratory' for other American states. He later served as member of the Industrial Relations Commission for the Federal Government, and took part in designing the Social Security Act of 1935, which established America's modern system of contributory old-age insurance. Finally, he wrote three major treatises in economic theory, *The Distribution of Wealth* (1893), *Legal Foundations of Capitalism* (1924) and

*Institutional Economics* (1934), which analysed the 'working rules' of 'going concerns' that translated individual action into collective action.

His was a theory of collective action conceived as a set of controls on conflicting private interests. By interpreting these controls as 'laws', in the broadest sense of the term, Commons was in fact placing jurisprudence at the centre of economic inquiry. Thus, he characterised the Supreme Court of the United States as 'the supreme faculty of political economy' for the nation. He was thereby the inventor of what has since been called the economics of law, which views the courts and judicial decisions as the arena for reconciling not just disagreements about the ends of economic policy but also for determining the appropriate means to achieve these ends. However, the new economics of law has not turned to Commons for inspiration, deriving its impetus rather from later work on the role of transaction costs and the economics of property rights. Commons' books were in fact stillborn and received little attention even at the time they were published. This is in large part because they are genuinely obscure; they bristle with specialised terms — 'transactions', 'working rules', 'going concerns' — which are manipulated at a high level of abstraction and then applied to the interpretation of judicial proceedings and legislative enactments. The entire style of reasoning was so foreign to that which passed as economic theory in the inter-war years that it is little wonder that the books fell on deaf ears. What is surprising, however, is that they have not been taken up subsequently by the new enthusiasts for the economic analysis of law.

Commons was born in 1862 in Hollandsburg, Ohio and attended Oberlin College as an undergraduate. He worked part-time as a printer to support himself and became interested in economics as a result of contact with trade unionism and the Henry George single-tax movement. After graduating in 1888, he attended Johns Hopkins University and fell under the spell of Ely (q.v.). He never completed his graduate studies and began teaching in economics at Wesleyan University in 1890. After leaving Wesleyan, he taught at Oberlin, Indiana and Syracuse before settling down at Wisconsin in 1904 where he remained until his retirement in 1934, taking frequent leaves of absence to act as a consultant for the state of Wisconsin. He died in 1945 at the age of 83.

*Secondary Literature*
L.G. Harter, *John R. Commons: His Assault on Laissez-Faire* (Corvallis, 1962); J. Dorfman, 'Commons, John R.', *International Encyclopedia of the Social Sciences,* vol. 3, ed. D.L. Sills (Macmillan Free Press, 1968).

# Cournot, Antoine Augustin (1801-1877)

Antoine Cournot, French mathematician, philosopher, economist, and university administrator, was the first writer to define and draw a demand curve and also the first to make serious use of calculus to solve a maximisation problem in economics. Indeed, reading *Researches into the Mathematical Principles of the Theory of Wealth* (1838) it is difficult to believe the date of publication: a mere 15 years after the death of Ricardo and 10 years before the appearance of Mill's *Principles of Political Economy* (1848). In Chapter 4 of the *Researches,* boldly entitled 'Of the Law of Demand', Cournot assumed as a matter of course that the sale of commodities is a decreasing function of their price. This assertion had nothing to do with utility theory but was based instead on casual observation of observed data; in other words, Cournot's demand function is not a Marshallian demand curve of the quantities consumers would buy at various hypothetical prices but quite simply a sales function. Writing $D = F(p)$ for the sale function and $pF(p)$ for what we would now call the total revenue function, Cournot went on to elucidate the price elasticity of demand (without using that term) by showing that a price increase may lower or raise total revenue, depending on whether demand is flexible or inflexible in response to a price change.

Instead of starting with the case of perfect or unlimited competition among many sellers and then ending up with monopoly (the case of a single seller), Cournot starts with monopoly and arrives at the competitive case by allowing the number of sellers to increase without limit. The monopolist faces a given total revenue function, $R = pF(p)$, and a marginal revenue function, $M = F(p) + pF'(p)$, the derivative of the total revenue function. These given revenue functions are then confronted with total and marginal cost functions. Cournot demonstrates that instantaneous profits are maximised when the monopolist produces an output at which marginal cost equals marginal revenue. Marshall (q.v.) adopted Cournot's analysis of profit-maximisation in his own *Principles of Economics* (1890) but expressed it in terms of a monopolist's *total* cost and revenue; in consequence, the concept of marginal revenue had to be rediscovered once again in the early 1930s by Joan Robinson and Roy Harrod.

Cournot not only developed the theory of monopoly but also gave attention to the case of duopoly (two sellers). As in the case of monopoly, he assumed that buyers name prices and that sellers merely adjust their output to given prices; thus, each duopolist estimates the demand function for his product and then sets the quantity sold on the assumption that his rival's output remains fixed. This assumption proves to be false. Nevertheless, as each duopolist successively adjusts his output to the changing output of the other, a determinate solution emerges in which further adjustments bring no improvement to the profits of each duopolist. This equilibrium position is characterised by a price lower than that charged by a monopolist and an output exceeding that of a monopolist. Cournot then proceeded to show that price declines and output rises still further as the number of sellers increases, reaching at last the competitive case in which price is at a minimum and output at a maximum given the level of demand and the technology for producing that commodity.

Needless to say, Cournot's book was totally ignored when it first appeared. He was so discouraged by its reception that he gave up economics for 25 years, returning to it in later works, *Principes de la théorie des richesses* (1863) and *Revue sommaire des doctrines économiques* (1877) in which he abandoned the language of mathematics in a vain effort to be more readable. In his own time, however, he was well known for a number of books on calculus and probability, as well as two philosophical treatises.

Cournot was born in central France in 1801, educated locally and was admitted in 1821 to the Ecole Normale Supérieure, Paris. In 1823, he entered the household of Maréchel Saint-Cyr as literary adviser and tutor to his son. He spent ten years there, obtaining a doctorate in science in 1829. After a brief professorship in mathematics at the University of Lyons, he held a number of high-level administrative posts at the Universities of Grenoble and Dijon. He retired in 1862 and died in 1877. By this time, he had been discovered by Jevons (q.v.), Walras (q.v.) and Marshall (q.v.) and was on the way to his eventual reputation as a major figure in the history of mathematical economics.

*Secondary Literature*
H. Guitton, 'Cournot, Antoine Augustin', *International Encyclopedia of the Social Sciences,* vol. 3, ed. D.L. Sills (Macmillan Free Press, 1968); R.D. Theocharis, *Early Developments in Mathematical Economics* (Macmillan, 2nd edn, 1983), Chapter 9.

# Cunningham, William (1849-1919)

William Cunningham was more responsible than anyone else for the establishment of economic history as an independent discipline in British universities: his *Growth of English Industry and Commerce* (1882) outlined its subject-matter, laid down its methods, and greatly stimulated teaching and research. When Marshall (q.v.) published his *Principles of Economics* (1890), the opening chapters of the book provided an outline sketch of the economic history of Europe together with a discussion of the relationship between economic theory and economic history. Cunningham called into question Marshall's competence to speak on such matters in 'The Perversion of Economic History', published in the *Economic Journal* in 1892. This was one of the few criticisms of his book to which Marshall replied, and in later editions he relegated the historical chapters to appendices while vigorously disclaiming any originality to his treatment of historical questions.

Cunningham and Marshall remained at daggers drawn over the place of economic history in the training of economists. Cunningham believed, like the members of the German Historical School, in 'the relativity of economic doctrine'; the study of economic history encouraged due attention to the facts and was thus the best possible introduction to the study of economics. Moreover, as a firm believer in Britain's national greatness and imperial responsibilities, Cunningham was not only a firm opponent of anything that smacked of *laissez-faire* but also a vigorous advocate of protectionism. His book on *The Rise and Decline of the Free Trade Movement* (1904) must have pained Marshall deeply and yet it is remarkable that Marshall studiously avoided open controversy with Cunningham (but then Marshall always avoided controversy!).

William Cunningham was born in Edinburgh in 1849, the son of a prominent Scottish solicitor. After a brief spell at the Universities of Edinburgh and Tübingen, Germany, he entered Caius College, Cambridge in 1869 to study moral science, graduating with distinction three years later. In 1873 he was ordained into the Anglican Church and from then on combined academic with clerical work, rising eventually to become an archdeacon. Between 1874 and 1878 he was a Cambridge University extension lecturer in the industrial cities of Northern England. In 1884, he returned to Cambridge as a lecturer in history. In 1891, he was appointed Tooke professor of economics at King's College, London, but continued to reside in Cambridge as a Fellow of both Trinity College and Caius College (thus, when he was disputing Marshall he was in fact his university colleague). He crossed the Atlantic twice in 1899 and 1914 to lecture on economic history at Harvard University. He was a founding member of the British Academy and served as President of the Economic Section of the British Association (1891, 1895) and the Royal Historical Society (1910-13). He died in 1919 at the age of 70.

*Secondary Literature*
R.M.Hartwell, 'Cunningham, William', *International Encyclopedia of the Social Sciences,* vol. 4, ed. D.L. Sills (Macmillan Free Press 1968).

# Davenant, Charles (1656-1714)

Charles Davenant was one of the leading economic pamphleteers of the 1690s, a decade that also saw the economic writings of Locke (q.v.), North (q.v.) and Gregory King. Son of a famous playwright and theatrical producer, he was himself the author of a play produced at the age of 19, a Commissioner of Excise under Charles II and James II, a Tory Member of Parliament under William and Mary, and Inspector-General of Exports and Imports under Queen Anne. All his pamphlets — *An Essay on Ways and Means of Supplying the War* (1695), *An Essay on the East India Trade* (1696), *Discourses on the Public Revenues, and on the Trade of England* (1698) and *An Essay Upon the Probable Methods of Making a People Gainers in the Balance of Trade* (1699) — were occasional pieces concerned with advancing a particular cause in which Davenant had a personal interest. In the course of his partisan arguments, however, he frequently developed general principles, some of which sound almost like the early writings of Adam Smith (q.v.). He was, however, a mercantilist in the sense that he underlined the advantages of a favourable balance of trade as a source of political power, favoured population growth and decried luxury spending. Nevertheless, he rejected an embargo on textile imports from India because 'trade is in its nature free', argued against writers who consider gold and silver 'the only and most useful treasure of a nation' and welcomed paper money as an addition to the metal coinage.

Davenant saw himself as a disciple of Petty (q.v.) whom he acknowledged in the *Discourses*, his most substantial work, as the founder of 'political arithmetic ... the art of reasoning by figures upon things relating to government'. Following on from Petty, he sought to calculate the national income as equivalent to national expenditure. He called the excess of income over expenditure a 'superlucration', that is, 'wealth or national stock'. It is easy to see how this advance over Petty's own conception of national income accounting must have influenced Adam Smith, who in fact cited Davenant's *Discourses* a number of times.

Davenant contributed to keeping political arithmetic alive not only by his own work but by quoting and reproducing Gregory King's careful quantitative estimates of national income, the growth of population, the value of capital and the rate of growth of capital, none of which estimates were published by King in his own lifetime (1648-1712). It included a famous schedule of the increase in the price of wheat following upon a reduction in the wheat harvest, which was said to be based on observations of over a century or more: whatever the size of the reduction in the harvest, the price always increases more than proportionately, thus suggesting not only that the demand curve for wheat is negatively-inclined but that (to use modern language) the demand for wheat is inelastic. This relationship, known as Gregory King's Law, was familiar to Adam Smith and to all the English classical economists.

*Secondary Literature*
D.A.G. Waddell, 'Davenant, Charles', *International Encyclopedia of the Social Sciences*, vol. 4, ed. D.L. Sills (Macmillan Free Press, 1968).

# Dupuit, Jules (1804-1866)

Jules Dupuit is one of the many engineer-economists of the nineteenth century who made signal contributions to economics — others are Dionysius Lardner (1793-1859), Charles Ellet, Jr (1810-62) and Wilhelm Launhardt (q.v.). At one time he was thought to have worked largely in isolation, but recent research has shown that he was part of an earlier tradition at the École des Ponts et Chaussées (School of Bridges and Mines) in Paris, applying economic analysis to the pricing of public works. He was born in Northern Italy in 1804 but was educated in France. He studied at both the École Polytechnique and École des Ponts et Chaussées, served in the Corps des Ponts et Chaussées and became its Inspector-General in 1855.

In a number of path-breaking articles, such as 'On Tolls and Transport Charges' (1842), 'On the Measurement of the Utility of Public Works' (1844), and 'De l'utilité et de sa mésure' (1853), he raised the question how to justify the public construction of roads, canals and bridges in terms of its social benefits. He realised that this social benefit was greater than that indicated by the price actually paid for the service, in as much as most people would be willing to pay more for the service than they actually do pay. Tacitly employing the concept of perfect price discrimination, he constructed a downward-sloping marginal utility curve for the collective good by supposing that the state charges the maximum toll for each additional unit of service, lowering the toll by small steps as it offers additional units. In this way, total receipts from the service are equal to the whole area under the marginal utility curve and the total utility derived from the existence of the facility is likewise equal to the whole area under the marginal utility curve. The 'relative utility', however, or what Marshall called 'consumers' surplus', is equal to the excess of total utility over marginal utility, multiplied by the number of units of the service supplied. If one identifies the marginal utility curve with a demand curve — a leap of thought that never troubled Dupuit — 'relative utility' is measured by the roughly triangular area under the demand curve above the price–quantity rectangle. Similarly, starting from any existing toll for a public facility, a reduction in the toll results in a net gain of consumer surplus, being the total gain to consumers of the price reduction minus the loss of receipts to the state. Without drawing a supply curve, Dupuit went on to consider the producer surplus from selling the services of bridges at a uniform price per unit as the excess of money receipts over the aggregate marginal costs of the industry. The total benefits of the bridge to the community, he realised, is the sum of consumer and producer surpluses.

When we compare Dupuit's papers with Marshall's refinement of the same concepts, we are struck by the inadequacies of Dupuit's discussion. Apart from the identification of utility and demand and the tacit assumption that the consumer surpluses of different persons are additive, Dupuit appeared to deny that public works are capable of generating external or spillover benefits to others than the consumers of such services. Nevertheless, Dupuit planted the concept of a negatively-inclined demand curve independently (so far as we know) of Cournot (q.v.) and was certainly the first writer to employ utility theory to develop some elementary theorems in the cost-benefit analysis of public projects.

Jevons (q.v.) was unaware of Dupuit's work when he wrote his *Theory of Political Economy* (1871) and even Marshall (q.v.) claimed to have known nothing of Dupuit when he developed his own ideas some time in the 1870s. Both writers, however, later paid ample tribute to Dupuit's pioneering efforts.

*Secondary Literature*
W.S. Vickrey, 'Dupuit, Jules', *International Encyclopedia of the Social Sciences,* vol. 4, ed. D.L. Sills (Macmillan Free Press, 1968); R.B.Ekelund, Jr and R.F. Hébert, 'Public Economics at the École des Ponts et Chaussées 1830-1850', *Journal of Public Economics,* 2, July 1973.

# Edgeworth, Francis Ysidro (1845-1926)

Francis Ysidro Edgeworth was an economists' economist: almost the whole of his literary output was addressed to his fellow economists, taking the form of elegant technical essays on taxation, monopoly and duopoly pricing, the pure theory of international trade and the theory of index numbers. He did venture one larger-scale work, *Mathematical Psychics* (1881), a quantitative application of utilitarian ethics to economic life, and its flowery and slightly old-fashioned prose, full of Greek quotations and passing allusions to classical literature, suggests a wider audience. In fact, however, it was a deep and elusive work, which even went over the heads of many of his colleagues. Its use of indifference curves caught on only slowly and that of the 'core' of an exchange economy has only recently attracted attention as a result of developments in games theory. His exposition was terse and obscure at the best of times and his personality was retiring, with the result that most of his ideas were and still are continually being rediscovered by those who arrive at them in their own way. Marshall (q.v.) for example, was decisively influenced by Edgeworth on a number of technical points and yet

Edgeworth always deferred to Marshall as the master at whose feet he sat. When the *Economic Journal* was founded in 1891 as the organ of the Royal Economic Society, Edgeworth became its editor, a task he carried on for 35 years. He was usually perfectly fair but on a number of occasions he did reject valuable articles which he thought might impugn the reputation of the Cambridge School headed by Marshall.

Edgeworth's contributions to economics are legion, and there is space to mention only a few of them: he was the first to define the laws of diminishing returns in terms of the decline of the *marginal* product of a variable factor, whereas everyone before him right back to Malthus (q.v.) and Ricardo (q.v.) always defined it in terms of the decline of the *average* product; he was the first to define a 'generalised utility function', the utility of a good depending not just on the quantity consumed of that good but on the quantities of all other goods consumed by the individual, thus bringing substitutability and complementarity between goods squarely within the purview of utility theory; he was also the first to introduce indifference curves, the loci of combinations of two goods conveying equal total utility (drawn upside down as compared with the way they are nowadays drawn), as well as the 'contract curve', the locus of tangency points of the indifference curves of different individuals. But his most beautiful contribution is the theory of the core of an exchange economy. Imagine a set of traders with certain initial holdings of goods setting out to exchange goods before there is anything like a market; these traders may act alone or they may form blocs or coalitions to improve their initial situation; everything is allowed but each and every trader must agree voluntarily to any final outcome from trade. Edgeworth then shows that in the limit, as the number of traders increases, the 'core' of the final distribution of goods resulting from unanimously agreed upon trade is the same as the set of equilibrium allocations of goods that would result from a price system under perfect competition. This insight has proved valuable to modern games theorists in proving the existence of general equilibrium à la Walras.

Edgeworth was born in 1845 in Ireland and educated at home until he was old enough to enter Trinity College, Dublin. From Trinity College he went to Balliol College, Oxford where he graduated in letters in 1865. After practising law in London and lecturing on English literature at Bedford College, London, he took up a post as lecturer in logic at King's College, London, followed by a professorship in political economy at King's in 1885. In 1891 he became Drummond Professor of Political Economy at Oxford, which then as now carried with it a non-teaching fellowship at All Souls College, Oxford. He retired in 1922 but went on editing *The Economic Journal* jointly with John Maynard Keynes (q.v.) until his death in 1926 at the age of 81.

Apart from *Mathematical Psychics*, he published a youthful book on ethics and a brief work on the measurement of utility, *Metrike* (1887), as well as several lectures on the economics of war during and immediately after the First World War. He collected his major essays and reviews together in a three-volume publication, *Papers Relating to Political Economy* (1925). Of all the great economists in this book, he is (apart from Bernoulli and Slutsky) the only one to have made original contributions to mathematical statistics. In the first programme of his television series, *The Age of Uncertainty* (1981), John Kenneth Galbraith remarked that 'all races have produced notable economists, except the Irish'. Had he forgotten the names of Cantillon, Longfield, Cairnes, Leslie and particularly Edgeworth?

*Secondary Literature*
J.M. Keynes, *Essays in Biography* (Macmillan, 1933); C. Hildreth, 'Edgeworth, Francis Ysidro', *International Encyclopedia of the Social Sciences*, vol. 4, ed. D.L. Sills (Macmillan Free Press, 1968); J. Creedy, 'F.Y. Edgeworth', *Pioneers of Modern Economics in Britain*, D.P. O'Brien and J.R. Presley (eds.) (Macmillan, 1981).

# Ely, Richard Theodore (1854-1943)

Richard Ely was not an original thinker or striking expositor but he was a great teacher and organiser who played a central role in the professionalisation of American economics in the last quarter of the nineteenth century. Born in up-state New York in 1854, he graduated from Columbia College in 1876. There was no such thing at the time in America as graduate work in economics and so, like John Bates Clark (q.v.), Ely decided to spend the next four years at the University of Heidelberg studying under Karl Knies (1821-98), a leading member of the 'older' Historical School. Upon returning to America in 1881, Ely joined the staff at the newly-founded Johns Hopkins University and rapidly produced a number of controversial books on socialism, the labour movement and fiscal reform. In a characteristic work, *The Past and Present of Political Economy* (1884), he drew a sharp contrast betweem the old orthodoxy of Ricardo and Mill, which he totally repudiated with the exception of Ricardo's theory of differential rent, and a 'new' political economy, involving an explicit ethical commitment to the welfare of the poor and increased use of inductive fact-gathering. At the University of Wisconsin, to which he had moved in 1892, his participation in reform movements led to a public denouncement for preaching strikes and socialism. After a widely-publicised inquiry, the regents of the university exonerated him and issued a declaration in favour of academic freedom that was to become a landmark in the history of American higher education.

Some years earlier in 1885, Ely and other advocates of the 'new' political economy founded the American Economic Association (AEA) with Ely becoming its first Secretary. At first, the Association, like the German *Verein für Sozialpolitik* (Union for Social Policy), was less a professional association of economists than an instrument of reform promoting a particular view of the social role of economists. But by the time Ely resigned his secretaryship in 1892, the AEA had acquired its present stance of academic neutrality, rapidly increasing its membership to embrace more or less all of the academic and business economists working in the United States. Although Ely served as president of the AEA from 1900 to 1902, his subsequent activity was largely confined to the state of Wisconsin. He became increasingly active in religious reform organisations, such as the Christian Social Union, and his popular elementary texts, *An Introduction to Political Economy* (1889) and *Outlines of Economics* (1893), struggled to show that the 'new' political economy was fully consonant with the social and political outlook of enlightened Christians. At the University of Wisconsin he gathered around him a host of ex-pupils such as Commons (q.v.) , Frederick Turner and Edward Ross, all of whom were later to make a name for themselves in economics, history and sociology, and he forged links with the state government of Wisconsin, led by the renowned progressive Governor, Robert La Follette. Ely's department of economics, political science and history became internationally famous for its work on labour legislation, land economics and public utility pricing, a reputation which survives to this day. Ely's fascinating autobiography, *Ground Under Our Feet* (1938) was written at the age of 84, capping a career of over 60 books and hundreds of articles. He died five years later in 1943.

*Secondary Literature*
A.W. Coats, 'Ely, Richard T.', *International Encyclopedia of the Social Sciences*, vol. 5, ed. D.L. Sills (Macmillan Free Press, 1968).

# Fetter, Albert (1863-1949)

Frank Albert Fetter was the leading exponent in the United States of the 'Austrian' point of view in economics. This did not mean that he slavishly adopted all of the ideas of the Austrian economists — on the contrary, he was a remorseless critic of Böhm-Bawerk's (q.v.) theory of interest — but that he attempted consistently to apply the subjective approach to all economic questions, deriving every aspect of the pricing process from the preferences of consumers.

Born in rural Indiana in 1863, he graduated from the University of Indiana in 1891, followed by an MA from Cornell University in 1892. Following in the footsteps of John Bates Clark (q.v.), Ely (q.v.) and so many other American economists of the period, he then went abroad to do graduate work, receiving his PhD from the University of Halle, Germany in 1894. Returning to America, he taught successively at Indiana (1895-98), Stanford (1898-1901), Cornell (1901-11) and finally Princeton (1911-33). He served as president of the American Economic Association in 1912 and was awarded the Carl Menger Medal of the Austrian Economic Society in 1927. He lived until the age of 86 and his last article appeared a few months before his death in 1949.

Although he published two treatises, *The Principles of Economics* (1904) and *Economic Problems* (1915), as well as a widely-read book on trust-busting, *Masquerade of Monopoly* (1931), his major contributions appeared in a long series of journal articles on interest and rent, stretching over a period of over 30 years from 1900 to 1937. Fetter's theory of interest laid exclusive emphasis on positive time-preference or what he called 'time-valuation' as the only cause of the payment of interest, and he never tired of attacking what he regarded as backsliding to a productivity theory of interest. Böhm-Bawerk had indeed tried to have his cake and to eat it too with his three grounds for interest. Fisher (q.v.), in *The Rate of Interest* (1907), had argued in general equilibrium terms for the determin-ation of the rate of interest in terms of both thrift and productivity, that is, a combination of Böhm-Bawerk's three grounds, the first two providing an explanation of the supply of capital and the latter doing as much for the demand for capital. But Fetter would have none of this: again and again he insisted that the fact that capital is physically productive cannot account for the rate of interest as a premium on present goods or discount on future goods; all it does is to make it possible to supply more goods in the future than are now available from the same volume of resources but if time-preferences were zero — if we were really indifferent about the date at which goods are available — this could not by itself create a premium on present goods. True enough, but the obverse does not follow — if capital were not physically productive, time-preference alone would not be capable of creating a positive rate of interest.

Despite hammering away at his time-valuation rate of interest in some 30 articles, Fetter never succeeded in persuading the rest of the profession that he had a case. The matter was finally laid to rest when Fisher updated and revised his earlier *Rate of Interest* into *The Theory of Interest* (1930), displaying the interest rate as the outcome of the interaction between 'the willingness principle' and 'the investment opportunity principle'. Fisher was content to show that individuals in receipt of income try to alter the successive amounts of income available for consumption at various times by means of saving and borrowing; the resultant price that is paid for income now rather than for income later is the rate of interest; it is usually positive but that is only because the amount of borrowing normally exceeds the amount of saving.

When Fetter was not attacking Böhm-Bawerk and Fisher, he was criticising Marshall (q.v.) whose *Principles of Economics* (1890) seemed to him to preserve all the worst outdated theories of the classical economists. He objected, in particular to Marshall's obeisance to the Ricardian notion that rent is a unique return to land as a non-reproducible factor in fixed supply. First, he rejected the notion that there was anything special about land as a factor of production; and, secondly, he insisted (along with John Bates Clark (q.v.) and Philip Wicksteed (q.v.)) that the concept of rent as an intramarginal surplus to a fixed factor of production is perfectly applicable to all the factors of production: rent, as he said, is the amount paid for the separable use of any durable agent entrusted by the owner to a borrower for a given period of time. He went on to argue that Ricardian rent theory always implied the Ricardian conclusion that rent is price-determined rather than price-determining, which in turn is based on the view that price in the long run is determined by 'real costs' of production. But like the true Austrian that he was, Fetter rejected any and all real-cost theories, insisting, after Wieser (q.v.), that costs of production are simply alternative opportunities forgone and hence dependent on the entire pattern of demand for consumer goods.

Although Fetter's critique on the contradictory rent theories found in Marshall's *Principles* hit the mark, it is true that he showed little appreciation for Marshall's continued interest in the dynamic forces that govern the growth of population and the accumulation of capital, which largely account for the strange mixture of comparative statics and economic dynamics in Marshall's *Principles.* Here too, Fetter was a true heir of the Austrian tradition, which invariably assumed a fixed supply of labour and capital and then focused the entire analysis on the question of the efficiency with which these fixed supply are allocated among alternative uses.

*Secondary Literature*
M.N. Rothbard, 'Introduction' to F.A. Fetter, *Capital, Interest, and Rent. Essays in the Theory of Distribution* (Sheed Andrews & McMeel, 1971).

# Fisher, Irving (1867-1947)

Irving Fisher was one of the greatest and certainly one of the most colourful American economists who ever lived. A writer and teacher of prodigious scope and power, his works are distinguished by their unusual clarity of exposition, the ideas being typically set out verbally, algebraically and geometrically with all the complications carefully deferred until the essential principles are established. In addition, they run the entire gamut from mathematical economics to mathematical statistics, from the theory of value and prices to the theory of capital and interest. The now familiar distinction between stocks and flows is almost entirely due to his masterpiece on *The Nature of Capital and Income* (1906). The modern theory of the real rate of interest stems from his *Theory of Interest* (1930), a revised version of an earlier book on *The Rate of Interest* (1907). His famous 'ideal index' of prices — a geometric mean of two indices in which prices are weighted by their base year and end-year quantities — was defended in *The Making of Index Numbers* (1922). Finally, *The Purchasing Power of Money* (1911) restated the old quantity theory of money in modern dress. In reading these books today one needs continually to remind oneself of the dates at which they were published because they read as if they were recently written and require almost no revision of any kind to accomodate later theoretical developments.

Irving Fisher was born in up-state New York in 1867 and took his BA in mathematics at Yale University in 1898, followed by a PhD in economics in 1901. For three years he taught mathematics at Yale, switching to the economics department in 1895 after establishing an international reputation with his startlingly original PhD thesis, *Mathematical Investigations in the Theory of Value and Prices* (1892), which contained, among other things, the design of a machine to illustrate general equilibrium in a multi-market economy. He remained at Yale until his retirement in 1935. He was director of Remington Rand (now the Rand Corporation), a founder and president of the Eugenics Research Association, the Stable Money League, the Econometric Society, the American Statistical Association and simply dozens of other companies and agencies.

The purpose of *The Nature of Capital and Income* was to provide a theoretical foundation for the science of accounting, both at the level of the individual enterprise and at that of the economy as a whole. Fisher defined 'capital' as any stock of wealth that yields a flow of services over time — land, machines, buildings, raw materials, natural resources, human skills — and 'income' as the surplus of that flow of services above those necessary to maintain and replace the stock of wealth. The link between capital and income is the rate of interest because the value of capital is nothing but the present value of the future flow of income from it, discounted, that is, at the going rate of interest. It is not capital that confers value on income but rather income that confers value on capital because economic activity is essentially forward looking. It follows that, strictly speaking, capital is the only factor of production, that all distributive income consists of interest, wages being merely the interest payments on the stock of human capital, and that national income consists entirely of consumption expenditure. It is evident that national income accounting eventually rejected the Fisherian notion of ignoring investment in the measurement of national income. Nevertheless, virtually every other element of this most brilliant of Fisher's many brilliant books has entered without qualification into modern economics.

*The Purchasing Power of Money* (1911), dedicated to Simon

Newcomb (q.v.), was organised around the 'equation of exchange': $MV + M^1V^1 = PT$, with M and $M^1$ standing for the stock of notes, currency and bank deposits in circulation, V and $V^1$ for their respective velocities of circulation, P for the level of prices (the reciprocal of 'the purchasing power of money') and T for the total volume of transactions, all variables being defined for an identical time period, say, one year. Fisher was fully aware that the quantity *theory* of money had frequently been defended by its advocates as a truism rather than a theory. As a theoretical proposition, PT is only brought into equality with $MV + M^1V^1$ by a transmission mechanism linking an increase in the stock of M or $M^1$ to the flow of expenditure. Thus, in what Fisher called 'transition periods' between two comparative static equilibria, the right-hand side of the equation of exchange is not equal to the left-hand side, and indeed it is this possibility of an inequality between them that allows us to speak of a quantity *theory* of money. He was always aware that much of the theory in question is hidden behind the quantity equation of exchange — for example, the role of the rate of interest in the so-called 'indirect mechanism' linking money to prices as distinct from the 'direct mechanism' which operates through the real value of the cash balances normally held by economic agents. Despite the fact that the book contains virtually no errors either of omission or commission, and despite Fisher's pioneering efforts to quantify the parameters of the equation of exchange, the balance of argument in the book was such as to suggest an intransigent defence of the quantity theory of money, minimising the weight of transition periods to the point where they practically disappear from view. The book never enjoyed the unqualified success of most of his other works and it failed altogether in resolving the great controversy over what was meant by the quantity theory of money. Even modern monetarists have found it necessary to start all over again in defining the problem of just how an increase in the supply of money affects prices.

Fisher's *Theory of Interest* made no claims to say anything new and its greatness as a book lies wholly in its outstanding pedagogic qualities. It was dedicated to 'the memory of John Rae and of Eugen von Böhm-Bawerk, who laid the foundations upon which I have endeavored to build', and amounted to the demonstration that the real rate of interest is determined by both demand and supply, by the demand for production and consumption loans on the one hand and the supply of savings on the other. Most of the book is devoted to theory of the determination of the real rate of interest but the distinction between the real and the money rate of interest is made at the outset of the volume and is taken up again in the closing chapters.

Three of Fisher's works were devoted to projects for monetary reform: *Stabilizing the Dollar* (1920), *Stamp Scrip* (1933) and *100% Money* (1935); and two others, *Booms and Depressions* (1932) and *Inflation* (1933), were designed to strengthen his proposals for monetary reform. *Stabilizing the Dollar* contained an ingenious scheme for stabilising the purchasing power of money under a convertible gold standard by varying the official price of gold inversely with an index of prices, a system which could be adopted by one country combined with a flexible exchange rate for its currency or by all countries operating with fixed exchange rates. *Booms and Depressions* and *Stamp Scrip* took up the old proposal of Silvio Gesell (1862-1930) of stamping notes each month at a post office without which stamp the notes cease to be legal tender; the object of the scheme was to discourage the hoarding of notes, which it would certainly succeed in doing if it was also extended to cover bank deposits, a point which Fisher quickly noted. *100% Money* was intended to show that business cycles are largely due to bank credit and the power of banks in a fractional reserve system to 'create money' at will. The solution was to insist on 100 per cent reserve backing for deposits held; depositors would pay charges to cover the cost of managing their deposit accounts and banks would then have to make loans with funds borrowed in the capital market. Fisher candidly admitted that the idea was as old as banking itself; in particular, he gave credit to a group of economists from the University of Chicago, including Henry Simons, Frank Knight and Paul Douglas, who had advocated a similar scheme only two years earlier; it is still supported by many economists today, principally Milton Friedman.

Having made a private fortune early in life from the invention of a visible card-index file system, Fisher spent most of it in later years compaigning for a great number of causes to which he was passionately devoted, including prohibition, preventive medicine, eugenics, world peace and 100 per cent deposit reserves. His enormous influence on the American economic profession (not to mention his private wealth) effectively came to an end in 1929: not only did he fail to predict the Wall Street crash but afterwards he went on insisting month after month that the upturn to a new boom was just around the corner. Nevertheless, he went on publishing until the age of 75, dying five years later in 1947.

Fisher never founded a school. He had many pupils but few disciples. Many of his later works were unfavourably received perhaps because the aura of a crank increasingly began to surround Fisher's name. It was difficult for fellow economists not to suspect the ideas of a man whose book on *How to Live: Rules for Healthful Living Based on Modern Science* (1915) had become a national best-seller, translated into 10 languages. Possibly if Fisher had been more cautious about the Great Depression, his reputation would not have suffered its extraordinary eclipse in the last two decades of his life.

*Secondary Literature*
J.A. Schumpeter, 'Irving Fisher 1867-1947', *Ten Great Economists from Marx to Keynes* (Oxford University Press, 1948); M. Allais 'Fisher, Irving', *International Encyclopedia of the Social Sciences,* vol. 5, ed. D.L. Sills (Macmillan Free Press, 1968).

# Galiani, Ferdinando (1727-1787)

Galiani was a leading critic of physiocracy and a major eighteenth-century proponent of the subjective theory of value. Born in the Kingdom of Naples in Italy, he received a classical education, took religious orders, but entered government service and spent almost a decade of his life in France as Secretary of the Neapolitan embassy in Paris. The remainder of his life was spent in Naples where he directed a number of government offices on behalf of the King. He wrote on a variety of subjects and corresponded with many of the leading intellectuals of the day: Diderot, Voltaire, Turgot and particularly Giambattista Vico, the great Italian historian and philosopher of history. It was from Vico that he derived his lifelong dislike of Cartesian rationalism – the attempt to deduce eternal truths valid in all ages and at all places solely from the power of reasoning and a few *a priori* postulates – choosing instead to stress the evolutionary development of society from which only historically relative truths can be derived.

At the age of 24, Galiani produced a remarkable, slender book, entitled *Della Moneta (On Money)* (1751), which was intended to form part of a general treatise of political science but which he never lived to write. Apart from some notable chapters on monetary theory, clearly based on a close reading of Locke's economic tracts, it contained some brilliant pages on the utility theory of value (admittedly only a sketch) with hints of diminishing marginal utility and even the price elasticity of demand. Galiani's treatment was based on the conflict between utility and scarcity, the subjective relationship between man's preferences and the availability of external goods, which had been at the core of value theory from the time of Aristotle. This conflict was fundamental to the theories of many of his predecessors but Galiani went beyond them in elaborating the concept of utility as 'the aptitude of a good to make us happy' that is, as an element that resides in our constantly changing preferences and not in the goods themselves. Turgot (q.v.) shared Galiani's view about the subjective nature of value and commended his book. A few decades earlier Law (q.v.) had also taught a subjective theory of value and in 1776, the year of the publication of *The Wealth of Nations,* Etienne Condillac (1714-80) in France similarly endorsed it. None of these four writers developed the utility theory of value into a fully-fledged price theory, failing in particular to illustrate its application to a variety of pricing problems. Nevertheless, when Adam Smith (q.v.) distinguished use value and exchange value and dismissed the former as a necessary but not sufficient reason for a good to have value, a reflection of physiological need rather than subjective preference, he successfully delayed the acceptance of a subjective theory of value for 100 years. No wonder that Galiani's *Della Moneta* was never translated in English and indeed remains to this day untranslated except in selected passages.

Twenty years after *Della Moneta,* Galiani produced a scintillating critique of the doctrines of Quesnay (q.v) and his School of Physiocracy, *Dialogues sur le commerce des blés (Dialogues on the Trade in Corn)* (1770). He attacked the physiocratic belief in the free trade of corn, not so much in general as on historical grounds as a policy that was inexpedient for the France of his day. His rejection of the confident dogmatism of the physiocrats and in particular their belief in universally applicable principles, showed the influence of Vico more than anything else he had previously written.

*Secondary Literature*
P.R. Toscano, 'Galiani, Ferdinando', *International Encyclopedia of the Social Sciences,* vol. 6, ed. D.L. Sills (Macmillan Free Press, 1968).

# George, Henry (1839-1897)

Who nowadays reads Henry George's *Progress and Poverty* (1879)? Not many because it is an old-fashioned book steeped in the terminology of Adam Smith, Ricardo and J.S. Mill. In its day, however, it was the most widely read of all books on economics; in the English-speaking world in the last quarter of the nineteenth century it was not Marx but Henry George who was the talking-point of all debates among fiery young intellectuals. George's lecture tours in Britain in the 1880s created a sensation; he was lionised wherever he went and filled the Free Trade Hall, Manchester and the Albert Hall, London. He narrowly missed being elected Mayor of New York in 1886, and public meetings to promote his idea of a 'single tax' followed the publication of *Progress and Poverty* in all the principal cities of America. The single-tax movement slowed down after 1900 but not before capturing some municipal statute books in America, Canada and Australia. To this day George still has disciples scattered around the world, particularly in Australia and New Zealand, who generally favour 'site value taxation' as the kernel of Georgism.

The essence of George's argument was entirely unoriginal, resting as it did on the old Ricardian theory of differential rent, and that is precisely why it was so effective. Ricardo had taught that land being a non-reproducible resource, fixed in supply and completely specialised in the production of crops, 'rent does not enter into price'; it is an intramarginal return to farmers who cultivate land of superior fertility. Rent being a 'free gift of Nature', it followed that rent was eminently suitable for taxation or even appropriation by the state since this had no effect on the marginal cost of producing agricultural goods. It was James Mill (1773-1836) who first drew the obvious conclusion from Ricardian rent theory that all 'future increments of unearned rent' could be taxed away without serious harm. Ricardo (q.v.) was not happy with this proposal but it remained an academic question in his lifetime. But with the publication of J.S. Mill's *Principles of Political Economy* (1848), a section of which reproduced his father's arguments, and the subsequent formation of the Land Tenure Reform Association under Mill's leadership, the idea caught on. All that George did in *Progress and Poverty* was to go a little further in proposing to confiscate all rents past and present and to claim that this would abolish all poverty and economic crises, the latter being simply the result of speculation in land values. This would be a 'single tax' — a phrase that George only adopted after publishing *Progress and Poverty* — because he thought that its proceeds would be sufficient to finance all government expenditure. His proposal was widely misunderstood as advocating the nationalisation of land. In point of fact, George only proposed to tax pure ground rent, exempting the returns from site improvements. In short, his single tax was designed to reduce the price of land as mere space to zero, leaving untouched the rentals of property on the land; it would put all property on the same basis irrespective of its location.

George was born in 1839 in Philadelphia. Leaving school at the age of 13, he tried his hand as a sailor, printer, publisher and journalist and, after years of dire poverty, settled in California where conditions soon convinced him that landlords were the passive recipients of an 'unearned increment' produced by the growth of population and technical progress.

When the success of his book turned him into a figure of worldwide fame, he returned to the eastern seaboard and launched the single-tax movement. During the 1890s, he left the advocacy of the single tax largely in the hands of others and devoted himself to writing and lecturing. He published two more books and died in 1879 having failed to complete *The Science of Political Economy* — an attempt to expound his doctrines in more up-to-date language — the book was published posthumously (1906-11).

All the leading economists of the turn of the century — Marshall (q.v.), Francis Walker (1840-97), Seligman (q.v.) and Ely (q.v.) — wrote extensive critiques of his ideas, not all of which were fair to the real merits of his case. But George's exuberant style, his repeated blending of positive and normative propositions, and his downright misconceptions about certain technical economic concepts, made it difficult for economists to treat him fairly; the very qualities in George that appealed to the general public alienated the sympathies of professional economists. Still, as Milton Friedman put it in 1978: 'In my opinion the least bad tax is the property tax on the unimproved value of land, the Henry George argument of many, many years ago.'

*Secondary Literature*
C.A. Barker, 'George, Henry', *International Encyclopedia of the Social Sciences,* vol. 6, ed. D.L. Sills (Macmillan Free Press, 1968); R.V. Anderson (ed.), *Critics of Henry George* (Fairleigh Dickinson University Press, 1979).

# Gossen, Hermann Heinrich (1810-1858)

If Hermann Heinrich Gossen had never existed, a Marxist would have invented him: an outline of an economic theory based entirely on utilitarianism; a total conviction that ruthless selfishness harmonises private and public interests in accordance with the wisdom of the Creator; a defence of private property (except in land) as a further manifestation of the Divine design; and the total rejection of anything and everything that smacks of communism and socialism, sum up his social message. The only fly in the ointment, however, is the date of publication of Gossen's only book, portentously entitled *Development of the Laws of Human Relationships and the Rules of Human Action Derived Therefrom* (1854), at which time Marx had published nothing on economics except an attack on Proudhon.

Gossen was born in the Rhineland in 1810, the son of a tax-collector. He was educated in a number of German towns and entered the University of Bonn in 1829, graduating in law and public administration in 1831. He continued his studies at Berlin and Bonn and entered government service in 1834. He seems to have disliked his bureaucratic duties and, after repeated failures to be promoted, resigned his office in 1847. Little is known of his private life after that. Bitterly disappointed at the poor reception of *Development of the Laws of Human Relationships* which, he had claimed, would do for economics what Copernicus had done for astronomy, he recalled all the unsold copies of the book and destroyed them. In consequence, when Jevons (q.v.) discovered the book in 1878, he and Walras (q.v.) only managed to trace a few copies still remaining. Walras was amazed to see that Gossen had not only formulated the principle of diminishing marginal utility and graphed it (with time along the X axis) but had also grasped the distinction, which Dupuit (q.v.) never did, between a negatively-inclined marginal utility curve and a negatively-inclined demand curve. Similarly, Jevons was astonished to find that Gossen had formulated a theory of the marginal disutility of labour strikingly similar to his own, including a virtual replica of his own diagram of the equalisation of the marginal disutility of work and the marginal utility of the product of work. Both of them were particularly struck by what soon came to be called Gossen's 'second law': 'Man obtains the maximum of life pleasure if he allocates his earned money between the various pleasures in such a manner that the last atom of money spent for each pleasure offers the same amount of pleasure.'

It is not easy to see who influenced Gossen. He may have read Adam Smith and Bentham but as he cites no sources the evidence for these influences is circumstantial. It is clear that he had studied Karl Heinrich Rau's *Lehrbuch der politischen Ökonomie (Manual of Political Economy)* (1826-37) and Rau (q.v.) was a follower of Smith. Nevertheless, he went so far beyond any of his sources that he has absolutely no equal for originality in the entire history of economic thought. He paid a high price, however, for his originality and his total isolation from other economists and from the economic literature of his times. The book was poorly organised without division into parts or chapters; it was written in a wooden and frequently preposterous style; and it abounded in algebraic formulae and lengthy arithmetical examples — not to mention 24 diagrams, at a time when there was still a deep antipathy to the mathematical treatment of social questions. That it was neglected is hardly surprising; even if it had been better written and more easily available, it was published at the wrong time and in the wrong country!

*Secondary Literature*
H.W. Spiegel, 'Gossen, Hermann Heinrich', *International Encyclopedia of the Social Sciences,* vol. 6, ed. D.L. Sills (Macmillan Free Press, 1968); N. Georgescu-Roegen, 'Introduction', *The Laws of Human Relations by H.H. Gossen* (MIT Press, 1983).

# Hilferding, Rudolf (1877-1941)

Eight years after Böhm-Bawerk (q.v.) published his trenchant attack on Marxian economics in *The Close of the Marxian System* (1896), Rudolf Hilferding, a German Marxist and prominent leader of the German Social Democratic Party, wrote the official reply entitled *Böhm-Bawerk's Criticism of Marx* (1904). Hilferding's work was a dogmatic defence of Marx in language taken almost directly from Marx and Engels. It was almost the first Marxist work to employ the unfortunate self-justifying argument that Marxian and bourgeois economics inhabit different 'paradigms' which make fruitful dialogue between them absolutely impossible. In other words, Böhm-Bawerk criticised Marx by his own standards and the only answer Hilferding offered was not to come to grips with Böhm-Bawerk's criticisms but instead to question his criteria.

It is not for this contribution that Hilferding is remembered, however. It is rather for his classic book, *Finance Capital* (1910), a highly original study of capitalism in the twentieth century, which sought to bring Marx up-to-date by placing monopoly and credit banking at the centre of the analysis. Hilferding depicted 'finance capital' as promoting cartels and other monopolistic restraints on competition among its industrial clients, while pressing for foreign investment outlets and inciting governments to imperialist rivalry. Nineteenth-century capitalism had stood for free trade but capitalism in its 'final stage' appealed to protective tariffs to enable domestic monopolists to charge high prices at home and to dump surpluses abroad, further strengthening the drive towards imperial expansion. The book, together with Hobson's (q.v.) *Imperialism* (1902), had a decisive influence on Lenin's *Imperialism the Highest Stage of Capitalism* (1916), the work which laid down the definitive version of the Marxist theory of imperialism. Lenin's definition of imperialism in terms of its five distinguishing features — monopolies, finance capital, the export of capital, international cartels and the territorial division of the world — was clearly derived from Hilferding's book with one or two elements borrowed from Hobson.

Hilferding's *Finance Capital* begins with a discussion of money and credit and represents one of the few attempts since Marx to develop and refine Marx's rather old-fashioned theory of money. After delineating the characteristics of 'credit money' (checking deposits as against coins and bank notes) Hilferding launched upon a discussion of the growing role of banks in the promotion of new enterprises, taking advantage of the increasing separation between ownership and control in joint stock companies. The close personal and organisational links between industrial and bank capital, marked by the ascendancy of bankers over industrialists, which Hilferding described as 'finance capital', undoubtedly characterised the economic development of Germany and Austria, but it is questionable whether it ever characterised the development of capitalism in any other countries. Thus, Hilferding's analysis was far from general and probably had little relevance for an understanding of economic trends outside Central Europe.

In the later chapters of his book, Hilferding discussed the role of economic crises and their relationship to the growing tendency towards imperialism. In his discussion of the Marxist theory of crises, Hilferding gave strong support to the 'disproportionality theory' — one of the two or three causes of economic crises mentioned by Marx in Volumes II and III of *Capital*. Marx had written down certain 'reproduction schema' representing the relationship between capital and consumer goods industries which had to be preserved if the capitalist system was to reproduce itself from year to year without breakdown. These equilibrium proportions between the two sets of industries were so strict, Marx argued, that capitalism was very likely to suffer from economic crises by violating them — hence, the 'disproportionality theory' of crises. Hilferding showed that the growth of monopolies and cartels made it even more likely that Marx's 'reproduction schema' would be violated. This argument attracted almost as much attention as Hilferding's theory of imperialism.

Rudolf Hilferding was born in 1877 in Vienna. He studied medicine at the University of Vienna and practised medicine for many years after obtaining his doctorate in 1901. Even as a medical student, however, he had taken an interest in economics and as soon as he graduated he began to contribute articles on economic subjects to *Die Neue Zeit*, the leading Marxist theoretical journal of that period, edited by Karl Kautsky (1854-1938), the doyen of Marxism after the death of Engels. He continued to lecture and write on socialism until the outbreak of the First World War, associating himself with the left-wing minority of the German Social Democratic Party who opposed the voting of war credits. After service on the Austrian front as a doctor during the war, he rejoined the Social Democratic Party in the early 1920s, became a German citizen, served as German Minister of Finance in two German governments in 1923 and 1929, and sat in the Reichstag from 1924 to 1933. After Hitler's coming to power, Hilferding went into exile, wandering all over Europe but ending up in 1940 in the unoccupied zone of France. Handed over to the Gestapo by the Vichy government, he died in captivity some time in 1941.

*Secondary Literature*
T. Bottomore, 'Introduction' to R. Hilferding, *Finance Capital* (Routledge & Kegan Paul, 1981).

# Hobson, John Atkinson (1858-1940)

John Hobson was all his life condemned as the great heretic: the advocate of an apparently fallacious theory of over-saving, a niggling critic of the orthodox theory of distribution, and a proponent of a theory of imperialism which was taken up by Lenin. And then in 1936 Keynes paid tribute in *The General Theory* to Hobson as anticipating his own theory that a society can, under some circumstances, save too large a proportion of its income, thrift then being a vice and not a virtue. Keynes was thinking principally of Hobson's first book, *The Physiology of Industry: Being an Exposure of Certain Fallacies in Existing Theories of Economics,* which he wrote together with A.F. Mummery, a businessman. As usual, however, Keynes was exaggerating because a close reading of the book does not suggest any anticipation of Keynes' own reasoning based on a distinction between planned saving and planned investment. Wedded to the old Adam Smith saving-is-spending theorem, Mummery and Hobson repeatedly defined saving to mean the same thing as investment. Like Malthus (q.v.) 70 years earlier, they held a peculiar version of the theory of under-consumption according to which there is too much saving and thus too much destruction of purchasing power at the very same time that the investment of these savings produces more capital goods that need purchasing power to be absorbed into productive employment: theirs is an under-consumption theory of the over-saving = over-investment type.

If we read the book sympathetically, we can discern an attempt at something like a Harrod–Domar growth model which the authors were unable to formulate. At any rate, there is continual reference (as there is in Malthus) to a vague notion of an optimal capital–labour ratio that cannot be exceeded if the economy is to stay on a viable growth path. There is no mention in this book of what was later to become an essential element in Hobson's under-consumption theory, namely, the unequal distribution of income which assigns a significant part of national income to low spenders and high savers in the upper tail of the income distribution. It make its first appearance in *The Problem of the Unemployed* (1896) and is prominent in his major work, *The Industrial System: An Inquiry into Earned and Unearned Income* (1909). But even in these works, Hobson continues to define saving as 'buying means of production', while denying the existence of hoarding as a normal occurrence in industrial societies. On the other hand, his advocacy of public works financed out of current taxation as a remedy to unemployment is clearly based on a comparison between the low marginal propensity to consume of the average taxpayer and the high marginal propensity to consume of the average beneficiary of public works spending. In short, without calling Hobson a true forerunner of Keynes it is true that there are hints of Keynes in almost everything that Hobson wrote.

*The Industrial System* also contained a wholesale condemnation of marginal productivity theory and the attempt to replace it by the concept of an 'unproductive surplus', an idea which bears a striking but unacknowledged resemblance to the recent book on *Monopoly Capital* (1966) by P. Baran and P.M. Sweezy. The problem with the notion of an 'unproductive surplus' over what is necessary to maintain the labour force and to provide for improvements and growth in the stock of both human and physical capital is of course where to draw the line. Hobson was full of suggestions for taxing away the surplus but, unfortunately, spoiled his analysis by candidly admitting the difficulties in practice of specifying precisely what portion of income is surplus. Nevertheless, one can trace in his many books a steady tendency to expand the concept of a disposable surplus — or rather to expand the sphere of appropriate government action beyond the 'surplus' category into the 'growth' and 'maintenance' categories. This was in part connected with his leaving the Liberal Party and joining the Labour Party in the early 1920s after which he drew closer to the interventionist style of thinking of the Fabians, supporting a widespread programme of nationalisation as the only lasting remedy to unemployment.

He was born in Derby in 1858 into a family that owned the local Liberal newspaper, thus assuring him of an adequate private income throughout his life. He studied classics at the University of Oxford, graduating in 1880. For some years he worked as a schoolmaster and from 1887 to 1897 he added to his income by acting as a university extension lecturer in both Oxford and London. Shortly after the publication of *The Physiology of Industry,* he lost both posts and even years later in his autobiography, *Confessions of an Economic Heretic* (1938), he blamed his dismissal on 'an Economics Professor who had read my book and considered it as equivalent to an attempt to prove the flatness of the earth'. As a matter of fact, the feeling of being an outsider, ridiculed by a dogmatic economic profession which does not tolerate dissent, is a constant theme of the autobiography. Oddly enough, there is absolutely no mention in *Confessions of an Economic Heretic* of Keynes' belated acknowledgement of the real merit of *The Physiology of Industry,* or for that matter of the Keynesian revolution which Hobson might have welcomed as a final vindication of his own views. But Hobson was 80-years-old when he wrote his autobiography and might perhaps be forgiven for not paying much attention to the latest developments in economic theory.

*Secondary Literature*
H.N. Brailsford, *The Life-work of J.A. Hobson* (Oxford University Press, 1948); R. Lekachman, 'Hobson, John A.', *International Encyclopedia of the Social Sciences,* vol. 6, ed. D.L. Sills (Macmillan Free Press, 1968).

# Hume,
# David
# (1711-1776)

If there is one economist before Adam Smith (q.v.) that some are tempted to place ahead of him in terms of analytical power, historical grasp and felicitous style, it is David Hume. However, he never wrote a systematic treatise on economics, confining himself to a series of essays on money, population and international trade, and of course the bulk of his writings were on philosophy, politics and history. Nevertheless, these essays, published as *Political Discourses* (1752), had such influence generally and in particular on his personal friend, Adam Smith, that they must rank among the major economic writings of the eighteenth century. Certainly, they have a sparkling quality that still makes them worth reading today.

Born in Scotland in 1711, Hume was educated at home and at the University of Edinburgh. After an unsuccessful attempt to work for a Bristol manufacturer, he left Britain for a protracted period of stay in France, having already completed his major work, *A Treatise of Human Nature* (1739). Apart from a brief period serving as a tutor to a Scottish nobleman, he spent the rest of his life in study. *Essays Moral and Political* (1741), *An Inquiry Concerning the Principles of*

*Morals* (1751) and *Political Discourses* (1752) established his reputation as a philosopher and *A History of England* (1754-62) did as much for his standing as a historian. Because of his profound scepticism about traditional Christian arguments in ethics and theology and his marked preference for the 'empirical method', a slight air of scandal surrounded all his views, such that when he died in the presence of Adam Smith and other friends, considerable pressure was exerted on them to admit that Hume had declared a belief in God and the after-life on his deathbed. Adam Smith resisted the pressure and denied that Hume had recanted his scepticism at the point of death.

Hume made three or perhaps four specific contributions to economic thought. The first was his statement of the so-called 'specie-flow mechanism', which constituted his answer to the mercantilist concern with the maintenance of a chronic surplus in the balance of payments. Employing the quantity theory of money, according to which the level of prices in a country vary directly with the supply of money and inversely with the volume of trade, Hume showed that an inflow of gold subsequent to a surplus of exports over imports will correct itself by raising domestic prices, thus discouraging exports and stimulating imports. In conditions of free trade, the balance of payments of each and every nation will in time achieve equilibrium, that is, an international distribution of specie in accordance with each country's level of economic development. For reasons still not fully understood, Adam Smith failed to mention that argument of Hume in his attack on mercantilist doctrine. Nevertheless, the specie-flow mechanism became an important element in the classical theory of free trade: it was expounded by Ricardo (q.v.), further elaborated by Senior (q.v.), and rehearsed once again by John Stuart Mill (q.v.).

The same cannot be said of Hume's advocacy of what we would now call the 'theory of creeping inflation'. To be sure, he denied that the absolute size of a country's money supply could make any difference to economic activity, but he conceded that a *gradual* increase in the money supply was capable of generating extra output and employment. The classical economists did their best to ignore this element in Hume's thinking because it conflicted with their war on all monetary panaceas, smacking, they thought, of the old mercantilist fallacies.

The third contribution is the notion that there is an inherent connection between the growth of political liberty in modern commercial societies and the individualism and political decentralisation brought about by the growth of commerce and manufacturing; in short, political freedom flows from economic freedom. To Adam Smith at any rate, this was so important a contribution that he cited it several times.

A final contribution was the famous proposition in *A Treatise of Human Nature* that, in modern language, 'you cannot deduce ought from is' — all the facts in the world cannot add up to a moral or ethical judgement. It is this philosophical clarification which lies behind the well-known distinction between positive and normative economics, which emerged explicitly as early as the 1830s in the writings of Senior.

*Secondary Literature*
E. Rotwein, 'Hume, David', *International Encyclopedia of the Social Sciences,* vol. 6, ed. D.L. Sills (Macmillan Free Press, 1968); 'Editor's Introduction', *David Hume: Writings on Economics,* ed. E. Rotwein (University of Wisconsin Press, 1955).

# Jevons, William Stanley (1835-1882)

William Stanley Jevons was one of the principal discoverers — or rather rediscoverers — of marginal utility theory, but he was also widely known in his own lifetime for his applied economic studies and his textbook on logic. In *The Coal Question* (1865), the book that made him famous, he treated coal as the essential resource for British industrial development and predicted its imminent exhaustion, the decline of Britain's industrial leadership and the rise of the USA as an industrial power. His other quantitative studies, collected posthumously in *Investigations in Currency and Finance* (1884), were concerned with seasonal and cyclical fluctuations in economic activity and included pioneer contributions to the technique of index numbers as well as a doomed attempt to trace business cycles to periodic variations in sunspot activity. His discovery of the mariginal utility concept, announced in a brief paper sent to the British Association in 1862 and published in 1866, was developed in some detail in *The Theory of Political Economy* (1871). Although the book provides only half of the entire field of microeconomics — the theory of consumer behaviour but not the theory of the firm — it, together

99

with the almost simultaneously published treatises of Menger (q.v.) and Walras (q.v.), must be considered as opening up a new period in economic theorising, marking what was later to be called the 'marginal revolution'.

It is hard to believe that Jevons had never read Lloyd, Longfield (q.v.) Dupuit (q.v.) Cournot (q.v.) and Gossen (q.v.) when he sat down to write *The Theory of Political Economy*, but so it was; the root of his inspiration was Bentham's 'felicific calculus' of pleasure and pain, supplemented by the works of Dionysius Lardner (1793-1859) and Fleeming Jenkin (1833-85), two British engineer-economists of the 1860s. It was only afterwards that he discovered how many forerunners there had been. The preface to the second edition of *The Theory of Political Economy* (1879), accompanied by a bibliography of early works on mathematical economics dating back to 1711, did much to teach the generation that came after him about the long history of utility theory and marginal analysis before 'the marginal revolution'.

Jevons was born in Liverpool in 1835 into a Unitarian family, the son of an engineer and iron merchant who had published a number of essays on economic and legal topics. After a year at University College School, London, he entered University College, London at the age of 16 to study chemistry and botany. His letters to his family in those early years already reveal a keen interest in social questions and a profound sense of mission in his life. The collapse of his father's business in the 1847 crisis forced him to interrupt his studies and to accept a post as assayer at the newly-established Mint in Sydney, Australia. He spent five years in Australia (1853-58), and it was there that he made his debut in print with articles on meteorology and railway pricing. Returning to England in 1859, he resumed his studies at University College, obtaining his BA in 1860 and his MA in 1862. In 1863 he took up his first academic post as tutor at Owens College, Manchester (now the University of Manchester), becoming professor of logic, moral philosophy and political economy in 1866. In 1876, he moved to London to a Chair in Political Economy at University College. He resigned this post because of ill-health in 1880. Two years later, he published a set of essays, on problems of economic policy, *The State in Relation to Labour* (1882) in which he roundly condemned the maxim of *laissez-faire*, opting for a purely pragmatic approach to government intervention. A few months later, at the age of 46, he was drowned while swimming, leaving behind him notes for a number of unfinished books, including parts of a *Principles of Economics* published posthumously by his son in 1905.

Jevons was very conscious of being a revolutionary attempting to overthrow 'the noxious influence of authority' of Mill and Ricardo. *The Theory of Political Economy* has marked iconclastic flavour and much of it is brilliantly written, and full of strikingly original passages. Nevertheless, its originality, and perhaps the haste with which it was written, produced an uneven quality in which many arguments are left incomplete. Thus, there is an extensive treatment of 'isolated' or barter exchange but market exchange is analysed by a sleight-of-hand and the law of diminishing marginal utility — or 'final degree of utility' as Jevons liked to call it — is in fact never employed to deduce a downward-sloping demand curve for commodities. Similarly, there is a famous discussion of the supply of labour in terms of the balance between the marginal disutility of labour and the marginal utility of its product; but the supply of capital is only treated sketchily and the role of firms in coordinating the factors of production is totally neglected. His famous tabular presentation of the determination of value clearly shows that he failed to grasp the mutual determination of values by both demand and supply:

> Cost of production determines supply;
> Supply determines final degree of utility;
> Final degree of utility determines value.

Jevons' book was not well received by his contemporaries: Cairnes (q.v.), Leslie (q.v.), Sidgwick (q.v.) and even Marshall (q.v.) gave it extremely cool reviews. Here was a 'revolution' that took over 20 years before it was recognised for what it was!

*Secondary Literature*
J.M. Keynes, *Essays in Biography* (Macmillan, 1933); T.W. Hutchison, 'Jevons, William Stanley', *International Encyclopedia of the Social Sciences*, vol. 8, ed. D.L. Sills (Macmillan Free Press, 1968); R.D. Collison Black, 'Introduction', *The Theory of Political Economy by W.S. Jevons* (Penguin Books, 1970).

# Jones, Richard (1790-1855)

Richard Jones was the first institutionalist critic of Ricardo and an historically-minded economist years before the emergence of the British and German Historical Schools. He was born in 1790 in Tunbridge Wells, and studied at the University of Cambridge, receiving his degree in 1819. At Cambridge, he became a friend of William Whewell, a philosopher and historian of science, and John Herschel, an astronomer and also historian of science, and there is some evidence that the three of them planned to revive Bacon's look-and-see method of inductive science in opposition to the deductive approach of Benthamite utilitarianism. After a brief spell as a clergyman, Jones turned to the study of economics, publishing his first and only completed work in 1831, entitled *An Essay on the Distribution of Wealth and on the Sources of Taxation, vol.1, Rent.* This led to his first academic post in 1833 at King's College, London. In 1835, he succeeded Malthus (q.v.) as professor of political economy at Haileybury College, operated by the East India Company. In the late 1840s he served as member of the UK Tithe Commission to reform the finances of the Church of England and may have had a hand in writing the final report. Apart from some pamphlets, he never published another work. His lectures and notes were published as *Literary Remains* (1859) by Whewell after his death in 1855.

It is clear from the opening pages of the *Essay* and from his *Literary Remains* that Jones saw himself as reconstructing the whole of economics on historical and evolutionary lines, creating what he called the 'Political Economy of Nations', an investigation of the structure of national economic systems in relation to changing forms of property relationships and social institutions. In fact, he failed to carry this ambitious programme beyond the field of rent theory. Rejecting Ricardo's method of basing the theory of rent on the prevailing land tenure system of Britain and then endowing so limited a vision with universal applicability, Jones began with a detailed classification of rents in different parts of the world and at different periods of history, depending upon who owned the land, who worked the land, and how the produce is divided between owner and tenant. The laborious description of *metayer* rents in classical Greece and Rome, *ryot* rents in India, cottier rents in Ireland, serf rents in Eastern Europe, and peasant rents in Central Europe takes up three-quarters of the volume, after which the analysis of farmer rents in Britain is not actually very different from that of Ricardo. Throughout the book he showed an amazing reluctance to generalise, even denying that the Malthusian theory of population, which he upheld, yielded any predictable relationship between changes in wages and changes in population.

John Stuart Mill quoted Jones several times in his *Principles of Political Economy* (1848) and this despite the fact that Jones' protectionism and deep revulsion of anything smacking of birth control must have irritated Mill. Marx too heaped praise on Jones as a forerunner of his own economic interpretation of history. Nevertheless, Jones' book sunk into oblivion and even the later advocates of historical economics in Britain, such as Cliffe Leslie, Thorold Rogers and Walter Bagehot, hardly ever refer to Jones. It is only in modern times that he has enjoyed something of a comeback.

*Secondary Literature*
N.T. Chao, *Richard Jones: An Early English Institutionalist* (Columbia University Press, 1930); W.L. Miller, 'Richard Jones's Contribution to the Theory of Rent', *History of Political Economy,* 9 (3), Autumn 1977.

# Juglar, Clément (1819-1905)

If anyone can be singled out as first establishing the phenomenon of periodic business cycles as an indisputable fact of economic life it is Clément Juglar in his largely descriptive study *Des crises commerciales et de leur retour périodique en France, en Angleterre et aux Etats-Unis (Of Commercial Crises and Their Periodic Return in France, England and the United States)*(1862). Of course, he was not the first to notice swings in the level of economic activity or even to suspect that they were marked by regular periodicity. After all, John Stuart Mill's *Principles of Political Economy* (1848) contained a discussion of 'periodic revulsions in trade'. Nevertheless, the periodic regularity of economic fluctuations remained a disputable phenomenon and, in particular, such fluctuations were typically explained by random, exogenous shocks to the economic system in the form of harvest failures or wars. Juglar not only showed that cycles in the three countries can be traced in a number of indicators all varying in tandem — such as wholesale prices, interest rates, bank discounts and advances, the note circulation and bank deposits — but that they varied consistently from five to nine years, with an average duration of six years. Moreover, he insisted that they were inherent in the capitalist system, an endogenous manifestation of the behaviour of economic agents, aggravated by, but fundamentally independent of, climatic and political events.

Clément Juglar was born in 1819, the son of a physician who followed in his father's footsteps by becoming a doctor himself. His background in medicine led to an interest in demography and from demography to the fluctuations of prosperity and depression influencing birth and death rates. After publishing an article on commercial crises in 1856, he entered an essay contest on the subject of commercial crises and won the prize with his 1862 book. He expanded it in 1889 into an historical survey of business cycles in the three countries from 1803 to 1882. He made only a modest attempt to generalise from his data and certainly cannot be said to have provided a theory of business cycles. Ever since Schumpeter's *Business Cycles* (1939), it has become common practice to refer to the modern 7-11 year business cycle as Juglar cycles as distinct from the shorter 3-5 year Kitchin cycle and the much longer 45-60 year Kondratieff cycle.

Juglar taught statistics in Paris at the École Libre des Sciences Politique, founded a statistical society, was voted president of the Société d'Economie Sociale, and is said to have amassed a considerable fortune as a predictor of turning-points in business activity.

*Secondary Literature*
A. Marshall 'Juglar, Clément', *International Encyclopedia of the Social Sciences,* vol. 8, ed. D.L. Sills (Macmillan Free Press, 1968).

# Keynes, John Maynard (1883-1946)

John Maynard Keynes is unquestionably the major figure in twentieth-century economics, and perhaps the only one who can stand next to Adam Smith (q.v.) Ricardo (q.v.), Marshall (q.v.) and Walras (q.v.) in the economists' Hall of Fame. His reputation does not rest solely on the *General Theory of Employment, Interest and Money* (1936), which initiated the so-called Keynesian Revolution, but also on his other writings, most notably *A Treatise on Probability* (1921) and *A Treatise on Money* (1930), as well as on his influential advice to the British Treasury, his central role in the Bretton Woods Conference of 1944 which created the International Monetary Fund and the International Bank for Reconstruction and Development, and his prominent place in the cultural and intellectual life of his day as a journalist and speaker.

His trenchant criticism of the peace treaty of Versailles (1919) with Germany in *The Economic Consequences of the Peace* (1919) made him famous overnight and effectively undermined public support for the treaty. His early economic work, as exemplified in *Indian Currency and Finance* (1913) and *A Tract on Monetary Reform*

(1923), was in the Marshallian tradition, but during the crises of the 1920s he came increasingly to identify conservative economic policies as the cause of Britain's economic problems. From this beginning, he developed a new theory of income determination, grounded in the concept of the 'consumption function', the 'liquidity preference theory of interest', and the inflexibility of money wages. The consumption function referred to a relationship between total consumer spending and national income, such that consumer spending always rises less than proportionately with income, leaving a savings gap that only private or public investment can fill. The liquidity preference theory of interest emphasised the role of the interest rate as the reward for doing without the advantages of money as the only perfectly liquid asset. The inflexibility of money wages, the most controversial of Keynes' leading principles, was grounded on a realistic appreciation of labour markets in a modern industrial economy. Full employment, Keynes concluded, could be maintained in a capitalist economy but only if the government were willing to incur counter-cyclical budgetary deficits to offset the inbuilt tendency towards private over-saving.

It is difficult nowadays to appreciate the bombshell effect of the *General Theory*. A myth has grown up in subsequent years that it was Keynes' radical views on economic policy that constituted the break with orthodoxy. According to this myth, all economists and governments stood helpless in the face of the 1929 crash, advocating balanced budgets and a cut in money wages, or else letting things run their course; only Keynes held out a realistic and effective solution to the Great Depression. But a glance at the *General Theory* shows that it is a severely theoretical book and that no more than 25 pages of it are devoted to the policy implications of the argument: it is a book about disagreements in the theory of how the economy works and not about disagreements of what ought to be done about the economy. In fact, many orthodox economists years before Keynes had advocated public works, monetary expansion and counter-cyclical budgetary deficits to deal with the unemployment.

What was new about Keynes was, first of all, the tendency to work almost exclusively with aggregate, macroeconomic variables and to reduce the entire economy to three markets for goods, bonds and labour; secondly, to concentrate on the short period and to confine the analysis of the long period, which had been the principal analytical focus of his predecessors, to asides; and thirdly, to throw the entire weight of adjustments to changing economic conditions on output or income rather than prices. Equilibrium for the economy as a whole now involved 'unemployment equilibrium', and the introduction of this apparent contradiction in terms involved a profound change in the vision of contemporary economists who had always believed that competitive forces do ultimately drive the economy automatically toward a steady state of full employment.

The gradual but increasingly widespread acceptance of most of Keynes' views in the immediate years after the Second World War raised Keynesianism for a while to the position of a prevailing orthodoxy. Price theory and microeconomics took second place to macroeconomics, long period analysis virtually disappeared, and demand management — the view that the government can achieve full employment and price stability by fine-tuning of the economy — commanded universal assent. In recent years, however, all these elements of Keynesianism have been repeatedly attacked and his star has definitely begun to wane. Even so, Keynes remains one of the three or four most influential economists that ever lived.

He was born in 1883, the son of John Neville Keynes (q.v.) himself a Cambridge economist and philosopher whose *Scope and Method of Political Economy* (1891) is a minor classic. After winning a scholarship in classics and mathematics at King's College, Cambridge, the young Keynes joined the civil service and became involved in the Bloomsbury Group, the literary circle which included such famous names as Lytton Strachey, Virginia Woolf and Bertrand Russell. In 1908 he gained a fellowship at King's and began working on Indian monetary conditions and the theory of probability. Shortly after the outbreak of the war he joined the Treasury and rose rapidly in the ranks to become the principal Treasury representative at the Versailles peace conference. After the war, he returned to Cambridge to teach, later becoming Bursar of King's College. He also began to speculate in foreign exchange, acted as an adviser to several business firms, assumed the chairmanship of a leading insurance company, wrote frequently for the *Manchester Guardian* and *The Nation,* and edited the prestigious *Economic Journal.* In 1930 he became a member of the Economic Advisory Council and of the Macmillan Committee on Finance and Industry. His amazingly active career nevertheless left him time to publish a series of elegantly written memoirs and biographies, notably *Essays in Persuasion* (1931) and *Essays in Biography* (1933). During the Second World War, he returned to the Treasury and the last years of his life were almost exclusively concentrated on working to establish a workable international monetary order. He was created Lord Keynes in 1942.

The Royal Economic Society, under the editorship of Austin Robinson, Elizabeth Johnson and Donald Moggridge, has been engaged since 1971 in publishing a complete edition of his published and unpublished writings in 30 volumes, which was only recently completed.

*Secondary Literature*
R.F. Harrod, *The Life of John Maynard Keynes* (Macmillan, 1951); M. Keynes (ed), *Essays on John Maynard Keynes* (Cambridge University Press, 1975); D.E. Moggridge, *Keynes* (Fontana/Collins, 1976); R. Skidelsky, *John Maynard Keynes, I — Hopes Betrayed 1883-1920* (Macmillan, 1983).

# Keynes,
# John Neville
# (1852-1949)

John Neville Keynes, the father of John Maynard Keynes, wrote only two books, one on formal logic and the other a textbook on the *Scope and Method of Political Economy* (1891), the first major statement on methodology from a British economist since Cairnes' *Character and Logical Method of Political Economy* (1857). Keynes spent his whole life at the University of Cambridge, first as a fellow of Pembroke College from 1876 onwards and then as university registrar from 1910-25; he was on intimate terms with Marshall (q.v.) The book was obviously written as a supplement to Marshall's *Principles* (1890) and reflected Marshall's view that the methodological controversies provoked by the criticisms of both the German and English Historical Schools could be papered over by a moderate exposition of the issues, rejecting the extreme views of the 'younger' historical economists who demanded a wholesale reconstruction of economics on an historical foundation but granting that effective applications of economic theory required an appreciation of the historical forces that disturbed the pure operation of economic laws.

On the fundamental question of whether economics was an

inductive or deductive science, however, Keynes was adamant that the direct induction of concrete facts, or what was called the method *a posteriori,* was not an appropriate starting point in a subject like economics. The right procedure was the *a priori* method of starting from 'a few and indispensible facts of human nature ... the physical properties of the soil, and man's physiological constitution'. The appeal to facts comes in, he argued, when we apply the purely hypothetical laws of economics to the interpretation of events: 'comparison with observed facts provides a *test* for conclusions deductively obtained and enables the *limits* of their application to be determined.' He was sympathetic to but not overtly enthusiastic about the use of mathematics and statistics in economics. Of course, the modern phase in the history of statistics, associated with such names as Karl Pearson, George Yule and Ronald Fisher, was just beginning in 1891. Keynes affirmed that statistics is essential in the testing and verification of economic theories but he provided not so much as a single example of any economic controversy that had ever been resolved by a statistical test, although such examples would not have been hard to find in the works of Cairnes (q.v.), Jevons (q.v.) and Marshall. In consequence, his readers were left with the overwhelming impression that since the assumptions of economic theory are generally true, the predictions of economic science are also generally true, and whenever they are not, diligent search of the facts will reveal some disturbing factors that must bear the blame for the discrepancy.

Thus, despite the fact that he commended Adam Smith (q.v.) as the ideal economist because of the way in which he combined abstract-deductive and historical-inductive reasoning, the book is basically concerned to vindicate the abstract-deductive view of economics of Ricardo (q.v.), a view which Keynes made more palatable by once again underlining the gulf that separated the positive science from the normative art of political economy. *The Scope and Method of Political Economy* was a great success. Its clear exposition of the issues and its deliberately uncontroversial prose were perfectly calculated to restore confidence in the methods of the 'new' economics. Indeed, it succeeded so well that it more or less killed off interest in economic methodology for more than a generation. It remained the last word on the philosophy of economics until Lionel Robbins responded to new controversies with *An Essay on the Nature and Significance of Economic Science* (1932).

John Neville Keynes seems to have narrowly missed a promising academic career — Marshall put him forward in 1890 for the Drummond Chair in Political Economy at Oxford and the editorship of the *Economic Journal* but in the event both positions were filled by Edgeworth (q.v.) — and to have settled instead for university administration. He published nothing after 1894 when he contributed some articles to *Palgrave's Dictionary of Political Economy.* He lived to the age of 97, long enough to attend the funeral of his own son in 1946.

*Secondary Literature*
D. Dillard, 'Keynes, John Neville', *International Encyclopedia of the Social Sciences,* vol. 8, ed. D.L. Sills (Macmillan Free Press, 1968).

# Kondratieff, Nikolai Dmitrievich (1892-1931)

Nikolai Kondratieff was one of the outstanding Russian economists and statisticians of the 1920s who wrote extensively on agricultural economics and problems of central planning. However, outside Russia he is known exclusively for one article, 'The Long Waves in Economic Life', first published in Russian in 1925, then in German in 1926 and finally in English in 1935. In response to criticism, Kondratieff later expanded the article into a slim book, *The Long Wave Cycle* (1928), which has only recently appeared in English. The idea that economic growth under capitalism is subject to periodic cycles much longer than those of the ordinary business cycle was not original: it had been conjectured by Aftalion (q.v.) and Spiethoff (q.v.) and had been discussed among Dutch and German Marxists before the First World War. Nevertheless, Kondratieff marshalled better evidence for the existence of long waves than any of these earlier writers, presenting 36 annual price, value and quantity series for the USA, the UK, France and Germany going back to 1840 and in a few cases 1780. He dated long waves as taking roughly 50 to 60 years in the following order: (1) from the 1780s to the mid-1840s, with a peak around 1815; (2) from the mid-1840s to the mid-1890s, with a peak around 1875; and (3) from the mid-1890s to a peak around 1918, with the decline stretching out to (presumably) the 1940s. He admitted that the smoothing of the data, eliminating trends by least squares regression, introduced a certain amount of spurious regularity in the evidence and he certainly did not claim that the dating of the turning-points in the four countries was anything but broadly similar give or take 5 years on either side. Nevertheless, he thought it very probable that long waves are an inherent feature of capitalist development.

Asserting the existence of long waves is one question: asserting that they are endogenously generated by the capitalist economy is another. Kondratieff had no real explanation of these long waves but he did suggest the effects of various exogenous shocks to the system, such as wars and gold discoveries, the only problem being to account for their more or less regular occurrence. Kondratieff's hypothesis became know to western readers largely as a result of Schumpeter's *Business Cycles* (1939) which contained a three-cycle model of economic fluctuations made up of the Kitchin inventory cycle (3-5 years), the Juglar investment cycle (7-11 years) and the Kondratieff long cycle (45-60 years) — three Kitchins making up one Juglar and six Juglars one Kondratieff. Schumpeter (q.v.) did have a coherent theory of long waves, namely, that pioneering innovations tend to be imitated by others with the result that innovations appear in swarms in different industries; precisely because they are widely imitated they soon cease to be profitable, which brings the innovative spurt to an end. Schumpeter failed to demonstrate, however, that the period required to digest these spurts is as long as 45-60 years. In consequence, interest in long waves died out in the 1940s. In recent years, however, there has been a new interest in the Kondratieff cycle. A prominent Belgian Marxist, Ernst Mandel, has taken it up seriously in his book on *Long Waves of Capitalist Development* (1980) — albeit seeking to fit it into a Marxist theory of capitalist growth. According to this view, we are now living in the downswing of the fourth Kondratieff, which started in 1945 and reached its peak in the early 1970s.

The central difficulty with Kondratieff's original evidence — and indeed with all evidence subsequently presented — is that it consists largely of time series on prices. But prices throughout the nineteenth century were dominated by agricultural rather than industrial prices and yet all the theories of long waves are about industrial innovations and echo-effects of capital formation in industry. The evidence on long swings in output and employment is either very thin or non-existent and in any case goes back only to the 1860s, except for Britain where there is some evidence going back to the 1790s. This implies that the inference of a Kondratieff cycle in the historical data is based largely on only one completed long wave, namely, the third from the 1890s to the 1940s; or to put it another way, it is an inference based on evidence for only five turning-points. It is a brave man, therefore, who would predict the next upturn of the fourth Kondratieff in the 1990s on the strength of only five observations. Nevertheless, there do seem to be something like long-term fluctuations in infrastructural investment at least in the twentieth century, but it is still an open question whether these Kuznets cycles of 15-25 years' duration are in effect what accounts for the occasional appearance of still longer Kondratieff cycles of 45-60 years.

Kondratieff was born in Moscow in 1892 and served briefly as Vice-Minister of Food in the provisional Kerensky government that bridged the months between the overthrow of the Tsar in May 1917 and the triumph of the Bolsheviks in November 1917. Kondratieff founded the Conjuncture Institute in 1920 and directed it until 1928 when it was disbanded by the authorities. In 1930 he was arrested as the alleged head of the illegal Working Peasants Party and deported to Siberia without trial. He died, as did so many Russian intellectuals of his generation, is an unknown place, at an unknown time, and for unknown reasons.

*Secondary Literature*
G. Garvy, 'Kondratieff, N.D.', *International Encyclopedia of the Social Sciences,* vol. 8, ed. D.L. Sills (Macmillan Free Press, 1968).

# Lange,
# Oskar
# (1904-1965)

Oskar Lange's career falls neatly into two phases: an American phase
before the Second World War during which he made important
contributions to mainstream economics without however disguising
his sympathies for Marxism; and a Polish phase after the war during
which he propagated an undogmatic version of Marxism, making full
use of modern economic tools. His most famous work was a two-part
paper 'On the Economic Theory of Socialism', published in 1936-37,
in which he sought to establish a model of market socialism in which
factory managers would follow the rule of maximising profits by
equating prices to marginal costs, while economic planners struggled
to balance demand and supply by a process of trial-and-error, the
combined effect achieving all the efficiency results of a perfectly
competitive economy, while avoiding the unemployment, monopolies
and social inequities of capitalism. This soon came to be regarded as
the decisive answer to the Mises – Hayek view of the impossibility of
rational planning under socialism, thus furnishing economists with
the comfortable doctrine that the standard theory of perfect
competition had in itself nothing whatever to do with the private or

public ownership of property. Lange's argument was not new: it had been stated 40 years earlier by such stalwart orthodox economists as Barone (q.v.), Pareto (q.v.) and Wieser (q.v.). The irony of all these developments was duly noted by Schumpeter (q.v.): the economic theory of socialism is to be found not in the writings of Marx, but in the writing of 'bourgeois' economists.

Later generations had increasing doubts about the Lange theory of market socialism, which, like the orthodox price theory from which it sprang, is extremely explicit about the nature of the final equilibrium state after all economic forces have spent themselves and totally implicit about the nature of the actual process by which an economy moves towards a final equilibrium. Why should managers maximise long-run profits rather than their own income, and who will finance the losses subsequent on poor investments? Lange himself had second thoughts after the war about his own earlier blueprint for a socialist state, realising that what is needed is not so much an economics of socialism as a *Political Economy of Socialism* (1958). Nevertheless, in *Political Economy* (1958), a post-war treatise addressed to readers in Eastern Europe, originally projected in three volumes of which this is the first, he attempted to demonstrate the continued relevance of marginalist principles to the analysis of centrally planned economies. When it was first published, this work was generally hailed as marking the first true joining of Marxist and 'bourgeois' economics, heralding the end of a generation of Stalinism in the economies of Eastern Europe. Alas, the book was never followed up either by Lange or by other economists in the Soviet bloc, economics in Poland, Hungary and Russia remaining as divorced from western economics in the 1980s as it was in the 1950s.

Lange was born in Tomaszow, Poland in 1904, obtaining his master's degree in law in 1927 and his doctorate in law in 1928, both from the University of Krakow. After a brief period of study at the London School of Economics (1929-30) he became a lecturer at the University of Krakow in 1931. He left Europe in 1935 to take up an appointment as a lecturer in the University of Michigan, marking his arrival with his first English article, 'Marxian Economics and Modern Economic Theory' (1935), a classic statement of the gulf that separates the two. In 1943, he became professor at the University of Chicago, publishing his last major contribution in English in 1944 under the title *Price Flexibility and Employment,* a theoretical work in which he attempted to treat Keynesian questions with the microeconomic tools of general equilibrium theory.

In 1945 the newly-created communist government of Poland appointed Lange ambassador to the United States and in the following year, delegate of Poland to the United Nations. However, when events in Poland took a sharp turn towards Stalinist orthodoxy in 1949, Lange was recalled to Poland and relegated to a minor academic post. By 1955, when the political atmosphere in Poland had changed once again, he was rapidly promoted to professor of statistics at the University of Warsaw and chairman of the Polish State Economic Council. These last years saw a number of publications in Polish and some *Essays on Economic Planning* (1963), dealing with planning problems in the Third World.

*Secondary Literature*
S. Wellisz, 'Lange, Oskar', *International Encyclopedia of the Social Sciences,* vol. 8, ed. D.L. Sills (Macmillan Free Press, 1968).

# Lauderdale, James Maitland (1759-1839)

James Maitland, eighth earl of Lauderdale (pronounced 'Lauerdale'), was an active member of the House of Lords all his life, beginning as a Whig at the age of 21 and ending as an extreme Tory and bitter opponent of the Reform Bill of 1832 in his seventies. He was well known in his day for his violent temper and eccentric opinions. In his only book, *An Inquiry into the Nature and Origin of Public Wealth* (1804), he repeatedly questioned the content of *The Wealth of Nations* and repudiated 'the superstitious worship of Adam Smith's name', but in House of Lords debates he was invariably found to invoke the principles of *laissez-faire* as admitting of absolutely no exceptions. Similarly, he always took a strictly orthodox position on monetary questions: he was a member of the Bullion Committee and strongly defended the Bullion Report (1810), which recommended the early resumption of convertibility of the currency into gold once the Napoleonic wars had been brought to a successful conclusion. It is doubtful that the unorthodox and convoluted arguments of the *Inquiry* were understood at the time, although they appear to have exerted some influence on Malthus's *Principles* (1820). With the

Keynesian Revolution in our own century, however, Lauderdale along with Malthus (q.v.) and Sismondi (q.v.) has been hailed as a forerunner of Keynes, in as much as he argued that over-saving was a distinct possibility and that public spending was required to offset private thrift if stagnation was to be averted.

Lauderdale broke not only with Smith's macroeconomics but also with his microeconomics. Labour, he held, is no measure of value because its own value varies. Likewise, Smith's distinction between productive and unproductive labour is untenable. Value depends on utility on the one hand and scarcity on the other. This implies a conflict between 'public wealth' and 'private riches' or social welfare and private welfare: if goods become scarcer, say, as a result of a harvest failure, public wealth would decline but private riches would increase. Adam Smith had greatly exaggerated the significance of the division of labour, which is not the cause of the introduction of time-saving and skill-saving machinery. Nor is capital adequately described as 'advances which set labour into motion', to quote Adam Smith. On the contrary, capital is always a substitute for labour, rendering services that labour cannot perform at all. Private thrift is not an undiminished blessing and capital may easily be accumulated to excess, given the prevailing cost of labour and the existing state of technology. In the light of these considerations, the government's determination to levy taxes to pay off the public debt is an error; it would be much better if tax proceeds were spent on goods and services because the average recipient of public expenditure is more likely than the average bond-holder to spend his extra income at once.

Whether this doctrine of the dangers of over-saving is truly Keynesian in flavour remains a matter of controversy. It appears that what Lauderdale — and for that matter Malthus — had in mind was an under-consumption theory of the over-saving type: aggregate demand is forever threatening to become insufficient to buy all goods and services produced at cost-covering prices not because planned saving exceeds planned investment, to use modern Keynesian language, but just because they are always equal and because investment creates not only income but also adds to productive capacity in the future; to absorb that extra capacity requires constantly increasing incomes but how are incomes to keep rising when every act of saving tends to cut down the demand for consumer goods even as the investment of these savings simultaneously adds to the supply of goods to be purchased? The resolution of this dilemma lies in a dynamic theory of the requirements for smooth growth from period to period and it is precisely because Lauderdale and Malthus were unable to emancipate themselves from the single-period static analysis of their times that they failed to communicate their concern about the adequacy of aggregate demand to contemporary readers. They were forerunners, not of Keynesian economics, but of Harrod – Domar growth theory. With the aid of modern growth theory, we can now make sense of their writings. No wonder, however, that without it, nineteenth-century readers simply found them incomprehensible.

*Secondary Literature*
B. Corry, 'Lauderdale, James Maitland', *International Encyclopedia of the Social Sciences,* vol. 9, ed. D.L. Sills (Macmillan Free Press, 1968).

# Launhardt, Carl Friedrich Wilhelm (1832-1918)

Wilhelm Launhardt was a pioneer of mathematical economics, an important early contributor to the pure theory of welfare economics, a major figure in the history of location theory, and one of the few German engineer-economists of his day to carry on the tradition laid down by Karl Rau (1792-1870), Wilhelm von Hermann (1795-1868), Gossen (q.v.), Mangoldt (q.v.) and Thünen (q.v.), which is sometimes called German Classical Economics because it was closer in spirit to the English School of Classical Political Economy than to the dominant German Stream of the Historical School. Launhardt spent his entire productive life in the city of Hanover as professor of highway, railroad and bridge construction at the Technische Hochschule (now the University of Hanover), eventually becoming its Director. This is just about all that is known about his life. His *magnum opus* was the still untranslated *Mathematische Begründung der Volkswirtschaftslehre (Mathematical Foundation of Political Economy)*. It was published in 1885, a decade after the appearance of the works of Jevons (q.v.), Walras (q.v.) and Menger (q.v.) but before the publication of the next round of great books, Böhm-

Bawerk's *Positive Theory of Capital* (1889) and Marshall's *Principle of Economics* (1891). It was written without knowledge of Cournot's path-breaking *Mathematical Principles of Wealth* (1838) and was based instead on a close study of the writings of Walras and Jevons, whose analyses of durable capital goods and labour supply it both restated and refined. Launhardt's main interests, however, lay elsewhere in the pricing policies of railways and the associated questions of the location of economic activity to which the whole of the last third of the *Mathematische Begründung* is devoted. It was here that he showed how much he had learned from Thünen, supplementing the latter's supply-determined theory of the location of agricultural activities by an analysis of the role of market sales areas in the location of industrial plants.

To anyone interested in the fascinating topic of multiple discoveries in science, and the associated question of why some figures are systematically neglected, Launhardt's case affords a rich example. His book on mathematical economics is riddled with original contributions, many of which he had published in even greater detail as early as 1872 in a book on railway economics as well as in 1882 in an article buried in an obscure German engineering journal. In these two publications, he invented the so-called 'law of market areas' (under certain specified conditions, the boundaries between the sales territories of competing firms takes the form of a hyperbola) and stated a complete solution to the famous 'three-points problem' of classical location theory (the optimal location spot of an industrial plant using raw materials located in two different places and serving a market located in a third place). Marshall actually stated the law of market areas in his *Principles* but wrongly attributed it to Thünen; it was rediscovered by Fetter (q.v.) in 1924 who was aware of Marshall but not of Launhardt. Similarly, when Alfred Weber (q.v.) published his great book, *Theory of the Location of Industries* (1909), he included a 'new' proof of the three-points problem in the belief that he was the first to have stated it. Right up to the 1930s, writers on the location of industry failed so much as to mention Launhardt's name and yet it is no exaggeration to say that, had his work been widely known, location theory might have saved itself roughly a quarter of a century spent in trying to integrate the demand side with the supply side in the analysis of the optimum location of business enterprises.

Another leading feature of Launhardt's work are his pronouncements in favour of the pricing of railways in accordance with marginal rather than average costs; in short, what was later to be called the 'marginal cost pricing' rule. The welfare of consumers is only maximised, he argued, if the additional revenue from an increase in railway freight equals the additional cost, which implies that the fixed or overhead costs of railways must be financed out of tax revenues. Private competition will never secure that result because railways are 'natural monopolies' in which maximum technical efficiency (lowest average unit costs) is only reached at a level of output that exceeds total market demand; so long as railways are left in private hands, competition will cease and railway freight charges will fail to maximise economic welfare. In short, railways must be subsidised and regulated if not owned by the state. His demonstration of this proposition unfortunately employed linear cost and demand functions for which marginal costs are equal to average costs, so that the marginal cost pricing rule failed to stand out in pristine clarity. Nevertheless, he drew the correct conclusion from his demonstration, namely, that marginal cost pricing always results in financial deficits when the industry in question is what Marshall called a 'decreasing-cost industry' or 'natural monopoly'. Launhardt thus stands first in the long line of economists from Dupuit (q.v.) in the 1830s to Abba P. Lerner in the 1930s who recognise that the pricing of public utilities presents a special problem, requiring public subventions if the welfare of consumers is to be served.

*Secondary Literature*
E.M. Fels, 'Launhardt, Wilhelm', *International Encyclopedia of the Social Sciences,* vol. 9, ed. D.L. Sills (Macmillan Free Press, 1968); J.V. Pinto, 'Launhardt and Location Theory: Rediscovery of a Neglected Book', *Journal of Regional Science,* 17(1), 1977.

# Law, John (1671-1729)

John Law was one of those extraordinary personalities in which the eighteenth century seemed to abound. Born in Edinburgh, the son of a prosperous banker and privately educated, he devoted his entire life to making proposals for the establishment of banks, both in Scotland and on the Continent, convinced as he was that the key to economic prosperity lay in augmenting the base of metallic currencies with paper money, particularly paper money backed by land holdings. His reputation as an economic theorist, however, rests entirely on a single tract, *Money and Trade Considered: With a Proposal for Supplying the Nation with Money* (1705); a later and even better *Treatise on Money and Commerce* (1706) remained unpublished in his own lifetime. Like Locke, Law held a demand-and-supply theory of value and, again like Locke, he treated the value of money or the determination of the average level of prices as only a special case of a general theory of value. Distinguishing between use value and exchange value, he notes that goods only have value because they are useful but how much value they have is determined by 'the greater or lesser quantity of them in proportion to the demand for them'. He illustrates the argument with the water-diamond paradox — the association of high use value and low exchange value in the case of water and the very opposite in the case of diamonds — which Adam Smith (q.v.) was later to adopt. But whereas Smith employed the paradox to demonstrate the irrelevance of use value to the determination of exchange value, Law uses it to show that scarcity is a coordinate influence on value because what matters is not use value but the intensity of demand in relation to the quantity of goods available to satisfy that demand. Smith cited Law's tract in *The Wealth of Nations* and one can only conjecture why he utterly failed to grasp the logic of Law's argument.

Law's numerous attempts to sell the idea of a land bank to Scotland, France and the Dukedom of Savoy in Italy finally met with success in 1716 when he persuaded the Duke of Orleans, Regent of France after the death of Louis XIV, to give him a charter for the first Bank of France. In the following year he formed a Company of the West (later renamed Company of the Indies) and began to sell stocks in France's North American colonies of Louisiana and Mississippi. Merging the operations of the central bank with those of his Louisiana concession, to which he added the royal privilege of tax farming, he completed what came to be called 'Law's system': the bank's note issue was greatly increased and much of it was used for bidding up the prices of the shares of the Company of the Indies. As France in 1719-20 plunged into the greatest speculative frenzy of her history, Law was promoted to Minister of Finance and stood at the pinnacle of his power. When the boom collapsed in the closing months of 1720 Law was forced to flee France, permanently discredited, and spent his declining years as a professional gambler in Venice. The collapse of the boom is the notorious Mississippi Bubble, which was employed for a century or more to frighten statesmen with the spectre of inflation based on the reckless issue of paper notes.

*Secondary Literature*
E.J. Hamilton, 'Law, John', *International Encyclopedia of the Social Sciences,* vol. 9, ed. D.L. Sills (Macmillan Free Press, 1968).

# Leslie, Thomas Edward Cliffe (1827-1882)

T.E. Cliffe Leslie is important not so much for his substantive writings on the land problem, particularly in relation to Ireland, as for his penetrating criticisms of the abstract-deductive methods of the English classical economists. Such criticisms had been heard before even in England, as for example from Richard Jones (q.v.), but Leslie's attack went deeper in denying the realism of both the assumptions and the predictions of classical doctrines. Thus, he repeatedly drew attention to the spread of wage rates for identical skills in local labour markets and the failure of population growth to outstrip the food supply either before or after free trade in 1846. Even his attack on the abstract assumptions of classical economics seized on elements frequently ignored by other critics, such as the presumption of perfect foresight of future economic opportunities.

Leslie's published work was entirely in the form of essays, most of which were later collected in book form, such as *Essays in Political and Moral Philosophy* (1879) and *Essays in Political Economy* (1879). Leslie was not alone in England in his rejection of the essentially Ricardian nature of contemporary economics. There was

Bagehot and John Ingram (1823-1907) and Arnold Toynbee (1852-83), all of whom were writing in the 1870s and likewise rejected the abstract-deductive method in favour of an institutional and historical approach, although of course differing among themselves as to what this implied for the scope and nature of economic science. These writers formed a band that almost amounted to an English Historical School, which seems, strangely enough, to have had almost nothing to do with the more flourishing German Historical School.

Leslie was born in County Wexford, Ireland in 1827 and was educated at Trinity College, Dublin. After graduating in 1847 he studied law at the University of London. He qualified as a lawyer in both England and Ireland but never in fact practised law. As a result of his early publications, however, he was appointed in 1853 to a professorship of jurisprudence and political economy at Queen's College, Belfast, a post he held until his death. His inaugural lecture on *The Military Systems of Europe Economically Considered* was published in 1856; it argued the merits of a volunteer army in preference to a conscripted army. Throughout the 1860s, Leslie's writings concentrated on the land question. Then in the 1870s he turned to the methodology of economics and continued to write on this subject until his death in 1882. Judging by the number of respectful references to Leslie by Marshall (q.v.) and John Neville Keynes (q.v.), his criticisms were taken seriously by the economists who came after him.

*Secondary Literature*
F.W. Fetter, 'Leslie, T.E. Cliffe', *International Encyclopedia of the Social Sciences,* vol, 9, ed. D.L. Sills (Macmillan Free Press, 1968).

# List, Friedrich (1789-1846)

Friedrich List is one of the earliest and most severe critics of the classical school of political economy. He denounced Adam Smith and his disciples as the 'cosmopolitan school' and held that universal free trade was an ideal that could be achieved only in the far distant future. For the time being, he argued, each nation should foster the development of its own manufacturers by import duties and even outright prohibitions. Only by such means could countries like Germany, Russia and the United States ever hope to achieve the industrial efficiency that would enable them to compete on equal terms with Britain.

List never used the term 'infant industry' but the infant industry argument is clearly what he had in mind because he specifically excluded agriculture from all his protectionist arguments and even conceded that global free trade was an ultimate desirable goal. He expressed his arguments very forcefully but not very precisely. Indeed, it is stated more precisely in one famous paragraph in John Stuart Mill's *Principles* (1848), with an acknowledgement to the writings of Rae (q.v.), than it is ever stated in pages and pages of

List's *Natural System of Political Economy* (1837) or the better-known *National System of Political Economy* (1841). It is even doubtful whether List understood the legitimate argument for his own conclusions. There is no evidence that he ever understood the theory of comparative costs underlying the classical doctrine of free trade he so much despised; Ricardo is never mentioned in the earlier book and only mentioned in the later one in relation to rent theory. Also, despite his withering critique of Adam Smith and Say (q.v.) for divorcing economics from politics, his own analysis of the ultimate transition from 'the policy of protection to the policy of as much free trade as possible' is hopelessly naive precisely on political grounds.

In recent times, List has been hailed not so much as a spokesman for protectionism as a champion of the ambitions of underdeveloped countries. No doubt he was one of the first to recognise the role of national power in the international division of labour and present-day advocates of the dependency school of economic development may legitimately regard him as a forerunner. Nevertheless, the actual content of List's development economics was pretty thin: he imputed virtually unlimited economic powers to government action and credited the prosperity of any country almost exclusively to the economic policies of the state. But perhaps List is one of those figures from the past who has been so constantly advertised and acclaimed in secondary sources that actually reading him is almost bound to lead to disappointment.

Whether he is a great economist must therefore remain a matter of doubt. There is no doubt, however, that (unlike most great economists) he led a fascinating life as civil servant, journalist, professor, railway promoter and political agitator in three different countries — Germany, France and the United States. Born in Württemberg in 1789, the son of a tanner, he was soon active in liberal politics as the editor of several periodicals and an advisor to leading statesmen. Elected to the legislature of Württemberg and a professorship at the University of Tübingen in 1820, he was nevertheless sentenced to 10 months' imprisonment for advocating the rationalisation of the civil service and greater publicity of judicial procedure. To avoid imprisonment he fled abroad. When he returned to Germany two years later, he was arrested and only released on the promise that he would emigrate to America.

Arriving in America in 1825, he worked first as a farmer, then as an editor of a German newspaper, next as an owner of a coal mine and a connected railroad, and finally wrote his first work, *Outlines of American Political Economy* (1827), for the Pennsylvania Society for the Promotion of Manufactures, the leading protectionist organisation in America. In 1832 he was active in the election campaign of Andrew Jackson and was rewarded by an appointment as American consul in Germany. He now embarked on a plan to organise a German railway system, which was partly successful but involved him in a financial scandal that drove him out of Germany again. After three years in Paris, he returned to Germany in 1840, published his *National System* (1841) and became editor of an influential review. But further financial failures and thwarted political ambitions led him to commit suicide in 1846.

*Secondary Literature*
E. Salin and R.L. Frey, 'List, Friedrich', *International Encyclopedia of the Social Sciences,* vol. 9, ed. D.L. Sills (Macmillan Free Press, 1968); W.O. Henderson, *Friedrich List. Economist and Visionary 1789-1846* (Frank Cass, 1983).

# Locke, John (1632-1704)

John Locke is a major figure in the history of political thought. He is a minor but nevertheless significant figure in the history of economic thought; and that for three reasons: his labour theory of property, expounded in his masterpiece, *Two Treatises on Government* (1690), provided the philosophical underpinning of the labour theory of value that was to emerge in the writings of Adam Smith and the classical economists that came after him; his pamphlets on *Some Considerations of the Consequences of the Lowering of Interest* (1691) and *Further Considerations* (1695) developed the implications of the quantity theory of money as a special case of the more general demand-and-supply theory of price determination; and his sophisticated defence of mercantilism affords a splendid opportunity to study the failure of some of the best minds in the seventeenth century to recognise the fact that a country is unable to accumulate gold indefinitely.

He was born in 1632 in a Somerset village, the eldest son of a small landholder, and entered Christ Church, Oxford in 1652 where he may have met Petty (q.v.) who, while only six years older, was already a professor of anatomy and a Vice-Principal of Brasenose College. In 1658 Locke was appointed senior student at Christ Church, teaching moral philosophy. After meeting Lord Ashley (later Lord Shaftesbury), the great Whig leader, he was drawn into politics and was soon spending more time in London than in Oxford. Becoming Secretary to the Council of Trade and Plantations in 1668, his career reached a peak when he was appointed to the well-paid post of commissioner for promoting colonial trade. When the 'Glorious Revolution' put an end to the reign of the Stuarts in 1683, Lord Shaftesbury was forced to flee abroad and Locke in his wake found himself deprived of his academic appointment and driven into exile. He found refuge in Holland where he spent six years studying and writing. He returned to England in 1689 already recognised as a major thinker and devoted himself for the remaining 15 years of his life to writing, while holding minor government offices and occasionally advising political leaders.

Locke's theory of property is grounded in the doctrine of natural rights: every man is endowed at birth with property in his own person and so is entitled to the products of his own labour; similarly, by applying his labour to the earth, he makes the fruits of the earth his property. Thus, labour is not only the origin of all property but also 'puts the difference of value on everything'. Whether Locke himself saw all the implications of this argument and whether he truly held a labour theory of *value* (relative prices are determined by the amount of past and present labour embodied in commodities) may be doubted, but he did argue that labour contributes far more to the value of goods than nature and it is a short step from this empirical assertion to the full-blown theory that labour alone determines value. Even Adam Smith (q.v.) did not take that step almost a century later but Ricardo (q.v.) probably and Marx (q.v.) certainly did. Elsewhere in his economic pamphlets, Locke repeatedly employs not the labour theory of value but a demand-and-supply theory or, in his own words, the relation between 'vent' and 'quantity'; thus, for example, he declares that air and water are useful but fetch no price 'because their quantity is immensely greater than their vent'.

Locke's monetary economics runs almost entirely in terms of a comparison between the ratio of one country's monetary stock to its volume of trade and that same ratio in another country. It is this ratio which determines international price levels and the entire argument is directed at the danger of prices at home falling below those abroad.

Although this sounds like the opposite of the mercantilist preference for low prices as a stimulus to exports, Locke turns it into a plea for a favourable balance of trade which will produce a constant inflow of gold. The resolution of this apparent contradiction lies in the fact that he assumed that the world's money stock is continuously growing, both absolutely and relative to the volume of trade. This notion of secular, worldwide inflation implies that a country that stands still will soon fall behind; in short, what is important is not the acquisition of gold as such but of more gold than is being acquired in the rest of the world. In this connection, he notes that the ratio between a country's monetary stock and its trade depends not just on the quantity of money but also on 'the quickness of its circulation'; he then proceeds to estimate crudely the velocity of circulation of money of different economic groups, such as labourers, merchants and landholders. Admittedly, one frequently has to read between the lines to make sense of Locke's extremely pithy reasoning. So often we, drawing on the modern identity $MV = PT$ (where $M$ = the money supply, $V$ = velocity, $P$ = the average level of prices, and $T$ = the volume of trade), can fill in the missing terms, in which case the reasoning usually hangs together. Nevertheless, it is fascinating to notice how totally unmindful Locke always is of the proposition that gold movements around the world cannot permanently get out of line with the trade flows between countries because of Hume's 'specie-flow mechanism'.

*Secondary Literature*
K.I. Vaughn, *John Locke. Economist and Social Scientist* (University of Chicago Press, 1980).

# Longfield, Samuel Mountifort (1802-1884)

Ever since the publication in 1903 of Edwin Seligman's famous article, 'On Some Neglected British Economists', a veritable treasure house of previously ignored forerunners, historians of economic thought have given due recognition to Longfield's *Lectures on Political Economy* (1834) for its consistent application of marginal concepts to the theory of value and distribution: the market price of commodities in Longfield is determined by 'that demand, which being of the least intensity, yet leads to actual purchases'; the rate of profit is determined by 'the profit of that capital which is naturally the least efficiently employed', which in turn is equal to 'the difference of the quantities of work which the feeblest labourer would execute with and without its use'. Subsequently, in his path-breaking *Studies in the Theory of International Trade* (1837), Jacob Viner showed that Longfield's *Lectures on Commerce* (1834) contains one of the earliest attempts to extend Ricardo's explanation of two commodities two countries international trade to the case of many commodities and many countries, to which may be added Longfield's discovery of the modern factor proportions theory of international trade, for which

Bertil Ohlin, the leading advocate of that theory in modern times, gave Longfield full credit. R.D. Collison Black went even further in an influential article published in *Economica* (1945), 'Trinity College Dublin and the Theory of Value 1832-63': he credited Longfield with the establishment of an Irish school of subjective value theory, which opposed the trend of received opinion in England right up to the 1870s. Still more recently, a book-length study of Longfield claims that he alone among all his contemporaries developed a theory of distribution that was a genuine alternative to the Ricardian theory. Be that as it may, Longfield was largely if not entirely neglected by the English classical economists, some of whom misunderstood him as defending rather than rejecting Ricardo.

Suffice it to say that Longfield's *Lectures* is an amazingly original if somewhat confusingly written book, which sketches a subjective theory of value and a marginal productivity theory of distribution — all this in 1834, 11 years after the death of Ricardo. Longfield had the idea of marginal demand price and favoured utility rather than labour as the basis of exchange value but he failed, like everyone before him, to discover the concept of marginal utility as the link between utility and demand. Curiously enough, even this link soon made its appearance in *Lectures on Population, Value, Poor Laws and Rent* (1831) by W.F. Lloyd (1795-1852), Senior's successor to the Drummond Professorship of Political Economy at Oxford. In other words, all the building-blocks and even some of the detail of the 'marginal revolution' of the 1870s were already at hand in 1837, which shows once again that 'there is nothing new under the sun'.

Longfield was born in 1802, the son of a vicar in County Cork, Ireland and was educated at Trinity College, Dublin, graduating in 1823. Richard Whateley (1787-1863), an Anglican divine who had published on economic questions, established the Whateley Chair of Political Economy at Trinity College, Dublin on becoming Archbishop of Dublin. Longfield was the first occupant of that Chair from 1832 to 1836. Disappointed by the reception of his *Lectures,* Longfield deserted economics for law in the 1840s. His experiences as Judge of the Landed Estates Court in Ireland led him to formulate interventionist views on economic policy that more or less reversed his earlier conservative beliefs in *laissez-faire.* In an 1872 paper to the Statistical and Social Inquiry Society of Ireland he advocated old age pensions, state education, free medical care and regulation of housing for the poor. He died in 1884 at the age of 82.

*Secondary Literature*
E. McKinley, 'Longfield, Samuel Mountifort', *International Encyclopedia of the Social Sciences,* vol. 9, ed. D.L. Sills (Macmillan Free Press, 1968); L.S. Moss, *Mountifort Longfield: Ireland's First Professor of Political Economy* (Green Hill Publishers, 1976).

# Luxemburg, Rosa (1870-1919)

Marx took a relatively sophisticated view of the breakdown of capitalism: he did not think that capitalism would collapse like a house of cards because of some flaw in its make-up but rather that it would be overthrown by the working class because its evolution involved periodic crises, unemployment and alienation which would necessarily encourage the rise of revolutionary class-consciousness among the have-nots. In the second volume of *Capital,* he set down a series of 'reproduction equations', which spelled out the conditions required for smooth, hitchless growth of a two-sector capitalist economy; these conditions were stringent and no doubt he meant to show how easy it would be to violate them. Nevertheless, they could also be used to demonstrate that continuous, steady-state growth is in principle possible for a closed capitalist economy. Marx did not live to polish these chapters for publication and we can only surmise just what he intended to show with the aid of the 'reproduction schema'. They were generally ignored by Marxists after his death but the publication of Rosa Luxemburg's *Accumulation of Capital* (1913) started off the great 'breakdown controversy' among German and

Austrian Marxists, which amounted in fact to an argument about what was implied by Marx's reproduction schema.

Rosa Luxemburg was in no doubt that it demonstrated the impossibility of a closed capitalist economy to sustain steady-state growth; growth under capitalism therefore required expansion into spheres of non-capitalist production either at home or abroad. With the increasing commercialisation of peasant agriculture in industrialised Europe and the exhaustion of the frontier in North America, capitalism was increasingly driven to exploit the under-developed countries of Asia, Africa and Latin America. Thus, she concluded, the inherent insufficiency of aggregate demand under capitalism is the essential cause of the international tensions and instabilities that characterise the modern world. It followed that the overthrow of capitalism would involve not just internal revolution, as Marx had predicted, but international wars and colonial struggles of liberation.

Luxemburg's reading of *Capital* was disputed by all the leading Marxists of the day, including Mikhail Tugan-Baranovsky (1865-1919), Karl Kautsky (1854-1938), Nikolai Bukharin (1888-1938) and Eduard Bernstein (q.v.), and she spent part of a jail sentence during the First World War writing a book to answer her critics, which has recently become available in English (R. Luxemburg and N. Bukharin, *Imperialism and the Accumulation of Capital,* ed. K.J. Tarbuck, Monthly Review Press, 1973). The debate raged on during the 1920s by which time she had also invited the enmity of Lenin by a pamphlet on the Bolshevik revolution of 1917, arguing that the much-acclaimed Leninist dictatorship of the proletariat was in fact a dictatorship of the Communist Party over the Russian proletariat. Upon her release from prison in 1918, she and Karl Leibknecht together founded the German Communist Party and participated in revolutionary activity that broke out all over Germany in 1919. They were both arrested and murdered under mysterious circumstances while in military custody.

Rosa Luxemburg was born in 1870 in Poland and spent her childhood and youth in Warsaw. She became active in the socialist movement while still at school and was forced to flee abroad to Switzerland in her teens. She entered the University of Zurich and took her doctorate in 1898 with a thesis on the industrial development of Poland; given the prevailing attitudes of the day towards the education of women, she may well have been one of the first women ever to have acquired a PhD in economics. Acquiring German citizenship in 1897 by a marriage of convenience, she moved to Berlin and joined Karl Kautsky in the fight against Bernstein's revisionism. She soon drew back from Kautsky's cautious policies, however, and placed herself at the head of the left-wing of the German Social Democratic Party. Beginning in 1907, she lectured regularly on Marxist economics at the party school in Berlin and published widely on questions of economics and political organisation. Her strident opposition to the war led, as we have said, to imprisonment for over three years, followed by her tragic death at the age of 49.

*Secondary Literature*
J.P. Nettl, *Rosa Luxemburg* (Oxford University Press, 1966); T. Kowalik, 'Luxemburg, Rosa', *International Encyclopedia of the Social Sciences,* vol. 9, ed. D.L. Sills (Macmillan Free Press, 1968).

# Malthus,
# Thomas Robert
# (1766-1834)

The most famous social scientist of the nineteenth century was not David Ricardo or Karl Marx but Robert Malthus. That fame rested on what was in effect a long pamphlet, *An Essay on the Principle of Population, As It Affects the Future Improvement of Society; With Remarks on the Speculations of Mr. Godwin, M. Condorcet, and Other Writers* (1798). Malthus was not the first writer to make the obvious point that the growth of population is ultimately limited by the food supply. He was, however, the first to bring it home to readers with the aid of a simple, powerful metaphor: population, when allowed to increase without limit, increases in a *geometrical* ratio, while the food supply can at best increase in an *arithmetical* ratio; so, whatever the plausible rate of increase of the food supply, an unchecked multiplication of human beings must quickly lead to standing-room only. The contrast that he drew between the two kinds of mathematical progression carried the hypnotic persuasive power of an advertising slogan. It was easy to see that even the smallest finite sum growing at the smallest *compound* rate must eventually overwhelm even the largest possible finite sum growing at the highest *simple* rate.

But the powerful impact of the *Essay* derived as much from its general implications as from the stark thesis itself. Rousseau, Godwin and Condorcet, to mention only three of the many writers Malthus had in mind, had argued that goodwill and education alone were capable of bringing about a perfect social order and the principal object of the *Essay* was to deny their contention. Poverty had its roots, not in social and political institutions, but in the unequal race between population and the means of subsistence. Moreover, nothing could stem the tide of numbers except the voluntary limitation of family size by the poor themselves. Thus, at one stroke, Malthus accounted for the existence of poverty, exposed the panaceas of visionary reformers, and provided a touchstone for every question of policy relating to the 'labouring poor'. No wonder then that Malthus achieved instant fame — but also instant vilification. Because the Malthusian theory of population rationalised the subsistence theory of wages to which all contemporary economists subscribed (wages will always tend to fall to the level required for the survival of workers because high wages stimulate population growth), Malthus came to typify the 'dismal science' of political economy, which so many reformers and writers despised. In consequence, when they attacked economics, it was frequently Malthus, and not Adam Smith or Ricardo, they regarded as the villain of the piece.

Malthus eventually converted his early 50,000 words essay into a full-scale treatise on demography running to some 250,000 words. In the course of doing so, he virtually abandoned his original thesis. Earlier, he had argued that population is normally prevented from increasing beyond the food supply either by positive checks (war, famine and pestilence that keep up the death rate) or by preventive checks (abortion and infanticide that hold down the birth rate) and both of these he labelled as manifestations of 'misery and vice'. Now, however, he granted that population could also be checked by 'moral restraint', meaning postponement of the age of marriage accompanied by strict sexual continence before marriage, and this particular preventive check was allowed to stand without any disapproving label. Although Malthus always remained profoundly pessimistic about the capacity of mankind to regulate its numbers by moral restraint, nevertheless the addition of this concept lightened the darker tones of his argument and also furnished him with a perfect escape clause against any adverse empirical evidence.

Malthus himself, like almost all figures of his day, regarded birth control devices as morally unacceptable, if not positively sinful. But within a few decades of his death, the birth control movement seized on his theory of population to justify their activities, calling themselves neo-Malthusians. And so, irony of ironies, the Malthusian theory of population eventually became a central tenet in the platform of almost all Victorian reformers. By the first quarter of the twentieth century, however, the Malthusian spectre of over-population gave way to the Keynesian spectre of under-population and Malthus's influence declined accordingly. Since the Second World War, the problem of underdeveloped countries has once again brought the Malthusian theory back into favour, giving it yet another lease of life.

While Malthus's fame in his own lifetime was based squarely on his theory of population, his modern reputation with economists rests more on his opposition to Say's law of markets and the contemporary Ricardian doctrine of the impossibility of 'general gluts'. Keynes hailed Malthus as a forerunner and there has been endless argument on whether Malthus's views on gluts — or as we would nowadays say, business depressions — in his *Principles of Political Economy* (1820) amounted to a simple confusion of ideas or an amazingly prescient appreciation of the problem of inadequate effective demand.

Robert Malthus was born in 1766, 10 years before the publication of Smith's *Wealth of Nations,* and he always regarded himself as a disciple of Smith. After being privately educated, he entered Jesus College, Cambridge, graduating in 1788 with a degree in mathematics. He took holy orders in 1797 and held a small curacy for a short period. He married in 1805 and shortly thereafter was appointed professor of modern history and political economy at the East India Company's College at Haileybury, the first appointment of its kind in England. He died in 1834, the year that saw the abolition of the old Poor Law and the passage of a new Poor Law that may be said to have been inspired by his writings. Besides his *Essay on Population* and his *Principles of Political Economy,* he published a number of minor but significant publications on strictly economic questions, such as *An Inquiry into the Nature and Progress of Rent* (1815), *The Measure of Value Stated and Illustrated* (1823) and *Definitions in Political Economy* (1827).

*Secondary Literature*
D.V. Glass (ed.), *Introduction to Malthus* (Watt, 1953); G.F.

McCleary, *The Malthusian Population Theory* (Faber & Faber, 1953); P. James, *Population Malthus: His Life and Times* (Routledge & Kegan Paul, 1979).

# Mandeville, Bernard (1660-1733)

One of the popular doctrines of the eighteenth century was the belief
that man's selfish impulses nevertheless work towards the general
good because an inherent sense of moral righteousness keep these
impulses at bay, not consciously but unconsciously as part of a Divine
Plan. This identification of private with public virtues was rudely
shattered by the publication of *The Fables of the Bees* (1714-29) with
a pointed sub-title *Private Vices, Public Benefits,* by Bernard
Mandeville, a Dutch physician who had moved to England at the age
of 29. Mandeville's scandalous argument was simply that self-interest
was indeed a moral vice, and yet that this vice conduced to economic
prosperity and thus to public benefits as an unintended consequence
of actions undertaken entirely for private and vicious reasons. In
short, there was a harmony of private and public interests but not
because of a Divine Plan but because of what Adam Smith was later
to call 'the invisible hand', which led each individual to promote 'an
end which was no part of his intention'.

Mandeville's satire — society as a beehive producing honey
although each bee is driven by greed and lust — was deliberately

designed to give offence so as to encourage the re-examination of traditional beliefs: conspicuous consumption of luxury goods, the fashionable display of foreign imports, crime, and even natural disasters like the Fire of London of 1666 all promote the 'division of labour' (Mandeville's term) and contribute to a brisk trade and full employment, whereas such supposed virtues as thrift and charity contribute to poverty and stagnation. *The Fable of the Bees* was widely read in the eighteenth century and criticised by all the leading thinkers of the day. There is no doubt that it was constantly in Adam Smith's mind as he wrote *The Wealth of Nations.* Nevertheless, he adopted the essence of Mandeville's doctrine of unintended social consequences, while rejecting much of its form. Mandeville had suggested that 'private Vices by the dextrous Management of a skillful Politician may be turn'd into publick Benefits' and in his writings a mercantilist belief in the importance of maintaining a favourable balance of trade drowns out the occasional hint of the principle of *laissez-faire.* Smith's view on the other hand was that it is the mechanism of competition rather than the wisdom of politicians which turns private vices into public benefits.

*Secondary Literature*
M.M. Goldsmith, 'Mandeville, Bernard', *International Encyclopedia of the Social Sciences,* vol. 9, ed. D.L. Sills (Macmillan Free Press, 1968); P. Harth, 'Introduction', *The Fable of the Bees by Mandeville* (Penguin Books, 1970).

# Mangoldt, Hans Karl Emil von (1824-1868)

Economic thought in Germany in the nineteenth century fell only gradually under the spell of the historical movement. In the first half of the century, there was room for the romantic nationalism of Adam Müller (1779-1829), the liberal nationalism of List (q.v.), the state socialism of Karl Rodbertus (1805-75) and Ferdinand Lassalle (1825-64), and the more abstract thinking of the German classical economists, such as Thünen (q.v.), Karl Heinrich Rau (1792-1870), Friedrich Wilhelm von Hermann (1795-1868) and the greatest of them all, Karl Emil von Mangoldt. This German classical school derived in part from Adam Smith (q.v.) and in part from the French eighteenth-century utility tradition of Galiani (q.v.); most of Ricardo's ideas were rejected but the Malthusian theory of population and the doctrine of comparative costs were retained; the concept of rent was generalised and held to apply to all the factors of production; factor rewards were judged to depend on marginal yields, as much for labour and capital as for land; and particular emphasis was laid on entrepreneurial profit as a special category of income alongside wages, interest and rent.

147

Mangoldt was born in Dresden in 1824. He studied law and political science at the Universities of Leipzig, Geneva and Tübingen, obtaining his doctorate from Tübingen in 1847. For some years he held a government post from which he was forced to resign for expressing liberal political opinions. He then edited a newspaper, which also led to a resignation for political reasons. The publication of his first important work, *Die Lehre von Unternehmergewinn (The Doctrine of Entrepreneurial Gain)* (1855), finally led to an academic post at the University of Gottingen. 'Unternehmergewinn' (entrepreneurship) was Thünen's term for certain unique components of profit and Mangoldt's monograph elaborated Thünen's anaylsis into an exhaustive classification of the different elements in entrepreneurial income. In 1862, Mangoldt moved to the University of Freiburg as professor of political science and political economy. A year later he published his major work, *Grundriss der Volkswirthschaftslehre (Outline of Political Economy)* (1863), of which only one chapter has been translated into English. It was a comprehensive but highly compressed work, which stands out not only for its path-breaking discussion of price formation but also for its liberal use of geometrical diagrams, including the Marshallian cross of demand and supply. No doubt, Cournot (q.v.), Dupuit (q.v.) and Gossen (q.v.) had been there before him but there is no evidence that Mangoldt knew anything of their writings.

Mangoldt drew a downward-sloping demand curve on the grounds that 'the use-value of each unit, will always be smaller, the more one adds'. He also drew three supply curves: a horizontal line representing the case of constant costs; a reverse L-shaped curve, representing the case of constant costs up to the limit of a rigidly fixed supply; and a U-shaped curve, representing the case of economies of scale, followed by diseconomies of scale. In the latter case, he went on to explain, the lower limit of the market price will be given by 'the costs of the last unit, or the highest necessary production costs'.

Mangoldt followed Thünen not only in his analysis of entrepreneurial profit but also in the use of marginal productivity theory to determine the rewards of factors of production: the level of wages is determined by 'the prospective return of the least productive, that is presumably the last, labour to be applied'; likewise, 'the net yield of the last unit of capital applied determines the level of interest'. Mangoldt's *Grundriss* also contained much advanced monetary economics, in particular an amazingly clear foreshadowing of

Wicksell's explanation of cyclical fluctuations in terms of the relationship between the 'natural' and the 'market' rate of interest. Mangoldt's book drew compliments from Edgeworth (q.v.) and Marshall (q.v.) but in his own country his writings fell into oblivion with the ascendency of the Historical School. Mangoldt died in 1868 at the age of 44 after a career as an economist that had lasted only 15 or 16 years.

*Secondary Literature*
E. Schneider, 'Mangoldt, Hans Karl Emil von', *International Encyclopedia of the Social Sciences,* vol. 9, ed. D.L. Sills (Macmillan Free Press, 1968); K.H. Hennings, 'The Transition from Classical to Neoclassical Economic Theory: Hans Von Mangoldt', *Kyklos,* 33(4), 1980.

# Marshall, Alfred (1842-1924)

Alfred Marshall is one of the most perplexing of all great economists. He was the dominant figure in British economics from the 1890s right up to the 1930s and his *Principles of Economics* (1890) still has the power to fascinate and excite the reader. On the other hand, his moral zeal and Victorian piety have always repelled some commentators and on the Continent his slighting of Walras (q.v.), Menger (q.v.) and Böhm-Bawerk (q.v.) was always deeply resented. He was an excellent mathematician — indeed a far better mathematician than such avowedly mathematical economists as Jevons (q.v.), Walras (q.v.) and Barone (q.v.) — but he hid his mathematics away in appendices and even relegated his elegant diagrams in footnotes because he hoped to be read by businessmen. He made many original contributions to static equilibrium theory and yet hankered all his life for a dynamic theory that he was unable to produce, even going so far as to proclaim that biology and not mechanics is 'the Mecca of the economist'. His one grand theme was that price is always determined by demand *and* supply, (cut by both 'blades of the scissors') and yet he struggled against all the evidence to argue that this had of course been well understood by the great classical economists before him — the history of economic thought was a seamless web and there never had been a 'marginal revolution'. He was a firm believer in private property and the merits of a market economy and yet he discovered some of the best arguments ever against the doctrine that free markets maximise economic welfare and always retained a sneaking sympathy for trade unions and even socialism. He never expressed an opinion, whether on pure theory or on questions of practical policy, without an almost endless list of qualifications. In short, he was a very complex, contradictory economist and perhaps that is the secret of his long-lasting appeal.

His life was relatively uneventful even for an academic. He was born in London in 1842 in a modest middle-class family and brought up by an extremely stern father in the expectation that he would become a clergyman. He rebelled against this plan, however, and went to St John's College, Cambridge to study mathematics, graduating in 1865 as 'second wrangler in the tripos', a super bachelor's degree. He was immediately elected to a fellowship in mathematics at St John's but was forced to resign the post in 1877 when he married Mary Paley, a former student of his (in those days, fellows at Oxford and Cambridge were required to be celibate like priests). He then spent five years as principal and professor of political economy at University College, Bristol (now the University of Bristol), a year as fellow of Balliol College, Oxford (the Oxbridge requirement of celibacy by then having been eliminated), returning to Cambridge in 1885 as professor of political economy. He remained at Cambridge until his retirement in 1908 when he was succeeded by his star pupil Pigou (q.v.).

By the time he published *Principles of Economics* (1890), he was already 48 years of age; apart from reviews and some articles, he had published little. Two early tracts on *The Pure Theory of Foreign Trade* and *The Pure Theory of Domestic Values,* both published in 1879, reworked some of the ideas of John Stuart Mill (q.v.) into rigorous diagrams; they showed Marshall in possession of the essence of marginalism but without a hint of utility theory. A slender book written jointly with his wife, *The Economics of Industry* (1879), again bore little sign of the new economics. In later years, he was fond of claiming that Cournot (q.v.), Dupuit (q.v.) and Thünen (q.v.) had supplied him with the discovery of marginal utility and marginal productivity in the 1860s well before the publication of the works of

Jevons, Menger and Walras. But this claim must be doubted. Nevertheless, by waiting so long to put the final touches to the *Principles,* he ensured its authoritative summing-up of the fruits of the 'marginal revolution', at the same time managing somehow to reconcile the old classical economics with the new neo-classical economics. He published two more tomes in later life, *Industry and Trade* (1919) and *Money, Credit and Commerce* (1923), but neither of these enjoyed the success of his *Principles.* Likewise, his many official memoranda and evidence given before Royal Commissions of Inquiry in the 1880s and 1890s were little known outside Cambridge.

Among many of Marshall's original contributions to economics, all of which he modestly disguised as part of the wisdom of the past, we may single out partial equilibrium analysis, the distinction between the market period, the short period and the long period, the improved discussion of demand curves, the idea of the price-elasticity of demand, the concept of consumer and producer surplus, the analysis of the conditions for stability of equilibrium, the distinction between increasing - and decreasing-cost industries, the distinction between internal and external economies of scale, the explicit recognition of the incompatibility of competition and long-run falling supply curves, culminating in the proposition that perfect competition does not maximise economic welfare because total welfare can always be increased by a fiscal policy of taxing increasing-cost industries to subsidise decreasing-cost industries, the concept of quasi-rents, the definition of the representative firm ... but enough. Some of these have become the bread and butter of economic textbooks, whereas others, such as his version of consumer and producer surplus, the tax-subsidy conclusion, and the concept of the representative firm, have been almost entirely discarded. Still others, like the distinction between increasing and decreasing costs and between internal and external economies, have been absorbed in the literature but so altered and refined as to render them almost unrecognisable as Marshallian in origin.

But even saying all that, there is still so much else left in the book that is classical in the double sense of the term, that is, of enduring value and of retaining the best of the classical tradition of political economy. So much of Jevons, Menger and Walras is based on the assumption that there is a fixed supply of resources in the economy, the only problem being how to allocate them among alternative uses.

Marshall, however, never lost sight of the fact that resources also grow through time and that therefore the growth of population and the accumulation of capital, not to mention technical progress, are genuine economic problems. Similarly, he found space for a discussion of 'the peculiarities of labour', those dynamic forces acting on the supply of labour that lead to cumulative disadvantages in labour's bargaining position in labour markets, thus adding what is perhaps the most penetrating contribution to labour economics since *The Wealth of Nations.* It is true that he said almost nothing about monetary theory (at least in the *Principles)* or about business cycles and macroeconomics and was therefore responsible for the pre-Keynesian view that these questions really belonged to the periphery of economics. And the way that he interlarded his static analysis with bits and pieces of dynamics and even historical processes sowed confusions that took the best efforts of a generation of economists to solve. But that is the price not so much of greatness as of too much influence; and Marshall had more influence, particularly in Britain, than any great economist deserves.

*Secondary Literature*
J.M. Keynes, *Essays in Biography* (Macmillan, 1933); B. Corry, 'Marshall, Alfred', *International Encyclopedia of the Social Sciences,* vol. 10, ed. D.L. Sills (Macmillan Free Press, 1968); D.P. O'Brien, 'A. Marshall', *Pioneers of Modern Economics in Britain,* D.P. O'Brien and J.R. Presley (eds.) (Macmillan, 1981); *Alfred Marshall: Critical Assessments,* ed. J.C. Wood (Croom Helm, 1983).

# Marx, Karl (1818-1883)

Karl Marx was born in Trier in the Rhineland, Prussia (now West Germany) of Jewish parents who had converted to Christianity for social reasons. He studied at the Universities of Bonn, Berlin and Jena, where he received his doctorate in philosophy at the age of 23. While a student he began to associate with the Young Hegelians, a group of intellectuals who were turning the conservative philosophy of Hegel into a weapon of fierce social criticism. The young Marx's articles soon wiped out the chances of an academic career and he turned instead to journalism. Forced to flee Germany in 1843 by the suppression of the newspaper he was editing, he settled first in Paris, then in Brussels, and finally in 1848 in London where he remained for the rest of his life. He had already struck up a friendship with Friedrich Engels, the son of a wealthy German cotton manufacturer with business interests in Manchester. The two began collaborating almost as soon as they met. Engels was well read in Adam Smith (q.v.) and Ricardo (q.v.) and persuaded Marx to take an interest in the theories of the English classical economists. This led to Marx's first published venture into economics, *The Poverty of Philosophy*

(1847), a critique of the then influential socialist ideas of Proudhon (q.v.). In 1848, the two men published *The Communist Manifesto* for the recently formed London Committee of the Communist League, perhaps the most influential political pamphlet ever written, whose pungent opening and closing sentences have rung in our ears ever since: 'The history of all hitherto existing society is the history of class struggles ... The proletarians have nothing to lose but their chains. They have a world to win. Workers of the world, unite!' Marx and Engels rarely wrote together after 1848 but they continued to confer and to collaborate until Marx's death in 1883. Marx did not hold a job after moving to London and was dependent all his life on financial handouts and eventually on a fixed annual settlement from Engels. Marx never lived to finish his great masterpiece, *Capital;* only Volume I was published in his lifetime in 1867. Engels spent over 10 years after Marx's death in preparing Volumes II and III for publication (1885, 1894). On Engels' death in 1895, Volumn IV, running to almost 1,000 pages — a history of economic thought from Petty to Mill — was left unedited; it was subsequently published by Karl Kautsky, a leading German Marxist. In short, Engels' friendship with Marx is one of the most extraordinary examples of unselfish intellectual devotion in the entire history of social science.

Marx spent over 20 years working up to the publication of *Capital.* Even before the appearance of *The Poverty of Philosophy* (1847), we can see from his private *Economic and Philosophical Manuscripts* (1844) and the later *Grundrisse der Kritik der politischen Ökonomie (Foundations of a Critique of Political Economy),* written in 1857-58 but only published in modern times, how deeply he had begun to study the economic literature of his day and age. There is still a lot of Hegel in these early works but even here Hegel is beginning to drop into the background and Ricardo is coming to the fore. Increasingly Ricardo, and particularly his qualifications of the labour theory of value, began to define the problem Marx had set for himself. Ricardo had demonstrated that, because capital and labour combine in different proportions in different industries, the labour theory of value is only approximately true: the proposition that the relative prices of commodities are determined by the labour time required to produce them could never be upheld strictly speaking. Ricardo was satisfied with the degree of approximation it afforded but Marx was determined to show that the labour theory of value was foolproof, not for each and every commodity taken in isolation but for the whole system of commodities taken together — macroeconomically, to use modern language. As a corollary it followed, thought Marx, that profits as the income of capitalists constituted nothing else but 'unpaid labour', a part of total output created by living labour but expropriated by the owners of the means of production. That was Marx's grand indictment of the capitalist system, an indictment grounded not in ethics or the rules of justice but in what he believed to be the strictly scientific principles laid down by the English classical economists.

*Capital* was deliberately designed in its construction to display the philosophical difference between the underlying 'essence' of things and their surface 'appearances'. In Volume I the labour theory is assumed to be strictly true at a deeper, essential level of understanding. Volumes II and III, however, show that the real world belies this 'essence' because prices are actually determined in the ordinary way by cost outlays plus a profit margin. Marx endeavoured to prove that these prices are actually transformed labour values. Unfortunately, he was not quite satisfied with his own proof and besides, never lived to finish these later volumes of *Capital*. No wonder that it took almost a quarter of a century of debate to get a clear view of what he was actually trying to do. Needless to say, there is not much agreement even now that he succeeded even when judged on his own terms.

The elaborate and intricate apparatus which Marx constructed to make his case has never made a socialist of anyone. What convinced were the occasional flashes of brilliant rhetoric, the pages that relieved the abstract tedium by vivid descriptions of the misery of the working classes under capitalism, and the apocalyptic vision that promised the demise of capitalism with all the confidence of a prediction in the natural sciences.

It has become popular to say that Marx was no mere economist but an all-round social scientist who integrated economics, sociology, political science, history and even anthropology; there are hundreds of books about Marx that hardly even mention his economic ideas. But Marx wrote no more than a dozen pages on the concept of social class, the theory of the state, and the materialist conception of history. He did write literally 10,000 pages on economics pure and simple; economics was the only social science which he professed to have mastered in all its aspects. And let there be no doubt, he was a great economist. Even if we reject the fundamental Marxist schema and many, if not all, of his central conclusions, the three volumes of *Capital* and particularly the second two contain a large number of remarkable pieces of analysis from which modern economists can still learn: the growth of large-scale enterprise, the separation of ownership and control that this entails, the functional role of unemployment as a method of disciplining workers under capitalism, the significance of changes in money wages in the course of the business cycle, the inherent periodicity of the business cycle, the effect of technical progress on the rate of profit, the capital saving nature of technical progress — the list could be extended indefinitely. We even get some modern growth theory, albeit of a simple kind. Marx *is* still worth reading. Yes, he is difficult, very difficult, but he is also rewarding as he explores an avenue or line of thought strictly for its own sake; at those moments, he revels like Ricardo or Walras in the abstract power of economic reasoning.

*Secondary Literature.*
M. Rubel, 'Marx, Karl', *International Encyclopedia of the Social Sciences,* vol. 10, ed. D.L. Sills (Macmillan Free Press, 1968); D. McLellan, *Karl Marx. His Life and Thought* (Macmillan, 1973); L. Kolakowski, *Main Currents of Marxism,* 3 vols. (Oxford University Press, 1978); M. Blaug, *Economic Theory in Retrospect* (Cambridge University Press, 4th edn, 1985), Chapter 7.

# McCulloch, John Ramsay (1789-1864)

John Ramsay McCulloch was Ricardo's most zealous disciple and was perhaps more responsible than any other man for Ricardo's enormous influence on the economic thinking of his times. For a quarter of a century, he wrote most of the economic articles in the *Edinburgh Review,* a widely-read quarterly journal throughout the first half of the nineteenth century; in addition, he authored a *Principles of Political Economy* (1825), a number of widely-read pamphlets, and an almost endless list of newspaper articles. Despite his reputation as a devoted disciple of Ricardo, however, he was no slavish, dogmatic follower. He soon admitted various defects in the Ricardian system and indeed openly disagreed with some of Ricardo's analyses as well as his opinions on policy questions. Unlike other members of Ricardo's circle, he did not subscribe to utilitarianism in philosophy and radicalism in politics; his outlook was that of a liberal Tory, optimistic but conservative. One may even detect a gradual shift in his writings from an early emphasis on the rigorous abstract approach of Ricardo to a later emphasis on the looser historical analysis of Adam Smith. Certainly he turned away from the exposition of economic theory to the collection of descriptive and factual material. His *Dictionary of Commerce and Commercial Navigation* (1832) and *A Statistical Account of the British Empire* (1837) demonstrated his encyclopaedic knowledge of the British economy; they remain authoritative reference works to this day. To his career as a publicist and fact-gatherer, he added that of a professional historian of economic thought. His *Discourse on the Rise of Political Economy* (1824) was virtually the first attempt in any language to project a formal history of economic doctrines. Subsequently, he edited *The Wealth of Nations,* the published works of Ricardo, numerous scarce seventeenth- and eighteenth-century pamphlets on economic questions, and an annotated catalogue of *The Literature of Political Economy* (1845) based on his own magnificent personal library.

He was born in Scotland in 1789, the son of a small landowner, and never lost his broad Scottish accent. He studied law at the University of Edinburgh but soon turned to journalism and political economy. When Ricardo's *Principles* appeared in 1817, McCulloch immediately supplied a masterful digest of the book for the *Edinburgh Review,* which won Ricardo's enthusiastic endorsement. In 1820 he went to London where he taught economics privately. After Ricardo's death in 1823, friends and admirers chose McCulloch to deliver the Ricardo Memorial Lectures. The lectures were then expanded into an outline on 'Political Economy' for the new edition of the *Encyclopaedia Britannica* (1824) in which Ricardo's brand of economics is equated with the science of political economy itself. Academic security eluded McCulloch all his life. His appointment in 1828 to a professorship at the newly-founded University College, London had to be abandoned because no patron came forward to endow the Chair. An earlier attempt to make him the first incumbent of a new Chair of Political Economy at the University of Edinburgh also failed. He finally obtained a lifetime sinecure in 1838 as Comptroller of Her Majesty's Stationery Office; he took little part in the activities of the department and, apart from abandoning occasional journalism, continued to publish books and pamphlets on economic subjects. He died in 1864 at the age of 75.

*Secondary Literature*
D.P. O'Brien, *J.R. McCulloch: A Study in Classical Economics* (Allen & Unwin, 1970); M. Blaug, *Ricardian Economics: A Historical Study* (Greenwood Press, 1973).

# Menger, Carl (1840-1921)

Carl Menger published his *Principles of Economics* in 1871, the same year in which Jevons published *The Theory of Political Economy*. Three years later Walras's *Elements of Pure Economics* (1874) appeared in print. All three authors rejected cost of production theories of value and each employed the principle of diminishing marginal utility as the keystone for a new style of economics. Somewhere around 1900, it became standard practice to group these three authors together in a triumvirate as the founders of 'the marginal revolution'. But the fact that Jevons, Menger and Walras published more or less simultaneously is purely coincidental because none had any knowledge of the others, and each drew on a totally different literature for inspiration. Moreover, their differences are almost as marked as their similarities: on the one hand, Walras stands apart for his consistent emphasis on the concept of general, multi-market equilibrium which is absent in both Jevons and Menger; and on the other hand, Menger stands apart for his continuous stress on the subjective element in economic activity, for his doubts about the very concept of equilibrium itself, insisting that many observed economic phenomena must be explained in disequilibrium terms, and for his misgivings about the use of mathematics in economic analysis. Jevons failed to establish an English school of followers; Walras soon attracted a few disciples but in Italy, and not in France or Switzerland; Menger, however, not only attracted disciples but aggressive disciples like Böhm-Bawerk (q.v.) and Wieser (q.v.) who built on his ideas and developed them in different directions, founding a united Austrian school of economics which for 50 years or more struggled for first place against the Cambridge School of Marshall and the Lausanne School of the Walrasians.

Menger was born in 1840 in Galicia, southern Poland (then part of the Austro-Hungarian Empire), one of three sons of a prosperous professional family. Such was the atmosphere at home that not only Carl but also his two brothers, Anton and Karl, eventually achieved academic prominence (Anton Menger became a legal philosopher and historian of socialism, and Karl Menger a celebrated mathematician). Carl Menger studied law at the Universities of Vienna, Prague and Krakow, receiving his doctorate in law from the University of Krakow in 1867. His first post was in the press section of the Prime Minister's Office in Vienna and it was here that he first began to study economics seriously. His *Principles of Economics* gained him a lectureship at the University of Vienna, followed in 1873 by a professorship. In 1876 he imitated Adam Smith (q.v.) by becoming a tutor to Archduke Rudolf, Crown Prince of Austria, travelling extensively with him through Germany, France and Britain. In 1879 he returned to the University of Vienna and set off the *Methodenstreit* (dispute on method) by publishing *Problems of Economics and Sociology,* an attack on the 'younger' German Historical School. When Schmoller (q.v.) replied to his criticisms, Menger redoubled his attack in a fiery pamphlet, *Die Irrthümer des Historisms in der deutschen Nationalökonomie (The Fallacies of Historicism in German Political Economy)* (1884). *Die Irrthümer* hardened attitudes on both sides and produced a deep cleavage between German and Austrian economics that was to last until almost modern times. In the early 1890s, he produced a number of articles on monetary economics, which laid the basis of later Austrian writings on the value of money, particularly the works of Ludwig von Mises (1881-1973). In 1903, he resigned his Chair at Vienna to devote himself to writing a great treatise that would bring his first work up-to-date. But he never lived to complete this task and such fragments of the manuscript that he bequeathed to his son on his death in 1921 were only published subsequently in bits and pieces.

The first half of Menger's *Principles* devoted to value theory, and particularly the first three chapters, make a striking contrast with the treatment of Jevons, *Theory of Political Economy*. Unlike Jevons, Menger developed his argument not in terms of maximising pleasure but in terms of satisfying subjectively-felt needs, eschewing the use of both diagrams and mathematical formulae. From the outset the valuation of producer goods ('goods of a higher order', as Menger called them) is treated in exactly the same way as the valuation of final consumer goods ('goods of the first order'), the only difference being that the latter satisfy needs directly while the former satisfy needs indirectly. Menger strongly emphasised the essential complementarity between both producer and consumer goods and laid the basis for a view of the structure of production as a series of successive layers or stages of complementary goods and services, which Böhm-Bawerk was later to work into a complete theory of capital and interest. Menger argued that needs are of different kinds and the attempt to satisfy them can only be graduated on a hypothetical scale, beginning with vital needs and descending to needs of lesser importance, until eventual saturation is reached. His well-known table to illustrate this argument implied that utility is measurable but failed to explain how, and only implies diminishing marginal utility, a principle which Menger did not even take the trouble to define.

He went on to express the value of producer goods in terms of a 'loss' principle: their value depends on the consumer goods that might have been produced by the withdrawal of the most productive unit of those producer goods now in actual use. Thus, according to this principle of 'imputation', the value of consumer goods is not determined by the value of the producer goods employed to manufacture them as the classical economists had believed, but, on the contrary, the value of producer goods is always determined by the prospective value of the consumer goods they serve to produce.

That was as far as Menger went in analysing the role of cost of production in determining value, stopping far short even of Jevons. Reacting sharply to the value theory of the classical economists, both developed their arguments on the basis of a given stock of goods whose costs incurred in the past are now irrelevant.

*Secondary Literature*
J.A. Schumpeter, 'Carl Menger, 1840-1921', *Ten Great Economists from Marx to Keynes* (Oxford University Press, 1951); F.A. Hayek, 'Menger, Carl', *International Encyclopedia of the Social Sciences,* vol. 10, ed. D.L. Sills (Macmillan Free Press, 1968).

# Mill, John Stuart (1806-1873)

Throughout the last half of the nineteenth century, during almost the whole of the Victorian age right up to the publication of Marshall's *Principles* (1890), the *Principles of Political Economy, With Some of Their Applications to Social Philosophy* (1848) by John Stuart Mill was the leading economic textbook of the English-speaking world. It drew its enormous appeal from its extensive coverage of contemporary economic issues, from its judicious blending of economic analysis and historical illustrations, from its masterful synthesis of Ricardian doctrine with many of the qualifications introduced by Ricardo's critics, from its radical tone contained within an orthodox framework, from its elegant style, and from the reputation of Mill as a logician, philosopher, political theorist and *belle lettrist.* Here was no mere economist but a leading Benthamite, a 'saint of liberalism', and a figure that towered over the intellectuals of his time in almost every area of debate.

He was born in London, the eldest son of James Mill, himself a leading disciple and friend of both Ricardo and Jeremy Bentham. His education at the hands of his father, beginning with Greek at the age of 3, Latin at the age of 8 and political economy at the age of 10, so movingly described in his remarkable *Autobiography* (1873), was designed to exemplify Bentham's radical ideas about education whereas it really illustrated the fact that Mill was an infant prodigy. Naturally, he soon became a convinced Benthamite. However, by the time he was 20-years-old, having followed his father into the service of the East India Company, he began to have doubts about Benthamism. Unable to shake off a severe mental depression, he turned to the poetry of Wordsworth and Coleridge and emerged by the age of 25 or thereabouts a qualified critic of Bentham who sought to marry the British empirical tradition in social and political philosophy with the organic, historical tradition of such French writers as Saint-Simon (q.v.) and August Comte. It was also at this time that he met Harriet Taylor, the wife of a London businessman, whom he subsequently married after waiting for 20 years for her to become a widow. This relationship eventually became the central event of his life: again and again he acknowledged not only her superior capacity for personal feelings but also her superior intellect, virtually crediting all his original contributions to her influence. Needless to say, commentators have ever since been divided between those who endorse Mill's high opinion of Harriet Taylor's talent and those who see it as one more example of the old adage that love is blind.

Mill's first major work was *A System of Logic* (1843), but earlier essays on 'The Spirit of the Age' (1831), 'On the Definition of Political Economy; and on the Method of Investigation Proper to It' (1836), on 'Bentham' (1838) and on 'Coleridge' (1840) had already established his reputation as a major thinker. *The Principles of Political Economy* (1848) was followed by his most famous contribution, a slim book entitled *On Liberty* (1859), which gave full vent to one of his major themes: the growth of mass conformism in social conventions and political opinions which tended increasingly to stifle the freedom of the individual. Further works on political theory appeared in 1861, namely, *Considerations on Representative Government* and *Utilitarianism,* followed by *The Subjection of Women* (1869), a remarkable early tract on feminism, *August Comte and Positivism* (1865) and the *Autobiography* (1873). And all this says nothing about literally hundreds of essays on logic, ethics, metaphysics, psychology and sociology. The University of Toronto edition of *The Collected Works of John Stuart Mill* now runs to 15 volumes and the end of the series is by no means in sight.

Mill's *Principles of Political Economy* is, like Marshall's *Principles,* so well written that its original features do not stand out, as a result of which the book is often dismissed as 'Ricardo all over again'. But although Mill presented himself as a pious disciple of Ricardo, the book is full of genuine theoretical innovations, of which the most lasting was the extension of Ricardo's doctrine of comparative costs to take account of the effects of reciprocal demand on the terms of trade in international exchange. In addition, he qualified Smith's theory of relative wages by the introduction of the concept of non-competing groups in labour markets, he restated the 'law of demand and supply' as an algebraic equation rather than an identity, he recognised the problems that joint production created for a labour theory of value, he showed awareness that all costs are essentially the costs of opportunities forgone, he noted the appearance of economies in scale in manufacturing — the list of new insights might be extended almost indefinitely. But even more startling were the policy implications which he drew from what remained an essentially Ricardian framework of economic ideas. He was a vigorous advocate of inheritance taxation, peasant proprietorship, profit-sharing, and producers' and consumers' cooperatives. In an early chapter entitled 'Of Property', he gave a surprisingly sympathetic account of socialist doctrines as embodied in the writings of Owen (q.v.), Saint-Simon (q.v.) and Charles Fourier (he showed no awareness then or later of Marx, whose *Communist Manifesto* had appeared in English in the same year), and in later chapters on the proper scope of government action he endorsed protectionism in favour of infant industries, the regulation of hours of work in factories, and compulsory education (but not compulsory schooling) for children, coupled with a state system of examinations to verify that a minimum level of competence had been achieved.

In one important respect, however, Mill's *Principles* is hopelessly dated, namely, the relentless insistence that every conceivable policy measure must be judged in terms of its effect on the rate of growth of population. Mill was an ardent and even maniacal defender of the Malthusian theory of population. But he escaped almost all the gloomy implications of the Malthusian doctrine by an optimistic belief, so different from Malthus's own, in the capacity of the working class voluntarily to limit the size of their families. He never tells us how this voluntary family limitation was to come about but, although he did not dare to advocate it publicly, we know in fact that he favoured the use of birth control devices among the poor.

*Secondary Literature*
V.W. Bladen, 'Mill, John Stuart: Economic Considerations', *International Encyclopedia of the Social Sciences,* vol. 10, ed. D.L. Sills (Macmillan Free Press, 1968); J.M. Robson, *The Improvement of Mankind: The Social and Political Thought of J.S. Mill* (University of Toronto Press, 1968); P. Schwartz, *The New Political Economy of J.S. Mill* (Weidenfeld & Nicholson, 1972).

# Mitchell, Wesley Clair (1874-1948)

Wesley C. Mitchell is usually grouped with Veblen (q.v.) and Commons (q.v.) as one of the co-founders of the American school of institutional economics. But in fact the three founding-fathers of institutional economics had so little in common as to throw doubt on any connection between them. Unlike Veblen and Commons, Mitchell showed little inclination for methodological attacks on the preconceptions of orthodox economics and even less for interdisciplinary forays into psychology, sociology and anthropology. His institutionalism took the form of compiling statistical data on the notion that these would eventually furnish explanatory hypotheses. He was the founder of the National Bureau of Economic Research (NBER) in 1920 and the chief spokesman for the point of view in economics that has been cruelly described as 'measurement without theory'. Actually, there is far more theory in Mitchell than meets the eye (as Milton Friedman once demonstrated in a fascinating essay in the *Journal of Political Economy,* 1950); it is just that it is hidden away in asides or tacitly incorporated in the very organisation of the statistical material.

Mitchell was born in Rushville, Illinois in 1874 and entered the University of Chicago in 1892 where he fell under the spell of Veblen, one of his teachers. However, it was another teacher, James L. Laughlin (1850-1933) who encouraged him to devote his doctoral dissertation to the causes of the price inflation during the American civil war. This led to his first publication, *A History of the Greenbacks* (1903), which Mitchell later extended into the post-civil war period in *Gold, Prices and Wages under the Greenback Standard* (1908), a book which remains the authoritative reference-work on the American monetary upheavals of the period 1862-78. Mitchell started teaching at the University of California, Berkeley in 1903 and spent 10 years there before moving to Columbia University in 1913, the year which saw the publication of his massive treatise on *Business Cycles*. The study of business cycles remained Mitchell's central concern for the rest of his life. Having founded NBER, he supervised a large number of studies by others of different aspects of the business cycle. The 1913 treatise relied on annual data for four countries over the relatively brief period from 1890 to 1911. In *Business Cycles: The Problem and Its Setting* (1927), the analysis was extended to quarterly and even monthly data for 17 countries over various periods between 1850 and 1925, supplemented by 'business annals' (reports by contemporary observers on business conditions in individual years) that in some cases went back to 1790. Even this study was superseded by *Measuring Business Cycles* (1946), co-written with Arthur F. Burns, which drew on 1000 monthly series in four countries to establish the extent to which different indicators of upturns and downturns coincide with one another.

Although the study of business cycles had been pioneered in the nineteenth century by Juglar (q.v.), Jevons (q.v.), Aftalion (q.v.) and Spiethoff (q.v.), Mitchell carried the analysis to the point where further work merely required up-dating: there was literally nothing new left to be done. Moreover, there emerges from Part 3 of the 1913 book, frequently reprinted as *Business Cycles and Their Causes* (1959), and from Chapter 2 of the 1927 book a definite picture — call it a theory — of how business cycles are generated in a capitalist economy. Both the boom and the slump are cumulative, self-generating movements in economic activity, which reverse themselves eventually, because selling prices lag behind buying prices and expenditures lag behind receipts. It is these lags in the responses of economic agents because of custom and contractual obligations that account for the regular and highly synchronised periodicity of output, employment and prices. In an intense boom, the limit is set by financial institutions but in most booms it is demand which places an effective limit on the volume of economic activity. Similarly, in prolonged slumps, the declining costs of borrowing plays a central role in the upturn but in most slumps, the role of money is passive. Thus, Mitchell's account succeeds admirably in reconciling real and monetary theories of the business cycle.

Mitchell continued to teach at Columbia University until 1919. He left to join others in organising the New School for Social Research, New York, founded in part to give a home to a number of American scholars whose pacificism during the First World War had placed their jobs in jeopardy. In 1922, he returned to Columbia University where he remained until his retirement in 1944. His popular lecture course on 'Types of Economic Theory' was transcribed stenographically and published posthumously as a lasting memorial to his effectiveness as a teacher of the history of economic thought. Mitchell died in 1948 before completing yet another major book on the causes of business cycles; *What Happens During Business Cycles: A Progress Report* (1951) is only a fragment of this last project.

*Secondary Literature*
V. Zarnowitz, 'Mitchell, Wesley C.', *International Encyclopedia of the Social Sciences,* vol. 10, ed. D.L. Sills (Macmillan Free Press, 1968).

# Moore,
# Henry Ludwell
# (1869-1958)

If econometrics is the use of statistical techniques to test the relationships asserted by economic theory, Henry Moore was the first econometrician. His quantitative estimates of demand and supply curves, the determinants of wage rates, and the causes of business cycles pre-date the founding of the Econometric Society in 1930 by almost two decades.

He was born in Charles County, Maryland in 1869, graduated from Randolph-Macon College in Baltimore in 1892, and received his PhD from Johns Hopkins University in 1896 with a thesis on Thünen's natural wage, the subject of his first published article in 1895. After attending the University of Vienna for a year, where he was taught by Menger (q.v.), he returned to his first teaching post at Johns Hopkins University in 1896. In 1897 he became professor of political economy at Smith College, moving to Columbia University in 1902, where he remained for the rest of his academic career. He retired in 1929 at his own request due to ill-health, but lived until 1958 dying at the age of 88.

His knowledge of mathematics and statistics was largely self-learnt, although he did spend two terms in London in 1909 and 1913 to attend courses by Karl Pearson. He made innumerable trips to Europe and met and corresponded with all the great European economists of the day: Walras (q.v.), Pareto (q.v.) and Bortkiewicz (q.v.). But at home he lived the life of a scholarly recluse and apart from a friendship with two colleagues, John Bates Clark (q.v.) and John Maurice Clark (q.v.), had little contact with other American economists. He was dogged by poor health all his life, much of which seems to have been psychosomatic in origin. His last book, *Synthetic Economics* (1929), a bold attempt to estimate a complete Walrasian system of general equilibrium, shows signs of frustration at his waning powers.

His first book, however, *Laws of Wages* (1911), was a pioneering attempt to test the marginal productivity of wages. His first problem was to discover what the theory actually predicted about wages. It is characteristic of the difficulties of testing economic theories that this first step was the most difficult part of the entire exercise and that at least one of the predictions — labour's relative share of the output of an industry varies directly with the capital–labour ratio in the industry — is not in fact implied by marginal productivity theory. Likewise, another prediction — that daily pay in coal-mining varies closely with the value of coal mined per day — follows from a large number of alternative theories of wage determination. Nevertheless, other findings (e.g. that wage rates for similar occupations in an industry vary directly with the size of the plant) have repeatedly been confirmed by later investigators. The book also contained a first attempt to measure the influence of unions on the outcome of strikes, with highly ambiguous results.

His next book, *Economic Cycles: Their Laws and Cause* (1914), attempted nothing less than a fundamental explanation of the cause of business cycles in terms of eight-year rain cycles. The argument was that rainfall cycles produce cycles of equal duration in yields per acre, which in turn produce cycles in both grain prices and the prices of industrial goods. Moore found it difficult to square declining crop yields with falling prices for industrial goods, and was therefore forced to assume 'a new type of demand curve', namely, a positively-sloped demand curve for pig iron as a representative industrial good. This effectively spoiled his theory of cycles but along the way he had produced some of the first statistical estimates of demand curves in the English literature. In a 1919 article he introduced the concept of the 'flexibility of prices' (the reciprocal of the price-elasticity of demand) and estimated it for a variety of agricultural products. He then extended the analysis to supply curves by correlating changes in acreage with percentage changes in prices a year earlier; this proved to be the source of later work on the so-called cobweb theorem in which prices converge on or diverge from their equilibrium values depending on how producers actually forecast prices.

Moore carried on in his earlier studies of cycle theory in *Generating Economic Cycles* (1923), dropping the new type of demand curve and attributing the eight-year cycle of prices to the eight-year transits of the planet Venus. This argument was greeted with ridicule and, in an almost exact parallel with Jevons' 11-year cycle of sun spots, effectively killed off any interest in his cycle theories.

The 1920s saw an extensive development of statistical studies of demand, carried out in almost every case by agricultural economists working at the US Bureau of Agriculture. Not at the Bureau of Agriculture but nevertheless the leader in this field was Henry Schultz (1893-1938), Moore's one true disciple whose *Theory and Measurement of Demand* (1938) was the crowning achievement of the work initiated by Moore 24 years earlier.

*Secondary Literature*
G.J. Stigler, 'Moore, Henry L.', *International Encyclopedia of the Social Sciences,* vol. 10,. ed. D.L. Sills (Macmillan Free Press, 1968).

# Mun, Thomas (1571-1641)

For those who want to read a single example of mercantilist writing, it is difficult to better Thomas Mun's *England's Treasure by Forraign Trade*, completed in 1628 and published posthumously in 1664. Adam Smith at any rate regarded it as perfectly representative of a vast body of similar literature: 'The title of Mun's book', he said, 'became a fundamental maxim in the political economy, not of England only, but of all other commercial countries'.

The leading features of mercantilism are well known: the balance of trade as *the* index of economic prosperity because the essence of wealth is 'treasure' or 'specie', that is gold and silver; the regulation of foreign trade to produce a chronic excess of exports over imports and hence a constant inflow of gold and silver specie; the promotion of domestic industry by inducing the importation of cheap raw materials and by placing protective duties on competing imported manufactured goods; the encouragement of exports in the form of finished goods because this maximises domestic employment; and the encouragement of population growth because it keeps wages and hence prices low. Adam Smith's answer to this set of ideas was to charge the mercantilists with the fallacy of equating money with capital. Like an individual, a country must spend less than its income if its wealth is to increase. But this surplus over consumption is capital, not money, and a positive balance of income over consumption permitting the accumulation of capital has nothing whatever to do with a favourable balance of trade promoting the inflow of gold and silver.

Other eighteenth century writers, such as Hume (q.v.), and the classical economists that followed Smith employed yet another argument against the mercantilists. Purely automatic forces, it was held, tend to establish a 'natural distribution of specie' between the trading countries of the world and such levels of domestic prices in different countries as to bring exports into equality with imports. Any additional mining of gold in one country will raise its price level relative to those of other countries; the resulting import surplus must be financed by an outflow of gold; this engenders the same response in the gold-receiving country; and the process continues until all trading nations have established a new equilibrium between exports and imports corresponding to the higher supply of gold. External trade and gold are akin to water in two connecting vessels that is constantly seeking a common level. Hence, a policy aiming at a favourable balance of trade is simply self-defeating.

Is Mun's book guilty, not only of committing the fallacy of equating money with capital but also of ignoring the specie-flow mechanism just described? Undoubtedly yes, although it must be said that he seems repeatedly to catch a glimpse of the flaws in his own reasoning. The notion that the balance of trade, by which he meant both visible and invisible items in the current account of the total balance of payments, is the 'rule' or 'touchstone' of national wealth is laid down in the opening pages of the book. Similarly, he moves on immediately in typical mercantilist fashion to decry luxury spending because of the high import content of luxury goods but qualifies it by conceding that England must import, lest she dries up foreign purchasing power to buy English exports. He commends the carrying trade over the exports of manufactured goods and the latter over primary products because the carrying trade is the most labour-intensive of all possible export industries. There follow some crude estimates of the price-elasticity of demand for different types of English exports in foreign markets in terms of which he lays down maxims for charging export duties. Being particularly concerned to defend the East India trade in which goods flowed to England paid for entirely by silver coin — a permanent *un*favourable balance of trade — he carefully distinguishes between the bilateral balance of trade with one other country and the multilateral balance of trade with the rest of the world: a bilateral balance may be unfavourable, reflecting triangular trade relations, but that matters little so long as the multilateral balance of trade is favourable.

All the elements of the specie-flow mechanism are to be found in his book but they are never put together to form a connected chain of reasoning. He is perfectly aware that an inflow of gold raises prices and that high prices reduce exports, thus leading to the conclusion that every favourable balance of trade will be short-lived. But he never drew this conclusion, possibly because it would have destroyed the whole of his central thesis but also because he kept his mind on the East Indies from which gold and silver never did return and thus never did raise prices in England.

After all this it will not come as a great surprise to learn that Mun was a prominent member of the East India Company and that his first work in economics, *A Discourse of Trade from England Unto the East Indies* (1621), was a defence of the East India Company against the specific charge that its trade with India had caused the economic depression of 1620 by draining England of silver. Nothing is known of Mun's education but it is probable that he served his apprenticeship in the Mediterranean trade and early on made a large fortune in the East India trade. He was the third son of a London trading family: his father and grandfather had both served as officers of the Royal Mint and his stepfather was one of the first directors of the East India Company. Mun eventually bought land and settled down as a country gentleman, where he died, aged 70.

*Secondary Literature*
R.W.K. Hinton, 'Mun, Thomas', *International Encyclopedia of the Social Sciences,* vol. 10, ed. D.L. Sills (Macmillan Free Press, 1968).

# Newcomb, Simon (1835-1909)

Well known during his lifetime as a leading American mathematician and astronomer, Simon Newcomb was also prominent in the mid-1880s as a defender of the old school of Ricardian economics against the criticisms of the new, German-inspired historical economists typified by the writings of Ely (q.v.). In popular books, like *The ABC of Finance* (1878) and *A Plain Man's Talk on the Labor Question* (1886), Newcomb took a stern line in favour of rugged individualism in opposition to the 'fallacies' of labour unionism and socialism. In an unsigned review of Ely's sympathetic *Labor Movement in America* (1886), he denounced his Johns Hopkins colleague as unfit to hold a University Chair. However, he always had a deeper, more professional interest in economic theory. As early as 1872, he was one of the few Americans to write a favourable review of Jevons' *Theory of Political Economy* (1871). Still earlier, his correspondence with the philosopher Charles S. Peirce shows a familiarity with Cournot's *Mathematical Principles of the Theory of Wealth* (1838).

In 1886, Newcomb published his highly original, but little noticed

*Principles of Political Economy,* which exerted considerable acknowledged influence on the later writings of Fisher (q.v.). Newcomb's book revealed a clear distinction between both stocks and flows and the circular flows of money and goods, culminating in an 'equation of societary circulation', VR = KP, which is identical to Fisher's 'equation of exchange', MV = PT, but for Newcomb's unmnemonic choice of symbols. He went on to analyse the demand for money, distinguishing between *ex ante* and *ex post* demand, and launched upon a sophisticated analysis of the effect of hoarding on employment and prices. Finally, his discussion of the determination of the rate of interest in terms of the demand and supply of loanable funds was as good as anything found in Fisher 20 years later. All in all, it was a remarkable performance, suggesting that Newcomb might have become a major American monetary economist if his real interests had not lain elsewhere.

He was born in humble circumstances in Nova Scotia, Canada in 1835 and received little formal education. Nevertheless, after a brief spell as a country schoolmaster, he obtained his first degree from Harvard University in 1858 while working part-time on the preparation of the *Nautical Almanac.* In 1861 he became a professor of mathematics in the US Navy and a professor of mathematics and astronomy at Johns Hopkins University, combining both posts with occasional lectures on economics at Harvard and supervision of the successive editions of the *American Ephemeris* and the *Nautical Almanac* until his retirement in 1897. He published widely, not only in mathematics, astronomy and economics, but also in politics, education, theology and psychic research. He remained active in the international scientific community until his death in 1909, aged 74.

*Secondary Literature*
A.W. Coats, 'Newcomb, Simon', *International Encyclopedia of the Social Sciences,* vol. 11, ed. D.L. Sills (Macmillan Free Press, 1968).

# North, Dudley (1641-1691)

Dudley North exerted little influence on the economic opinions of his times because his one brief pamphlet, *Discourses Upon Trade* (1691), was published shortly after his death in so few copies that it quickly disappeared from circulation. Why then treat him here as a major economist? In part because North's only pamphlet was rediscovered in 1818 by James Mill and reprinted by McCulloch (q.v.) in 1822 as a revelation which fully confirmed their own "new" views in favour of free trade; for the rest, because the pamphlet represents a unique example of the capacity of certain thinkers to emancipate themselves almost totally from the prevailing preconceptions of the times in which they are writing. In fact, reading it now it seems almost impossible to believe that it was published at about the same time that Locke (q.v.) was writing on economic questions.

For one thing, there is not a hint of the mercantilist concern with a favourable balance of trade. On the contrary, North argues, international trade like inter-regional trade is best left unhampered by regulation. Besides, countries grow wealthy not by regulation but by active industry, the supply of money being kept to an adequate level by the ebb and flow of market forces. The total volume of world trade is not fixed, so that the gains of one country come at the expense of another, but all foreign trade is a 'commutation of superfluities', an exchange of 'conveniences'. For another, the argument is conducted at a high level of abstraction, free from all moralising and ethical overtones. North deliberately fails to address concrete problems, such as are emphasised in all other economic tracts of the period, and insists on treating trade 'philosophically' on the basis of 'principles indisputably true', a method of reasoning, he adds, introduced by 'Descartes's excellent dissertation *De Methodo*'. Such methodological self-consciousness was extremely rare in economic writings until the nineteenth century.

Sir Dudley North, the offspring of an old and notable family of merchants and statesmen, appears to have been largely self-taught. He failed at school at the age of 12 and was sent to Turkey at the age of 19 to try his luck in the Levant merchant trade. He returned to England in 1680, retired from business, and spent the remainder of his life first as Commissioner of the Customs and later as a Commissioner of the Treasury.

*Secondary Literature*
D. Vickers, 'North, Dudley', *International Encyclopedia of the Social Sciences,* vol. 11, ed. D.L. Sills (Macmillan Free Press, 1968).

# Owen, Robert (1771-1858)

No one would pretend that Robert Owen was a great economist, but his writings and particularly his practical work as an enlightened businessman, leader of trade union agitation and founder of cooperative communities had an electrifying effect on those who lived through the industrial revolution in Britain: to Ricardo (q.v.), Torrens (q.v.) and Senior (q.v.) socialism meant Owenism and even John Stuart Mill (q.v.) as late as 1848 coupled him with St-Simon (q.v.) and Charles Fourier as *the* socialist thinker of his time. His belief in the value of cooperation rather than competition and his optimistic faith that education was capable of totally transforming self-interest into a concern for others were first stated in *A New View of Society: Or, Essays on the Principle of the Formation of the Human Character* (1813) and then expanded in a number of pungent essays, particularly *Report to the County of Lanark* (1821). In later years, when he was active in America in setting up self-supporting 'villages of cooperation', he advocated the abolition of money backed by a metallic standard and replacing it by tickets expressed in units of labour time which would be paid for work done on a *pro rata* basis.

Although this idea was the practical expression of the then widely-held labour theory of value, he never troubled to explain its operation or to provide it with some sort of theoretical support; one searches in vain in his later writings for any coherent discussion of labour money. Nevertheless, the notion has ever since had a powerful appeal to producer cooperatives organised on socialist or communist principles; it is practised today in parts of China, Kampuchea and Ethiopia, although rarely without subsidies from the outside for capital equipment.

Owen was born in 1771 in Newtown, Wales, the son of a prosperous Welsh farmer and merchant. His career shows three well-marked phases: an early phase from 1799-1824 when he was a respectable owner of a new type of cotton mill in Lanark, Scotland, accompanied by cheap housing for his workers and a school for their children, and struggled to convince the rich and the powerful of the wisdom and practicality of his plans for a new social order; a phase of unsuccessful community building in Indiana, USA, which lasted from 1824-29; and from 1829 onwards, when he was increasingly drawn into British working-class politics, culminating in the formation of the Grand National Consolidated Trades Union in 1833, the first attempt anywhere in the world to form a national federation of trade unions. When this failed within a year, Owen went back to community experiments, in Britain this time. The Rochdale cooperative movement, which flourished in Britain in the 1840s, was undoubtedly inspired by Owenite ideals but the Rochdale cooperatives were consumer not producer cooperatives and thus fell short of Owen's own vision of social redemption. Owen lived until the age of 87, a venerated but nevertheless disillusioned man.

*Secondary Literature*
A. Briggs, 'Owen, Robert', *International Encyclopedia of the Social Sciences,* vol. 11, ed. D.L. Sills (Macmillan Free Press, 1968).

# Pareto, Vilfredo (1848-1923)

Vilfredo Pareto succeeded Walras (q.v.) to his Chair at the University of Lausanne in 1893 and for long regarded himself as a disciple of Walras. But Walras was not always happy with the younger man's social and political ideas and Pareto grew increasingly disenchanted not just with general equilibrium theory but with economics in general, choosing instead to work within the wider framework of political sociology. His really formidable knowledge of mathematics and his early training as an engineer were displayed in all his major economic writings, *Cours d'économie politique* (1896-97), *Manual of Political Economy* (1906) and the important essay on 'Mathematical Economics' (1911) for the *Encyclopédie des sciences mathématiques*. He was interested in Marx as early as the 1890s and published a powerful non-mathematical critique of socialist thought including Marxism in three volumes in *Les systèmes socialistes* (1902-3). A massive work in four volumes, *The Mind and Society: A Treatise on General Sociology* (1916) crowned the last decade of his active life.

He was born in 1848 in Paris, his father having been exiled from Italy. He began his education in France but continued it in Italy, specialising in mathematics and classical literature. He graduated from the Polytechnic Institute in Turin in 1869 and then spent more than 20 years working as an engineer and director of two Italian railway companies. He did not come to the study of economics until 1890 at the age of 42. He taught economics at Lausanne for only seven years, resigning in 1900 when he inherited a substantial fortune. He spent the rest of his life in Switzerland, wholly devoted to his studies and writings. Shortly before his death in 1923 he was appointed a member of the Italian senate by the new government of Mussolini.

Both the *Cours* and the first two chapters of the *Manual* contain a remarkable discussion of the methodology of economics, which shows Pareto to have been better read in the then received literature on the philosophy of science than any other economist of the period. The uneven and poorly organised *Cours* contained, among its many historical and statistical illustrations, the so-called Pareto's law of income distribution, according to which the slope of the line connecting the percentage of income received above a certain level to the percentage of relevant income-receivers is a constant, thus demonstrating that the distribution of income in all countries and in all ages conforms to an invariant pattern. The *Manual* is famous for at least three ideas: the unsuccessful attempt to banish the term 'utility' and to replace it by 'ophelimity', a word coined by Pareto to denote the power of goods to satisfy wants; the clear distinction between cardinal and ordinal utility and the demonstration, via Edgeworth's indifference curves, that ordinal utility or the mere ranking of preferences is sufficient to deduce all the important propositions of demand theory; and the apparently innocent, non-controversial definition of an economic optimum as that configuration of prices that commands unanimous approval — any other configuration might make some better-off but only by making at least one person worse-off — the notorious concept of Pareto optimality, coupled with the not altogether successful attempt to show that a perfectly competitive economy in fact achieves a Pareto optimum, and vice versa. Despite the intimidating use of some fairly advanced mathematics, it is doubtful that Pareto's theory of consumer behaviour advanced the subject much beyond Edgeworth's *Mathematical Psychics* (1888) and Fisher's *Mathematical Investigations in the Theory of Value and Prices* (1892). Even the concept of Pareto optimality already appears in Edgeworth, although admittedly not in a way that one would notice it if one did not know it already from Pareto. The *Manual* also contained a much misunderstood section on the theory of production, which seemed to deny marginal productivity theory as erroneous, but in fact placed more weight on the complementarity between factors of production than on their substitutability.

Pareto is a difficult author to read: too many of his tersely expressed ideas are jumbled together on the same page, many thoughts are left incomplete to be taken up again at a later date, and his mathematical notations are frequently inconsistent. His influence made itself felt only very gradually and it was not until the late 1930s that he actually entered English-speaking economics, in part because even then not a single book of his had been translated into English. (The *Manual* finally appeared in English in 1971, *Mind and Society* having appeared in 1963.) Even now it is difficult to get a bearing on his entire output and particularly his later sociological writings, with their pessimistic picture of man driven by irrational sentiments, thinly disguised by residues of rational argument and locked in perpetual social struggle barely held at bay by 'circulating élites'.

*Secondary Literature*
J.A. Schumpeter, *Ten Great Economists from Marx to Keynes* (Oxford University Press, 1951); M. Allais, 'Pareto, Vilfredo', *International Encyclopedia of the Social Sciences,* vol. 11, ed. D.L. Sills (Macmillan Free Press, 1968).

# Petty, William (1623-1687)

The only major work of Petty's that was published during his lifetime was *A Treatise of Taxes and Contributions* (1662). All the others — *Political Arithmetic, Verbum Sapienti, Political Anatomy of Ireland* and *Quantulumcunque Concerning Money* — were published in the decade after his death. Each of them is focused on some practical question of the times: war finance, monetary reform, relief for the poor, the relative strength of England compared to her rivals, etc. His statements of general principles always emerge incidentally to his discussion of concrete problems. Nevertheless, these works represent a veritable cornucopia of terms and concepts that came to dominate economic thinking for the next three centuries: 'full employment' and *'ceteris paribus'* — these are Petty's own terms; the idea of national income as identical to national expenditure; public works as a method of dealing with unemployment; land and labour as the only primary factors of production — 'Labour is the Father and active principle of Wealth, as Lands are the Mother'; the notion of a 'par' or common unit of measurement with which to convert the product of land into that of labour; the price of land as the discounted present value of expected future rentals, and likewise the 'value of man' as the present value of expected earnings; population growth as the touchstone of national prosperity; the advantages of low wages because the supply curve of labour is backward-sloping; the theory that the supply of money adjusts itself automatically to the 'needs of trade' via adjustments in the velocity of circulation; the argument that taxes should be proportionate to spending and not to income and that they should be neutral with respect to the prevailing distribution of wealth; the evaluation of the gains from foreign trade in terms of the benefits of specialisation and the territorial division of labour — there is simply no end to the versatility of Petty's mind throwing off ideas in all directions.

His greatest contribution, however, was the invention of what he called 'political arithmetic', the quantitative estimation of both the stock of national wealth and the flow of national income for purposes of determining the appropriate base for taxation. Lacking adequate data and unaware of any statistical techniques other than the concept of the arithmetic average, Petty employed short-cuts which invited the ridicule of later generations. Thus, to estimate the population of England he began by calculating the population of London; multiplying the known number of burials in London by 30 on the assumption that one Londoner out of 30 dies every year, he then multiplied the London estimate by a factor of 8, this being the proportion in which the assessed taxable value of the whole of England stands to that of London. No wonder Adam Smith declared, 'I have no great faith in political arithmetic.' Nevertheless, Petty's methods were developed and elaborated by other late seventeenth-century writers, such as Davenant (q.v.) and Gregory King, whose social accounting methods were surprisingly modern. After this promising start, it is difficult to understand why work on the measurement of national income in England came to a complete halt at the beginning of the eighteenth century. Possibly it may have been due to the continued inadequacy of the statistical data and the relaxation of international tension. But whatever the reason, the quantitative approach to economics in general and national income estimation in particular had to wait until the early nineteenth century for a new start.

Dazzling as are Petty's writings, his own life was even more dazzling. Born in 1623 of a poor Hampshire clothier, he acquired Latin and Greek at a local school. Going to sea as a cabin boy at the age of 14, he was put ashore on the Normandy coast after breaking a leg and talked himself into admission at the Jesuits' college of Caen. From there he went to the Netherlands to study medicine and then to Paris where he assisted Thomas Hobbes, the famous political philosopher, in anatomical studies. In 1647 he returned to England, entered Oxford University and in a few years received his Doctor of Physic. He then enrolled at the London College of Physicians and eventually became Vice-Principal of Brasenose College, Oxford and a professor of anatomy. The English civil war between the King and Parliament being in full swing, he left England for Ireland in 1651 to serve as physician-general to the English army under Cromwell. Within two years of his arrival in Ireland he had assumed the immense task of surveying the forfeited estates of the Irish rebels so as to distribute them among the soldiers of Cromwell's army. The survey, for which he was partly paid in land, placed him in a privileged position to purchase still more land from other claimants, thus laying the foundation of what was to become a substantial fortune. Petty returned to London in 1659 and from then on he moved back and forth between Ireland and England. He served as a Member of Parliament, became a charter member of the Royal Society (whom he frequently addressed on a variety of topics), advised Charles II, who overlooked his past connections with Cromwell and knighted him in 1661, worked on many inventions (a two-wheeled conveyance, an early water closet, and a twin-hulled ship), and started to write a series of books of which, as we have said, only one was published in his own lifetime. On James II's accession to the throne in 1685, he became an advisor to the new king: he died in 1687, a year before James II was dethroned.

*Secondary Literature*
P. Deane, 'Petty, William', *International Encyclopedia of the Social Sciences,* vol. 12, ed. D.L. Sills (Macmillan Free Press, 1968).

# Pigou, Arthur C (1877-1959)

Arthur Pigou, professor of political economy at Cambridge University from 1908 to 1943, is best known for his authoritative statement of the theory of the old economic welfare. His *Theory of Unemployment* (1933) furnished Keynes in *The General Theory* (1936) with the best example of the classical economics Keynes so decisively rejected. Having unfairly served as Keynes's whipping-boy, Pigou nevertheless managed in old age graciously to acknowledge that Keynes had been largely correct.

In his fundamental work, *The Economics of Welfare* (1920), Pigou elaborated Marshall's invention of the concept of externalities into a general economic theory of government intervention. Externalities occur when the actions of one economic agent unintentionally harm or benefit others, as a result of which the *private* costs or benefits of an activity diverge from their true *social* costs or benefits. Such cases of market failure, he argued, require government intervention in the form of taxes or subsidies to close the gap between private and social cost-benefit ratios. This liberal theory of state action in the economic sphere has been with us so long and has entered so deeply into the fabric of political life in the twentieth century that its obvious weaknesses may not be immediately apparent. It is only in recent years that economists have come to realise that market failure as such is an insufficient reason for government intervention since taxes and subsidies themselves generate a divergence between the private and the social calculus: there is 'government failure' as well as 'market failure'.

*The Economics of Welfare* was old welfare economics, in the sense that Pigou was perfectly happy to employ definite interpersonal comparisons of utility as if they had 'scientific' standing. Thus he concluded that any increase in national income which did not involve a shift from the income of the poor to the income of the rich was to be defined as an improvement ·in economic welfare; naturally, he left himself free in any particular case to decide for himself who were the poor and who were the rich.

Pigou was born at Ryde in the Isle of Wight in 1877, the son of a retired army officer. He won a scholarship at an early age to the famous public school, Harrow, from which he won another scholarship to King's College, Cambridge, graduating in 1901 with a thesis on *Robert Browning as a Religious Teacher,* his first published book. He began lecturing on economics at Cambridge in the same year, a task which he carried on without interruption until the Second World War. In these early days he was a brilliant lecturer, and his repeated insistence to students that 'It's all in Marshall' was largely responsible in the interwar years for the Marshallian orthodoxy of Cambridge economics. His early books — *Tariffs* (1903), *Industrial Peace* (1905) and *Import Duties* (1906) — do little to explain his accession in 1908 to Marshall's Chair in Economics at the early age of 30. But *Wealth and Welfare* (1912) and *Unemployment* (1914) give a first hint of his true powers, the later *Economics of Welfare* (1920) being a reworking of *Wealth and Welfare. Essays in Applied Economics* (1923), *Industrial Fluctuations* (1927) and *A Study in Public Finance* (1928) were other major contributions.

From 1927 onwards ill-health undermined the liveliness of his lecturing and the vigour of his writing. He gave up mountain-climbing, the full-time hobby of his youth, and gradually became the academic recluse of later years, famous for his absentmindedness and slovenly appearance. His stream of output, however, never lapsed. The notorious *Theory of Unemployment* (1933) was succeeded by *The Economics of Stationary States* (1935), *Employment and*

*Equilibrium* (1941), and a whole series of short popular expositions: *Socialism versus Capitalism* (1937), *Income: An Introduction to Economics* (1946), *Lapses from Full Employment* (1947), *The Veil of Money* (1949), *Keynes's General Theory: A Retrospective View* (1950) and *Essays in Economics* (1952).

Pigou has probably been more underrated than any other major economist, and he has only recently been adequately defended against Keynes's abuse in *The General Theory*. It is indeed impossible to discover Keynes's description of Pigou's ideas in Pigou's own *Theory of Unemployment* — in particular, that the only cure for the Great Depression was to force real wages down; Pigou, like Keynes, did not believe it feasible to reduce real wages substantially and looked to public works to relieve unemployment. On the other hand, it is difficult to discover any coherent, operational theory of unemployment in what is actually one of Pigou's most abstract and complicated books. Many of Pigou's other works contain remarkable hints of things to come in economics, particularly in monetary theory; for example, in *Unemployment* (1913) he provided an exposition of the concept of the 'balanced budget multiplier' that Keynes might have envied 23 years later, and in an essay on 'The Value of Money' (1917), he all but spelled out the 'real balance effect' that Patinkin was to make his own in his famous *Money, Interest, and Prices* (1956). But Pigou's crowning achievement remains that of the monumental *Economics of Welfare*.

*Secondary Literature*
A. Robinson, 'Pigou, Arthur Cecil', *International Encyclopedia of the Social Sciences,* vol. 12, ed. D.L. Sills (Macmillan Free Press, 1968); D. Collard, 'A.C. Pigou, 1877-1959', *Pioneers of Modern Economics in Britain,* D.P. O'Brien and J.R. Presley (eds.) (Macmillan, 1981).

# Proudhon, Pierre-Joseph (1809-1865)

Although Owen (q.v.), St-Simon (q.v.) and Charles Fourier were renowned early socialists, none achieved the wide readership of Proudhon, particularly in France in the years before and after the revolution of 1848. Moreover, Proudhon was the first socialist to engage orthodox economists in an active dialogue. Marx was not misguided when he chose Proudhon as the target for one of his famous polemical assaults in *The Poverty of Philosophy* (1847).

What made Proudhon so influential was not the power of his ideas but the caustic eloquence of his writing. *What is Property?* (1840), his principal work, contained the immortal answer, 'Property is theft'; but in fact all his writings are full of quotable lines. In these respects, as well as in many others, he departed from most socialists of his time. He deplored feminism, free love and common-law marriage and extolled the nuclear family; most of his social views were those of the artisan or *petit bourgeois* shopowner. On the other hand, he was an atheist and an anti-semite, typical of nineteenth-century socialists. But where he differed most radically from other socialists was in his views on government. He did not hesitate to call himself an anarchist and denounced the very existence of the state. What he wanted to put in its place was 'mutalisme', that is, a set of voluntary agreements between large-scale agricultural industrial communities, a federal system with strict representation whose constitution he set out with considerable care. Applying a crude version of the labour theory of value, he contemplated the disappearance of all 'unearned' profits and rents in these communities, while a 'people's bank' would freely monetise the products of their labour and advance funds for investment. Marx had great fun ridiculing Proudhon's puerile economic ideas, and it must be confessed that Proudhon's economics was not his strong point.

Most socialists of the day were sons of the middle or even upper classes, whereas Proudhon was the son of a local brewer who went bankrupt. He spent his childhood in abject poverty (as he constantly reminded his later readers) and was only to finish secondary education by working as a proof-reader and printer's foreman. He was 29-years-old before he was admitted to an institution of higher education; and he failed to graduate. After working for a small shipping company in Lyons, he moved to Paris and was elected to the National Assembly in 1848. By this time, he was already known as a formidable journalist and author. He was sentenced to three years' imprisonment in 1849 for publishing slanderous articles in the newspaper he was editing. He went on writing even in prison and was subsequently exiled to Belgium. In 1862, he was pardoned and returned to France. He died in poverty in 1865.

*Secondary Literature*
M. Prélot, 'Proudhon, Pierre-Joseph', *International Encyclopedia of the Social Sciences,* vol.12, ed. D.L. Sills (Macmillan Free Press, 1968); E. Hyams, *Pierre-Joseph Proudhon: His Revolutionary Life, Mind and Works* (Taplinger, 1979).

# Quesnay, François (1694-1774)

François Quesnay is one of those economists that students and even many of their teachers must leave unread: so intricate is his reasoning, so convoluted are his calculations, and so steeped is his every word in the outdated political philosophy and economic circumstances of eighteenth-century France that only years of study can make any sense of his writings. What everybody knows about Quesnay is the bizarre zig-zag diagram or *Tableau Économique,* the proposition that only agriculture generates a positive 'net product' and that industry is 'sterile', the recommendation of a 'single tax' on ground rent, and the slogan *laissez-faire, laissez-passer* — that, and the fact that he was the first to found a school of economists called the 'physiocrats', which enjoyed an immense vogue in France for about a decade in the 1750s. The problem is what all these ideas have to do with one another and, indeed, why they proved so successful.

There were many later economists who admired Quesnay, such as Smith (q.v.), Marx (q.v.) and Schumpeter (q.v.), but what they admired was not the detail of his arguments but the vision that tied them together. Smith was excited by the physiocratic distinction between the 'productive' classes, which are instrumental in the capacity of the economy to reproduce itself from period to period, and the 'unproductive' classes, which merely produce articles for consumption in this period. Marx was excited by Quesnay's belief that economic analysis must pinpoint the source of the surplus over the subsistence requirements of workers that is generated by a viable economic system. Schumpeter, on the other hand, admired the underlying physiocratic conception of a circular flow of goods in one direction and money in the other direction, the income payments of this period becoming the spending flows of the next.

In Quesnay's own time, however, it was the idea that agriculture, and not merchandising or manufacturing, is the engine of economic growth that proved to be the key to the appeal of physiocratic ideas. Even after the influence of the physiocrats had waned and the industrial revolution had begun, an emphasis on the importance of agriculture was always followed by a reference to the writings of Quesnay.

Quesnay was born in 1694, the son of a small landowner. He appears to have had no formal education but nevertheless succeeded in teaching himself enough medicine to practise as a doctor and even to write several medical treatises. He did eventually acquire a medical degree but even before that he had moved to Versailles and, under the patronage of Madame de Pompadour, became a consulting physician to Louis XV.

His first publications in economics appeared as articles for the *Encyclopédie* in 1756 and 1757 when he was 60-years-old. In 1758, he published a brief pamphlet, *Tableau Economique* (1758), which contained the famous zig-zag diagram, a sort of input – output table expressed in terms of money flows. Unfortunately, he reworked the diagram three or four times in later publications and the original version was printed in so few copies that it was subsequently lost: this increased the mystery of its meaning and later led to a large literature attempting to unravel its message. The clearest statement of physiocratic doctrine is contained in a book entitled *Philosophie rurale* (1763), which Quesnay wrote with one of his disciples, the Marquis de Mirabeau (1715-89). But it was another collection of his writings, edited by yet another disciple, Du Pont de Nemours (1739-1817), and published under the title *La Physiocratie* (1768), which gave a name to the followers of Quesnay.

Physiocracy was a reform movement *par excellence*. Quesnay had no interest in economics for its own sake but only as a means of improving the parlous state of the French economy, catching up with England which had had its agricultural revolution, and reforming the tax system which stifled French farmers. The great enemy for Quesnay was mercantilism or *Colbertisme,* which for so long had given special privileges to French manufacturing at the expense of agriculture. Thus, the practical programme of the physiocrats was to eliminate the vestiges of mediaeval tolls and restrictions in the countryside, to rationalise the fiscal system by reducing the maze of taxes to a single levy on rent, to amalgamate small-holdings into large-scale agricultural estates, to free the corn trade from all mercantilist restrictions — in short, to emulate England. Placed in its historical context, these were eminently reasonable views. It was only the effort to provide these reforms with a watertight theoretical argument that produced some of the forced reasoning and slightly absurd conclusions that invited ridicule even from contemporaries.

*Secondary Literature*
R.L. Meek, *The Economics of Physiocracy* (Allen & Unwin, 1962); B.F. Hoselitz, 'Quesnay, François', *International Encyclopedia of the Social Sciences,* vol. 13, ed. D.L. Sills (Macmillan Free Press, 1968).

# Rae, John (1796-1872)

John Rae wrote one great book, *Statement of Some New Principles on the Subject of Political Economy* (1834), which came to the attention of both Senior (q.v.) and John Stuart Mill (q.v.). Mill quoted it frequently in his *Principles of Political Economy* (1848), and yet the book remained largely unread; so much so that when it was reissued in an abridged revised edition in 1902, under a new title, *The Sociological Theory of Capital,* it was hailed by such leading neo-classical economists as Böhm-Bawerk (q.v.), Wicksell (q.v.) and Fisher (q.v.) as a revelation; Fisher indeed was so impressed that he subsequently dedicated his masterpiece on *The Theory of Interest* (1930) to 'The memory of John Rae and of Eugen von Böhm-Bawerk who laid the foundations upon which I have endeavored to build.' What struck everyone was the uncanny extent to which Rae had foreshadowed the two pillars on which the Austrian theory of capital was later constructed — the idea that extra capital only increases output by 'lengthening' the process of production, and the notion that postponed output is always valued less than the same output available now because of time preference, being respectively a supply-side and a demand-side view of the determinants of the rate of interest. In addition, he embedded his analysis of these two elements in a rich treatment of the social and cultural forces that determine the 'effective desire of accumulation' as a race between technical process and time preference. In short, there was some justification for labelling his book 'a sociological theory of capital'.

The neglect of Rae's book, despite Mill's praise of it, is to some extent explained by the fact that it was written in Canada, published in America, and appeared from its subtitle ('Exposing the Fallacies of the System of Free Trade and of Some Other Doctrines Maintained in the Wealth of Nations') to be another rejection of classical economic doctrines.

John Rae was born in Scotland, studied at the Universities of Edinburgh and Aberdeen without acquiring a final degree, and emigrated to Canada in 1822 to work as a schoolmaster. In 1848 he moved to California and from there to Hawaii, teaching, practising medicine, and writing articles for newspapers and magazines. In 1871 he returned to America where he died within a year in New York.

His experiences in frontier societies gave him a healthy respect for the influence of government on economic activity. In his book he argued that governments are perfectly capable of promoting the 'effective desire for accumulation' by patents legislation, taxation of luxury goods, banking controls, state-subsidised education, and the protection of infant industries. His reasoning at this point was not dissimilar from that of List (q.v.), writing at just about the same time and likewise preoccupied with the development problems of agrarian frontier countries.

*Secondary Literature*
R.W. James, *John Rae, Political Economist: An Account of His Life and a Compilation of His Main Writings* (University of Toronto Press, 1965); J.J. Spengler, 'Rae, John', *International Encyclopedia of the Social Sciences,* vol. 13, ed. D.L. Sills (Macmillan Free Press, 1968).

# Ricardo, David (1772-1823)

With the possible exception of Karl Marx, no great economist of the past has received so many divergent and even contradictory interpretations as David Ricardo. No sooner had his *Principles of Political Economy and Taxation* (1817) appeared, but he attracted a number of ardent disciples who hailed him as the founder of a new rigorous science of political economy. However, these were soon followed by an even larger number of detractors, who struggled (not always successfully) to escape from the grip of Ricardo's overwhelming influence on the economic thinking of his times. The leading economic textbook of the mid-nineteenth century, John Stuart Mill's *Principles of Political Economy* (1848), paid tribute once again to Ricardo's genius and secured his reputation with yet another generation of students. With the onset of the 'marginal revolution' in the 1870s, Ricardo's star finally began to wane, and many now agreed with Jevons (q.v.) that he had 'shunted the car of economic science onto a wrong line'. The fact that Marx hailed Ricardo as his intellectual mentor served if anything to accelerate the anti-Ricardian trend, and even Marshall's charitable effort in his *Principles of*

*Economics* (1890) to make the best case for Ricardo failed to save his declining reputation.

Ricardo has staged a comeback, however in our own times. One of the many features of Ricardo's thinking that had puzzled generations of readers was his habit of expressing all his economic variables in terms of an 'invariable measure of value' — a hypothetical yardstick which even he admitted did not and could not exist as such. But in 1960, Piero Sraffa published a slim volume entitled *Production Commodities by Means of Commodities,* which purported to show that Ricardo had been right all along to measure prices with the aid of a yardstick that makes relative prices invariant to changes in profits and wages. This appeared to rehabilitate Ricardo as having put his finger on a vital truth: it is possible, contrary to modern teaching, to divorce the determination of commodity prices from the determination of factor prices; and there is even a sense in which it may be said that, logically, the latter precedes the former. Coming from an author who was himself the editor of *The Works and Correspondence of David Ricardo* (1951-55), Sraffa's reinterpretation of Ricardo could not be ignored.

It took little time for Marxist economists to perceive the significance of this Sraffian reading of Ricardo. The history of economic thought, they say, reveals two great branches: a general equilibrium branch leading down from Jevons, Walras and even Marshall to the Samuelsons and Friedmans of today, in which all relevant economic variables are mutually and simultaneously determined, and a Ricardo – Marx – Sraffa branch in which distribution takes priority over pricing and in which all economic variables are causally determined in a sequential chain, starting from the real wage and hence the power relationships between capital and labour. Thus, 160 years after his death, Ricardo, that most bourgeois of all bourgeois economists, is back in business as one of the founding fathers of Marxian economics. Such are the strange twists and turns of intellectual history.

Ricardo was born in London, the third child of a Sephardic Jewish family that had emigrated from Holland in 1760. At the age of 14 he started working for his father, who had become a successful member of the Stock Exchange. At the age of 21 he married the daughter of a Quaker against the wishes of his parents, who promptly disinherited him. Striking out on his own, he soon accumulated a small fortune as a stock-jobber and loan contractor. In 1814, at the age of 42, he retired from business, purchased an estate, Gatcomb Park, in

Gloucestershire (now owned and occupied by HRH the Princess Anne) and began to devote himself to literary pursuits.

Ricardo's interest in economics dated back to 1799, when by chance he came across a copy of Adam Smith's *Wealth of Nations.* Ten years later he made his debut in print with a newspaper article on the bullion controversy, subsequently expanded into a vigorous pamphlet entitled *The High Price of Bullion: A Proof of the Depreciation of Bank Notes* (1810). The Bullion Committee Report, which appeared the following year, agreed with Ricardo that the current inflation was due to the Bank of England's failure to restrict the issue of bank notes. The fame of the committee's report lent prestige to Ricardo's tract, so much so that later commentators incorrectly credited Ricardo with inspiring it.

In 1814 he turned his attention to commercial policy and a year later published the important *Essay on the Influence of a Low Price of Corn on the Profits of Stock* (1815), which laid down what was soon to become one of the cornerstones of classical political economy — the law of diminishing returns to increments of capital and labour applied to acres of land. Two years later, he expanded this pamphlet into a major treatise, *On the Principles of Political Economy and Taxation* (1817). In 1819 he obtained a seat in the House of Commons and for the next few years took an active part in parliamentary discussions of current issues. He died of a cerebral infection in 1823, leaving a wife, seven children, and an estate valued at £750,000 (the equivalent of about £75 million today): Ricardo may or may not be the greatest economist that ever lived, but he was certainly the richest.

Ricardo's intellectual appeal then and now rested on his remarkable gifts for heroic abstractions: he seized hold of a wide range of significant problems with a simple analytical model that involved only a few strategic variables and yielded, after a few elementary manipulations, dramatic conclusions of a distinctly practical nature. In short, he was the first to master the art that later brought success to Keynes. It was a style of thinking markedly different from that of Adam Smith and it set an entirely new standard for economic discourse.

At the heart of Ricardo's argument is the notion that economic growth must sooner or later peter out owing to a scarcity of land. In the simple version of his model, as expounded in the 1815 *Essay,* the whole economy is conceived as a giant farm, distributing its produce among landlords, tenant-farmers and hired workers. The Malthusian tendency of population to increase to the limits of the food supply provides an unlimited supply of labour that can be employed at a constant real wage fixed in terms of corn (or wheat). This of course is the notorious 'iron law of wages', which Ricardo hedged about with ample qualifications. Every worker is equipped with the same amount of fixed capital (say, a spade), which combines with every worker in the same proportion, and hence can also be expressed in terms of corn. In other words, corn is the only output of the giant farm and it is also the only input in the form of seeds and foodstuffs to maintain workers. As the labour force grows, extra corn to feed the extra mouths can only be produced by extending cultivation to less fertile land or by applying additional capital and labour to land already under cultivation with diminishing returns. The difference between the net corn output of a worker on the least fertile land and his constant wage goes to the tenant-farmer as profit. Since farmers outbid each other for the best land, the real advantage of working superior land accrues to the landowner in the form of rising rents. As more land is taken up, the net product per worker falls, whereas the real wage remains the same; obviously, profits per worker decline. At the same time, the corn value of the capital of each worker increases because corn is continually becoming more expensive to produce in terms of real resources used. Divide the falling profits per worker by the rising capital per worker, and it follows that the rate of profit on capital, which supplies the motive for investment, declines.

In the *Principles,* this simple one-sector model was replaced by a three-sector model, but the argument and the conclusions reached were essentially the same. The root of the trouble being the declining yield of wheat per acre of land, it is evident that the short-run solution is to import wheat from countries better endowed with fertile land in exchange for domestically-produced manufactured goods. No wonder then that Ricardo vigorously attacked the existing corn laws, which protected British wheat farmers by prohibiting foreign wheat except in years of famine price.

Eager to show that Britain would benefit from specialising in manufactured goods and importing the bulk of its food supply, he hit upon the doctrine of comparative cost, which marked his most lasting contribution to economics: under free trade, each country will find it profitable to export, not just goods which it can produce more cheaply than other countries, but goods which it can produce more cheaply *compared* with the goods which it imports; even when it produces everything more expensively than anyone else, there are still benefits to be obtained from international trade, not just for the country in question, but for all countries taken together. Here is the fountainhead of all nineteenth-century free trade doctrine! Although the corn laws were not in fact repealed suntil 1846, 23 years after Ricardo's death, his writings helped to make free trade a popular objective of British policy. Unwittingly, Ricardo provided the theoretical justification for the long-run solution to the growth problem which Britain actually adopted in the nineteenth century: Britain became the 'workshop of the world' and bought most of her food abroad.

*Secondary Literature*
O. St Clair, *A Key to Ricardo* (Augustus M. Kelley, 1957); M. Blaug, *Ricardian Economics. A Historical Study* (Greenwood Press, 1973); B. Gordon, *Ricardo in Parliament, 1819-23* (Barnes & Noble, 1977); S. Hollander, *The Economics of David Ricardo* (University of Toronto Press, 1979).

# Robertson, Dennis Holme (1890-1963)

Born in 1890 in Lowestoft, the son of a country parson and schoolmaster, Dennis Robertson went to Eton at the age of 12 and from there to study classics at Trinity College, Cambridge. Despite a brilliant performance in classics, he switched to economics, gaining a first class degree in 1912. He was taught at Cambridge by Pigou (q.v.), and by a young tutor, John Maynard Keynes (q.v.), who was his senior by seven years. This marked the beginning of a friendship and collaboration between Robertson and Keynes which lasted until the mid-1930s when it was shattered by Robertson's failure to endorse the Keynesian revolution.

Robertson gained a teaching fellowship at Trinity with his first major work, *A Study of Industrial Fluctuations* (1915), and spent the rest of his academic life at Cambridge, interrupted only by army service during the First World War, a single year as professor of banking at the London School of Economics in 1938, and several years as economic advisor to the Treasury during the Second World War. He succeeded Pigou to the Chair of Economics in Cambridge in 1947 and retired in 1957. From 1944 to 1946 he was a leading member of the Royal Commission on Equal Pay and in 1957-58 he was the only economist on the three-man Council on Prices, Productivity and Incomes set up by the Conservative government as a half-hearted attempt at an incomes policy. Although he won many honours, including a knighthood in 1953, his later years at Cambridge were embittered by disputes with Keynes's disciples, who closed ranks against him as a traitor to the cause and conducted an almost personal vendetta against him.

*A Study of Industrial Fluctuations* was a remarkable book, which effectively imported into the British literature the Continental European analysis of the non-monetary causes of business cycles. Robertson went on to direct his attention to the monetary side in *Money* (1922) and to the integration of real and monetary forces in *Banking Policy and the Price Level* (1926). *Money,* with its chapters headed by apposite quotations from *Alice in Wonderland,* became one of Robertson's best-known works: it was frequently revised, endlessly reprinted, and translated into many languages. His mastery of the English language and his simple but elegant style is best displayed in this gem among his 15 books.

*Banking Policy and the Price Level,* on the other hand, was too difficult and too idiosyncratic — revelling in specialist terminology such as 'automatic stinting' and 'induced lacking' — to command a readership, and it remained largely unread then as now. In retrospect, however, it emerges as one of the most important breakthroughs in twentieth-century economics: it was almost the first book to try to pin down the meanings of such terms as saving and investment, and to explore the relationship between the two, employing a step-by-step, period-to-period method of analysis. Indeed, it is not extravagant to claim this work and not Keynes's *General Theory* as the fountainhead of modern macroeconomic dynamics.

At this stage in Robertson's career, he and Keynes saw eye to eye. But with the publication of Keynes's *Treatise* (1930) and even more with that of Keynes's *General Theory* (1936), their paths increasingly diverged. Robertson rejected Keynes's short-period equilibrium analysis, his definitions of saving and investment, and his liquidity-preference theory of interest, becoming for a while the principal opponent of the Keynesian revolution. He insisted that it was contradictory to define both saving and investment as functions of *this* year's income, thus treating them as two identical sides of the same coin, and at the same time to regard the change in this year's income as bringing saving and investment into equality in the very same time-period. Likewise, he doubted that the liquidity demand for the *stock* of money was a useful way of analysing the determination of the rate of interest, which he regarded as a variable equilibrating the *flow* of loanable funds, made up of private and business savings plus net credit creation by the banks on the supply side and investment and the hoarding of money on the demand side. His criticisms of the Keynesian system were contained in numerous articles, most of which are collected in *Essays in Monetary Theory* (1956).

In the 1950s, he was similarly disinclined to join the bandwagon in favour of the new welfare economics, reverting instead to Marshall on this and other matters. *Utility and All That* (1952), *Economic Commentaries* (1956) and a delightful set of *Lectures on Economic Principles* in three volumes (1957-59) convey the full flavour of his irreverence. One of his last publications, *Growth, Wages, Money* (1961), took him back to the theme of his youth, business cycles, now re-examined with the hindsight of the Keynesian revolution.

*Secondary Literature*
S.R. Dennison, 'Robertson, Dennis Holme', *International Encyclopedia of the Social Sciences,* vol. 13, ed. D.L. Sills (Macmillan Free Press, 1968); J.R. Presley, 'D.H. Robertson, 1890-1963', *Pioneers of Modern Economics in Britain,* D.P. O'Brien and J.R. Presley (eds.) (Macmillan, 1981).

# Roscher, Wilhelm Georg Friedrich (1817-1894)

Wilhelm Roscher was one of the principal founders of the German Historical School. Bruno Hildebrand (1818-78) and Karl Knies (1821-98) and Roscher are frequently linked together as the 'older' Historical School to distinguish them from Schmoller (q.v.) and Sombart (q.v.), the 'younger' Historical School of the following generation. All three shared the belief that the clear exposition of the aims and methods of economic inquiry must take precedence over the development of substantive doctrines; that all economic truths are purely relative and valid only for a specific set of national and historical circumstances; that economics must therefore proceed via the history of economic thought by ruthlessly criticising the ideas of the past; that economic development reveals definite stages of growth similar to the biological cycle of infancy, youth, manhood and old age; and that a variety of social policies are required to ameliorate the conditions of the working class and to stem the rising tide of socialism. Roscher was closer to the ideas of the English classical economists than were Hildebrand and Knies, and he alone of the three carried out fundamental research in the history of economics, best represented by his still valuable *Geschichte der Nationaloekonomik in Deutschland (History of Political Economy in Germany)* (1874).

Roscher was born in Hanover in 1817, the son of a judge. He studied history and political science at the Universities of Göttingen and Berlin, and lectured on both these subjects at the University of Göttingen from 1840 onwards. In 1843, he launched the Historical School with a programmatic publication, *Grundriss zu Vorlesungen über die Staatswissenschaft nach geschichtlicher Methode (Outline of Lectures on Political Economy Based on the Historical Method)*. In 1848, he became a professor of political economy at the University of Leipzig and set to work on writing *Principles of Political Economy* (1854), a work which he kept expanding and revising right up to the year of his death in 1894. It became perhaps the most widely-read textbook of economics in Germany in the second half of the nineteenth century.

Compared with what was promised, what Roscher actually delivered was very modest, amounting in fact to a critical restatement of the conventional economics of his time with a wealth of examples and illustrations of the so-called 'laws' of historical development, which somehow he never succeeded in stating explicitly. A studious disinclination to enter into anything smacking of normative economics kept him from spelling out the policy implications of his ideas.

*Secondary Literature*
E. Salin, 'Roscher, Wilhelm', *International Encyclopedia of the Social Sciences,* vol. 13, ed. D.L. Sills (Macmillan Free Press, 1968).

# Saint-Simon, Claude Henri de Rouvroy (1760-1825)

Everyone has heard of St-Simon but very few have ever read him; no wonder because he never wrote a single enduring work and his voluminous articles and essays move with bewildering speed from one forgotten issue to another, lacking order, coherence and clarity. Nevertheless, he attracted disciples who systematised and reshaped his ideas, notably Auguste Comte his one-time collaborator, and for a while in the 1830s and 1840s a movement formed in his name attracted many of the outstanding young intellectuals of the day, including Thomas Carlyle and John Stuart Mill. Karl Marx later attacked St-Simon, together with Owen (q.v.) and Charles Fourier (1772-1837) as 'utopian socialists'. 'Utopian reformer' would be a better label for St-Simon, who never subscribed to the collectivisation of the means of production and relied on the rulers of society to relinquish their power voluntarily as they became persuaded of the inevitability of social change.

Three powerful ideas underlie all of St-Simon's works, which were effectively disseminated throughout Europe despite the opaqueness of his writings. The first is an awareness of the unique scientific and technical revolution of his own age (he coined the term 'industrialisation') whose potentials he appreciated better than most of his contemporaries. He projected a future society in which poverty and war would be eradicated through large-scale industrialisation under the planned scientific guidance of scientists, engineers and business managers. The second is the belief that the methods of natural science can be extended into the social sphere and that this 'positive' science, as he called it, could be taught to the masses, thus serving as a new form of secular religion to bond society together. The third is that history is marked by definite stages of development, which are fundamentally stages in ideology. Thus, Graeco-Roman civilisation had a polytheistic religion, a slave economy and monolithic political rule. This was supplanted in the middle ages by Catholicism, feudal property relations and decentralised political control. Then, in the fifteenth century, a new era began founded on science, industry and parliamentary democracy. His own efforts were designed to complete this third stage of history by a managerial and ideological revolution designed to unleash the forces of production. It was a garbled mixture of ideas which nevertheless exerted an extraordinary influence on the intellectual climate of Europe in the second quarter of the nineteenth century.

He was born in Paris in 1760, the son of a declassed nobleman, and he led a chequered career as a soldier fighting in the American Revolution and a speculator in confiscated church lands. He was imprisoned during the Reign of Terror of 1793-94, and narrowly escaped a death sentence. Having amassed a considerable fortune as a speculator, he ran through his money in 10 years and from 1804 to his death in 1825 he lived a hand-to-mouth existence as a journalist and pamphleteer. After his death, his followers continued to develop his ideas but they soon degenerated into a religious cult which was disbanded by the authorities.

*Secondary Literature*
M.V. Martel, 'Saint-Simon', *International Encyclopedia of the Social Sciences,* vol. 13, ed. D.L. Sills (Macmillan Free Press, 1968); K. Taylor, *Henri Saint-Simon* (Croom Helm, 1975).

# Say, Jean-Baptiste (1776-1832)

Jean-Baptiste Say is almost unread today, and yet he is famous as the originator of Say's law, which Keynes in *The General Theory* (1936) pinpointed as the source of all later thinking, asserting the automatic tendency of competitive markets to achieve full employment. Alas, Say did not originate Say's law of markets. He did say in his *Treatise on Political Economy* (1803) that 'products are always exchanged for products', but it was James Mill, in his *Commerce Defended* (1808), who turned this into 'supply creates its own demand' and who drew from it some of its implications; for example, gluts or trade depressions are never due to over-production and that the role of money is of secondary importance in accounting for the phenomena of exchange. Once Mill — and Ricardo after him — had shown the way, Say expanded his earlier statements until they resembled Mill's formulation. Moreover, neither Say nor Mill nor Ricardo ever read as much into Say's law as Keynes did. For them, it was essentially an argument against monetary panaceas and the fear the economy might permanently stagnate from an absolute glut of goods; it never implied any denial that depressions would occur and that when they did, they might last for several years.

Say's reputation as a discoverer of Say's law is therefore misplaced. Similarly, he is sometimes credited with the concept of entrepreneurship in contradistinction to Adam Smith and Ricardo who alway identified the role of the capitalist as owner of an enterprise with the essentially different creative role of the entrepreneur. But a close reading of Say shows that he emphasised the role of the entrepreneur as a coordinator of the factors of production and largely neglected the more important function, emphasised long ago by Cantillon (q.v.), of buying inputs at a certain spot price in order to sell output at an uncertain forward price. Even the role of the entrepreneur as the innovator of new products and processes of production, which Schumpeter (q.v.) was later to make the centrepiece of his own theory of entrepreneurship, is present in Say only with hindsight. Thus, history was once again too kind to Say.

All in all, throughout a number of works, the quality of Say's theorising is inferior to Smith in historical sweep, to Ricardo in analytical rigour and to Malthus in perceptive criticisms. His importance, particularly for French economics, was to popularise the ideas of Adam Smith, to disseminate English classical political economy on the Continent and to keep alive an emphasis on utility and demand in contrast to the English overemphasis on costs and supply.

Say was born in Lyons in a Protestant merchant family and came eventually to run a cotton plant himself in Northern France. In his youth he worked for an insurance company, then edited a journal, and eventually became a member of the Tribunate under the Consulate of Napoleon. In 1815, after the fall of Napoleon, he began to teach the first public course of political economy ever given in France and two years later he was appointed to a professorship in industrial economics at the Conservatoire des Arts et Métiers, succeeding in 1830 to the first Chair of Political Economy in France at the Collège de France in Paris. He visited England many times in his career and was a close friend of both Ricardo and Malthus, which did not however imply total agreement with all their teachings.

*Secondary Literature*
G. Leduc, 'Say, Jean-Baptiste', *International Encyclopedia of the Social Sciences,* vol. 14, ed. D.L. Sills (Macmillan Free Press, 1968).

# Schmoller, Gustav von (1838-1917)

The 'younger' German Historical School, standing on the shoulders of Roscher (q.v.), Hildebrand and Knies, was led by Gustav von Schmoller, who literally presided over all that passed for economics in Germany in the last quarter of the nineteenth century. The younger German historical economists continued to believe in the merits of an historical approach to economic questions, but abandoned the aim of providing comprehensive laws of historical development, confining themselves to illustrative monographs on particular subjects. In addition, they gave much greater prominence to piecemeal social reform by public action than had the earlier historical economists, forming an influential *Verein für Sozialpolitik* (Union for Social Policy) in 1872 to give expression to their political ideals. They came to be know, ironically, as *Katheder Sozialisten* (academic socialists) but were in fact highly conservative social reformers, close to the Crown and ministers in the Prussian civil service.

Schmoller was born in Württemberg and educated at the University of Tübingen from which he graduated in 1860. He became a professor of political science and political economy at the Universities of Halle (1864-72), Strassbourg (1872-82), and finally Berlin (1882-1913). Schmoller made his debut in print in 1870 with a book on the history of small-scale industry in Germany and published prolifically in the 1870s and 1880s on a variety of methodological and historical questions. His only work translated into English is *The Mercantile System and its Historical Significance: Illustrated Chiefly from Prussian History* (1897), a justification of mercantilism as a system of state-building perfectly reasonable for its day and age. Schmoller's views on the scope and method of economics were criticised by Menger (q.v.) in his *Problems of Economics and Sociology* (1883). Schmoller replied to these criticisms in his own journal, *Jahrbuch für Gesetzgebung,* whereupon Menger bore down on him in full fury in a famous pamplet, *Die Irrthümer des Historismus in der deutschen Nationalökonomie (The Fallacies of Historicism in German Political Economy)* (1884). Schmoller rebutted the charge and it is this debate which has gone down in history as the *Methodenstreit,* giving the methodology of economics a bad name for unproductive acrimony that lasts to this day.

It is not easy even with hindsight to pin down what the two were arguing about. Menger upheld what Marshall was to call 'partial equilibrium analysis' based on the abstract-deductive method. Schmoller, on the other hand, held a more complex and indefinite position, regarded most of traditional economics as irrelevant rather than wrong, and the abstract-deductive method as appropriate to a future phase of economic thought that would succeed decades and perhaps generations of painstaking fact-gathering. His own encyclopaedic *Grundriss der allgemeine Volkswirtschaftslehre (Outline of General Political Economy)* (1900-4) was actually a fairly traditional work, differing only from, say, Marshall's *Principles* by the extent to which the statistical and historical material outweighed the analytical sections. But whatever Schmoller's intentions, the effect of his methodological pronouncements was to throttle the development of economic theory in Germany right up to the 1920s and 1930s.

*Secondary Literature*
W. Fisher, 'Schmoller, Gustav', *International Encyclopedia of the Social Sciences,* vol. 14, ed. D.L. Sills (Macmillan Free Press, 1968); T. Veblen, 'Gustav Schmoller's Economics', *The Place of Science in Modern Civilization* (Viking Press, 1919).

# Schumpeter, Joseph A (1883-1950)

Schumpeter is one of the giants of twentieth-century economics whose majestic vision of the entire economic process can rank with that of Adam Smith or Karl Marx. In an astonishing book, *Theory of Economic Development* (1912), written at the early age of 28, he replaced Marx's greedy, blood-sucking capitalist by the dynamic, innovating entrepreneur as the linchpin of the capitalist system, responsible not just for technical progress but the very existence of a positive rate of profit on capital. Distinguishing between 'inventions' and 'innovations', he stressed the fact that scientific and technical inventions amount to nothing unless they are adopted, which calls for as much daring and imagination as the original act of discovery by the scientist or engineer. Furthermore, the 'innovations' that count for economic progress consist of much more than the new machines that capture popular attention: they take the form of new products, new sources of supply, new forms of industrial and financial organisation just as much as of new methods of production.

The entrepreneur is frequently also the capitalist; nevertheless, in principle there is a world of difference between doing things in a new

215

way and providing the capital required to finance a new venture. The capitalist earns 'interest', but the entrepreneur earns 'profit' and without the dynamic change created by the entrepreneur, the rate of profit would soon fall to zero. Schumpeter was scathing about the great classical economists of the early nineteenth century for continually confusing the role of the capitalist with that of the entrepreneur and he was no less scathing of his immediate contemporaries for losing sight of the pivotal role of the innovating entrepreneur in their obsessive concern with the static properties of final equilibrium states. His theory of the entrepreneur has ever since been the starting point for every subsequent discussion of entrepreneurship.

Born and educated in Austria, and briefly Minister of Finance of Austria in the years following the First World War, he emigrated to America in 1932, where he established a new career for himself as a brilliant teacher. A prominent member of the department of economics at Harvard University in its golden decade of the 1930s, he published a massive two-volume study of *Business Cycles* (1939), in which once again the entrepreneur was placed at the centre of events. Schumpeter's explanation of the business cycle in that book was not perhaps particularly original but he coupled his account of the ordinary 7-11 year Juglar cycle of output and employment with an explanation of Kondratieff long cycles over a period of 45-50 years in terms of swarms of innovations, succeeding one another until the super-profits of the original innovator are fully eroded by later imitators. This was one of his least successful books: it struck many of his colleagues as being too glib and, moreover, moved too quickly over the causes of the then prevailing depression; besides, Schumpeter had no time for Keynes and *Business Cycles* was published just when the Keynesian revolution was hitting its stride.

In 1942, however, Schumpeter produced what has ever since come to be regarded as his masterpiece: *Capitalism, Socialism and Democracy,* a book which was as much addressed to intelligent laymen as to his fellow economists. In this work, he paradoxically rejected the Marxian diagnosis of the imminent breakdown of capitalism and, at the same time, predicted the almost inevitable arrival of socialism as a result of the betrayal of capitalist values by the intellectuals of the western world. Paradox was always his principal weapon and in this book he absolutely revelled in the picture of an economic system being gradually undermined, not by its enemies, but by its friends. It is true that his predictions have not, so far, come true. Nevertheless, reading it now, over 40 years later, it still sounds uncannily pertinent to the ills of the day.

After the popular success of *Capitalism, Socialism and Democracy,* Schumpeter spent the remainder of his life converting a youthful book on the history of economic thought, *Economic Doctrines and Method* (1914), into a stupendous *History of Economic Analysis* (1954), which was published posthumously as a finished work except for its last chapter. This work of old age, with its hundreds of scholarly footnotes, its unbelievable breadth of coverage, its startling conclusions — downgrading Adam Smith (q.v.) as unoriginal, damning Marshall (q.v.) as confused, and upgrading Walras (q.v.) as the greatest economist that ever lived — has continued to inspire historians of economic thought as a pinnacle of achievement they can only hope to approximate.

Born in Triesch in the Austro-Hungarian Empire in 1883, the son of a high-ranking army officer, Schumpeter graduated from the University of Vienna in 1904. He began teaching in 1909 at the University of Czernowitz (now in the USSR) and then moved to the University of Graz in Austria. After a brief spell as Minister of Finance of Austria (1919-20), he became president of a small German bank in the years 1920-2. He first visited the United States in 1924, returning to Europe in 1925 to become professor of public finance at the University of Bonn. With the rise of Hitler in 1932, he left Europe to take up a professorship at Harvard University, where he remained until his retirement in 1950. He was founding member and president of the Econometric Society in 1938, and president of the American Economic Association in 1948.

A sample of Schumpeter's many articles are bound together in *Ten Great Economists* (1951) and *Essays of J.A. Schumpeter,* R.V. Clemence (ed.) (1951). Earlier essays on *The Crisis of the Tax State* (1918) and *Imperialism and Social Classes* (1919), are still worth reading.

*Secondary Literature*
S.E. Harris, (ed.), *Schumpeter: Social Scientist* (Harvard University Press, 1951); W.F. Stolper, 'Schumpeter, Joseph A.', *International Encyclopedia of the Social Sciences,* vol. 14, ed. D.L. Sills (Macmillan Free Press, 1968); A Heertje (ed.), *Schumpeter's Vision: Capitalism, Socialism and Democracy After 40 Years* (Praeger, 1981); H. Frisch (ed.), *Schumpeterian Economics* (Praeger, 1981).

# Seligman, Edwin, Robert Anderson (1861-1939)

Edwin Seligman was an expert on public finance, member of innumerable tax commissions, a notable bibliophile and historian of economic thought, and a key figure in the professionalisation of American economics. Among his many books and essays on taxation, *Progressive Taxation in Theory and Practice* (1894) and *The Income Tax: A Study of the History, Theory and Practice of Income Taxation at Home and Abroad* (1911) are still worth reading as early examples of the application of marginal analysis to the incidence of what was then a relatively new idea — the direct taxation of earned income. Seligman was among the many to think out the import of marginal utility theory for the ability-to-pay theory of taxation, in the course of which he crossed swords more than once with Edgeworth (q.v.), who usually had the best of the argument. Seligman's remarkable personal library of books and pamphlets on the history of economic thought (now the Seligman Collection in Columbia University), formed the basis of his path-breaking article, 'On Some Neglected British Economists' (1903), which drew attention to such forgotten writers as Lloyd and Longfield (q.v.) as forerunners of marginal utility theory.

He helped Ely to form the American Economic Association in 1885 and succeeded Ely as its president from 1902 to 1904. He also helped to establish the American Association of University Professors (AAUP), served as its president from 1919 to 1920, and chaired the AAUP committee that wrote the *Report on Academic Freedom* (1915) that still furnishes the AAUP to this day with a fundamental statement of principles.

Early in his career he also published an influential study of *The Economic Interpretation of History* (1902), which sought in vain to extract the nugget of truth in Marx's many confusing pronouncements on the philosophy of history. Reading it today, one can only marvel at the state of historical debate at the turn of the century that made it necessary to underline the obvious as Seligman did. In the last decade of his life, he crowned his busy career by co-editing the first English-language *Encyclopedia of the Social Sciences* (1930-35) in 15 volumes. Although it is now superseded by the *International Encyclopedia of the Social Sciences,* edited by D.L. Sills (1968) in 18 volumes, the old *Encyclopedia* is still worth referring to for a number of biographies and for some of its classic articles by leading experts of the day.

Edwin Seligman was born in New York City in 1861 into a prominent banking family. He was tutored at home until the age of 11 and entered Columbia College at the age of 14, graduating in 1879 at the age of 18. In the fashion of the period, he spent three years attending the Universities of Berlin, Heidelberg and Paris before joining the first cohort of graduate students in economics at Columbia University. In 1884 he received both an MA and an LLB, and in the following year his PhD. He immediately joined the newly-formed faculty of political science at Columbia University, where he remained until his retirement in 1931, becoming a professor of political economy and finance in 1890. He died in 1939 at the age of 88.

*Secondary Literature*
C.S. Shoup, 'Seligman, R.A.', *International Encyclopedia of the Social Sciences,* vol. 14, ed. D.L. Sills (Macmillan Free Press, 1968).

# Senior, Nassau William (1790-1864)

Nassau Senior was a minor but highly original classical economist in the era between the publication of Ricardo's *Principles* (1817) and Mill's *Principles* (1848). He published his own textbook, *An Outline of the Science of Political Economy*, in 1836, being a collection of lectures delivered at the University of Oxford where he held the Drummond Chair of Political Economy. In these and other lectures published separately, he made original contributions to the theory of value, rent, population, money and international trade. His most famous, almost notorious, novelty was the abstinence theory of profits — profits are a reward to the capitalist for abstaining from the present consumption of his own capital — which invited some of Marx's strongest jibes about the apologetic nature of 'bourgeois economics'. But his statement of the principle of diminishing marginal utility, unconnected however to a theory of demand, his generalisation of the Ricardian rent concept to any factor in fixed supply, and his demonstration that equilibrium in the balance of payments implies predictable inequalities in international wages and prices, are more deserving of praise. He also promoted greater methodological sophistication among Ricardo's followers by attempting to derive all the propositions of political economy from four axioms about economic motivation and the technology of industry and agriculture. Lastly, he hammered away at the fundamental distinction between the 'science' and the 'art' of political economy; or, as we would now say, between positive and normative economics.

The distinction was of great personal significance for him for he was the first economist to spend years acting as an economic advisor to politicians — namely the Whig Party of his day, in and out of office. He worked on the laws relating to trade unions, the reform of municipal corporations, the administration of poor relief in Ireland and he served on four Royal Commissions — the Poor Laws 1834, the Factory Acts 1837, the Distress of Hand-loom Weavers 1841, and Popular Education 1857 — in each case writing all or large parts of the commissions' reports. His work on the Poor Law Inquiry Commission of 1834, which succeeded in abolishing outdoor relief to the able-bodied and replacing it with a new system of indoor relief for the sick, aged and destitute, was the crowning achievement of his efforts as policy-maker: not only did he write the whole of the influential report of the commission but he organised the inquiry that lay behind the report and lobbied ruthlessly to persuade Parliament to enact its recommendations. The abolition of the old Poor Law with its provision of locally-administered unemployment compensation had been one of Malthus's favourite deductions from the theory of population. Senior agreed with Malthus's indictment of the old Poor Law but he was otherwise unsympathetic to the Malthusian population theory. Indeed, his *Two Lectures on Population* (1829) is one of the first criticisms of the Malthusian theory, based on the argument that the theory is refuted by empirical evidence about rising living standards despite the growth of population.

Senior was born in 1790, the eldest son of a Wiltshire vicar. He was educated at Eton, Magdalen College, Oxford and Lincoln's Inn, London. In 1817 he became a certified conveyancer and in 1819 he was called to the bar. Throughout the 1820s, he combined the practice of law with the teaching and writing of economics, and in the 1830s he added to these his efforts as a policy-maker. With the fall of the Whig administration in 1841, Senior turned back to theoretical economics. In 1847 he was appointed for a second time to the Drummond Professorship at Oxford. He published a few more lectures and wrote large parts of a treatise on political economy which he never finished. He began to travel widely and kept a series of travel journals, some of which he published himself but many of which were only published after his death in 1864 at the age of 74.

*Secondary Literature*
M.Bowley, *Nassau Senior and Classical Economics (A.M. Kelley, 1949);* M. Bowley, 'Senior, Nassau William', *International Encyclopedia of the Social Sciences,* vol.14, ed. D.L. Sills (Macmillan Free Press, 1968).

# Sidgwick, Henry (1838-1900)

Henry Sidgwick was the last British political philosopher to make a contribution to economics. Like Locke, Hume and John Stuart Mill, Sidgwick devoted some years to economics but his main interests were elsewhere in *The Methods of Ethics* (1874) and *The Elements of Politics* (1891). Nevertheless, his *Principles of Political Economy* (1883) laid the basis for some of the principal features of Marshall's more influential *Principles of Economics* (1890) and thus served to fashion what was soon to become the Cambridge School of neoclassical economics: an eloquent, non-technical style, addressed as much to the general reader as students of the science; an emphasis on the continuity of economic thought and hence a deliberate attempt to pour some of the newer elements of marginal analysis into a mould set by Ricardo and Mill; a marked insistence on the distinction between the 'science' and 'art' of political economy; an utterly utilitarian approach to all acts of government intervention, including fiscal measures designed to equalise the distribution of income; a recognition of externalities in production (the famous example of the lighthouse) as a source of 'market failure', hinting at a perfectly general theory of government intervention based on divergences between private and social benefits; and a sympathetic but sceptical attitude to socialism. The first two of the three books of Sidgwick's *Principles* are fairly traditional, although marked by a new clarity and incisiveness of exposition, but the main thrust of the work comes in Book III dealing with the art of economic policy almost as if there were little point in the science unless it promoted better prescriptions for the state in organising economic life.

Sidgwick was born in 1838 at Skipton, the son of an Anglican clergyman. He graduated from the University of Cambridge in both classics and mathematics in 1859 and was immediately elected to a fellowship at Trinity College. He spent the rest of his life at Cambridge and became a leading figure in the curriculum reforms of the 1870s that opened the doors to women, broke with the religious vows that were previously imposed on fellows, and upgraded the status of social science and other vocational subjects. He died in 1900. Marshall once said of Sidgwick: 'He was so to speak my spiritual father and mother.' It was a well-deserved compliment.

*Secondary Literature*
B. Corry, 'Sidgwick, Henry', *International Encyclopedia of the Social Sciences,* vol. 14, ed. D.L. Sills (Macmillan Free Press, 1968).

# Simons, Henry Calvert (1899-1946)

Henry Simons was one of the founders of the Chicago School, whose modern representatives are Milton Friedman, Gary Becker and George Stigler. Many of the central ideas of modern Chicagoans are set out in his essays of the 1930s, collected together in *Economic Policy for a Free Society* (1948), such as the belief that the role of government in economic life is essentially to maintain a framework in which free enterprise can operate, that is, monetary policy, fiscal policy, trust-busting, and little else; that monetary policy should be abandoned in favour of a non-discretionary rule governing the supply of money; that banks should be forced to maintain reserves at 100 per cent of their deposit holdings; that unions are an even greater threat to the competitive order than big business; and that the trend towards big business would soon be reversed but for the fact that government regulations are constantly tending explicitly and implicitly to support monopoly.

Simons' important writings, such as his famous essay, 'A Positive Program for *Laissez-Faire*' (1934), began to appear at the depth of the Great Depression and were naturally concerned to uphold the free enterprise system at a time when it appeared to be failing. Believing as he did that the Depression was basically the result of monetary mismanagement, he was an early advocate among American economists of monetary expansion by means of budgetary deficits as the remedy to mass unemployment. Thus, whereas in Keynes the argument was that fiscal policy is the means to recovery precisely because monetary policy is relatively ineffective in a depression, in Simons the argument is that fiscal policy is required to give effect to monetary policy if only because the way in which the budgetary deficit is financed can have a potent effect on the money supply.

Among the many causes which Simons made his own, the one to which he gave the most detailed attention was reform of the tax system. In two slim books, *Personal Income Taxation* (1938) and *Federal Tax Reform* (1943), he spelled out the implications of a few basic ideas which were central to his reform proposals. He defined 'income' for tax purposes in the manner of Fisher (q.v.) as the sum of consumption expenditures and the change in the value of net assets owned and insisted that the calendar year was too short a period of time over which to assess income. He therefore suggested that even if income was taxed as it accrued, the tax bill ought to be adjusted every few years for income carried forward over a number of years. With the aid of such principles, he examined all the outstanding issues in the taxation of capital gains, corporate profits, inherited income, and the like. Although the emphasis in all his proposals was to maximise the freedom of individuals to spend their post-tax income as they preferred, it is a striking fact that he did not neglect expenditure policies motivated by the goal of social equality. Indeed, his point was that the case for more expenditure on social welfare activities remained weak so long as such expenditures were either wholly or in part financed by the prevailing unreformed tax system.

Simons was born in Virden, Illinois in 1899. He graduated from the University of Michigan in 1920 and began teaching immediately after graduation at the University of Iowa. In 1927, he moved to the University of Chicago where he remained for the rest of his life. He died at the early age of 47 in 1946. Simons wrote relatively little in his active years — two books and less than a dozen articles — and his influence made itself felt more as a teacher than as a writer. He was surrounded by an unusually brilliant set of colleagues — Jacob Viner (1882-1970), Frank Knight (1885-1972), Henry Schultz (1893-1938), Paul Douglas (1892-1976) and many more — among whom he held his own, supplying some of the essential philosophical ingredients of the unique Chicago outlook on economic affairs.

*Secondary Literature*
H. Stein, 'Simons, Henry C.', *International Encyclopedia of the Social Sciences,* vol. 14, ed. D.L. Sills (Macmillan Free Press, 1968).

# Sismondi, Jean Charles Leonard Simonde de (1773-1842)

Simonde de Sismondi, born in Geneva, the son of a Calvinist clergyman, historian and economist, was the first critic of industrial capitalism. He was no socialist and might be better described in the words of Lenin as an 'economic romantic': he deplored the costs which industrialisation imposed on the 'proletarians' (his own term), and yearned for the simple, personal relationships characteristic of the rural economy of bygone days. His critique emerged only slowly as a result of the severe depression that set in after the end of the Napoleonic wars. An early work, *De la richèsse commerciale* (1803), was a perfectly traditional exposition of the doctrines of Adam Smith. He then devoted 10 years of his life to a mammoth 16-volume history of the Italian republics, which he later followed by an even vaster history of France in 31 volumes. *Nouveaux principes d'économie politique* (1819), untranslated into English to this day, marked his turn-around to a more critical attitude to free trade, *laissez-faire* and industrial capitalism. Convinced that the new industrial system was doomed to suffer recurrent depressions and a chronic tendency towards under-consumption, he was particularly struck by the labour-saving bias of technical progress to which he saw no answer except government intervention of a far-reaching kind, including a guaranteed minimum wage in and out of work, a ceiling on hours of work, a floor and ceiling on the age of work, and the introduction of profit-sharing schemes.

Sismondi met Ricardo (q.v.), Malthus (q.v.) and Say (q.v.), was cited by Malthus (q.v.), McCulloch (q.v.), Torrens (q.v.) and John Stuart Mill (q.v.), but only to be generally condemned by everyone except Malthus. As a matter of fact, it is evident that *Nouveaux principes* had a profound influence on Malthus's own *Principles of Political Economy* (1820). The same emphasis on what we would now call insufficient aggregate demand, and the same tendency to break out of the mould of comparative statics and to view the problem of aggregate demand in dynamic terms as a question of reproducing the income flows of this period in the next period are at work in both books. Indeed, the Keynesian flavour is even stronger in Sismondi than in Malthus, and it is he and not Malthus whom Keynes should have hailed as his forerunner. Sismondi may also be regarded as a genuine forerunner of Marx, not only in singling out the working class as the victims *par excellence* of the factory system but in perceiving that workers and owners are locked into a perpetual 'class struggle' — another term he coined.

Sismondi spent his life living alternately in Switzerland, France, Italy and England and carried on a wide correspondence with contemporary historians, economists and statesmen. He was twice offered academic posts, which he twice declined. He continued to be read, particularly by socialists, throughout the nineteenth century — as late as 1896 Lenin thought him important enough to attack in one of his two economic works, *A Characterization of Economic Romanticism: Sismondi and Our Native Sismondists* (1896).

*Secondary Literature*
G. Sotiroff, 'Simonde de Sismondi', *International Encyclopedia of the Social Sciences,* vol. 14, ed. D.L. Sills (Macmillan Free Press, 1968); T. Sowell, 'Sismondi: A Neglected Pioneer', *History of Political Economy,* vol.4(1), Spring 1972.

# Slutsky, Eugen (1880-1948)

When John Hicks and Roy Allen in 1934 introduced their new theory of consumer behaviour based on the concept of indifference rather than marginal utility, one of the claims for the new theory was that it neatly decomposed the effect of a change in price on demand into an 'income effect' and a 'substitution effect', which usually act additionally to produce a negatively-inclined demand curve but which can, under certain well-specified circumstances, cancel each other out so as to produce a positively-sloped demand curve. This solved Marshall's old puzzle of 'Giffen goods' — or what Hicks and Allen called 'inferior goods' — and in addition led to a straightforward explanation of negatively-sloped supply curves of labour, which had similarly puzzled previous observers.

It was more than two years after writing the 1934 article that Allen discovered that it had all been said before both verbally and mathematically by Eugen Slutsky, a Russian economist and statistician, in an unnoticed Italian article published 20 years earlier in 1915. Allen immediately drew attention to Slutsky's pioneering effort, giving him full credit for the whole of the Hicks–Allen theory, but for their now familiar geometric diagrams of indifference curves.

This was not the only time that Slutsky led the field unnoticed by everyone in it. In 1913 he published a paper in the *Journal of the Royal Statistical Society* on the criterion of goodness of fit of regression lines, which bore a striking resemblance to a paper on the same subject published nine years later by R.A. Fisher, the famous statistician. Slutsky's subsequent publications were all in the area of probability theory and the theory of stochastic processes; his interest in economics seems to have died with the 1915 article.

Slutsky was born in Russia in 1880, the son of a schoolteacher. He entered the University of Kiev to study mathematics in 1899 but was expelled three years later for revolutionary activities. In 1903 he entered the Institute of Technology in Munich to study engineering, but returned to Russia in 1905 before completing his course. In 1911, he finally obtained a degree in law from the University of Kiev and obtained a second degree in 1918, this time in economics. In other words, his famous article of 1915 was published only a year or two after beginning to study economics. He joined the Kiev Institute of Commerce in 1918 as a professor of political economy, moving in 1926 to the Conjuncture Institute in Moscow which was directed by Kondratieff (q.v.). From 1931 to 1934 Slutsky was a member of the Central Institute of Meteorology in Moscow and from 1934 to his death in 1948 he held an appointment at the Mathematical Institute of the Academy of Sciences of the USSR.

*Secondary Literature*
R.G.D. Allen, 'The Work of Eugen Slutsky', *Econometrica,* 18 July 1950; A.A. Koms, 'Slutsky, Eugen, *International Encyclopedia of the Social Sciences,* vol. 14, ed. D.L. Sills (Macmillan Free Press, 1968).

# Smith, Adam (1723-1790)

Until comparatively recently, Adam Smith was known only as the author of a single book, *An Inquiry into the Nature and Causes of the Wealth of Nations,* published in an easily remembered year, 1776, the year of the American Revolution; this book that is said to have established economics as an autonomous subject and, at the same time, to have launched the doctrine of free enterprise upon an unsuspecting world. It is true that he also published another major treatise, *The Theory of Moral Sentiments* (1759), a work about those standards of ethical conduct that hold society together, but this was a book that economists generally left unread; those that did read it found it superficially inconsistent with *The Wealth of Nations* and were puzzled by Smith's failure ever to relate the two books to each other. It is also true he wrote many essays on philosophical and literary subjects and over the years the discovery of his lecture notes on justice and rhetoric suggest that he may have been working towards a complete system of social science, which he never lived to complete. Nevertheless, these essays and lecture notes were hard to come by and were usually dismissed as being of peripheral interest.

However, the publication of the *Complete Works and Correspondence of Adam Smith* (1976-81) by the University of Glasgow has thrown a new light on his total output, suggesting indeed that he was no mere economist but a system-builder on a grand scale and, furthermore, a thinker thoroughly steeped in eighteenth-century traditions, being less 'modern' than he is usually made out to be. Nevertheless, *The Wealth of Nations* is the record of his most mature thought. It was the most comprehensive attempt up to his own time to analyse the workings of a 'commercial society' (as it was then called) or the 'capitalist economy' (as it is now called). It laid down a mode of treating questions of value and distribution that shaped the entire course of economic thinking until the 'marginal revolution' of the 1870s, founding, in fact, a distinct School of English Classical Political Economy. And its crusading attack on existing economic policies — the vestiges of what he labelled the 'mercantile system' — set a pattern of involvement in the affairs of the day that characterises economics to the present day. That is precisely what is meant when we call Adam Smith a *political* economist; alas, for him the term meant, not a policy-oriented kind of economics, but the economic policies of a nation.

Adam Smith was born in Kirkcaldy, a small fishing and mining town across the Firth of Forth from Edinburgh. He was the only son of a Comptroller of Customs who died shortly after Adam Smith was born. Smith lived with his mother whenever he was in Scotland until her death in 1784. He never married and, so far as we know, was never seriously involved with any woman. He entered the University of Glasgow at the age of 14, which was common practice in Scotland in those days, graduating at the age of 17 with an MA. He then spent six years at Balliol College, Oxford on a fellowship, an experience which left him with a lifelong disdain of the ancient English Universities of Oxford and Cambridge. On his return to Scotland, he gave several successful series of public lectures on the strength of which he was elected to the professorship of logic at the University of Glasgow in 1751, followed almost immediately by election to the more prestigious professorship of moral philosophy.

His reputation firmly established by the publication of *The Theory of Moral Sentiments* in 1759, he resigned his Chair in 1763 to accompany and tutor the young Duke of Buccleuch on a Grand Tour of the Continent. He spent almost three years in France and met all the leading figures of his day, including Quesnay (q.v.), Turgot (q.v.),

Jean-Jacques Rousseau and Voltaire. Returning to England in 1766, he retired to Kirkcaldy to work on *The Wealth of Nations,* financed by the life pension he had been awarded by the Duke of Buccleuch. Two years after publishing *The Wealth of Nations,* he was appointed a Commissioner of Customs for Scotland and promptly undertook to suppress smuggling, although he had extolled smuggling in *The Wealth of Nations* as a legitimate protest against 'unnatural' legislation! He died in Edinburgh in 1790, shortly after supervising the burning of almost all his unpublished manuscripts, said to run to 16 folio volumes.

Much of *The Wealth of Nations* strikes a modern reader as stretching the bounds of economics to encompass history, political theory and even anthropology. The work is organised in five books and it is only the first two which genuinely inspired subsequent generations. It is here that he introduced the fundamental 'cause' of the wealth of nations — namely, the division of labour — explained the equally fundamental distinction between the 'natural' and the 'market' price of commodities, and developed his theories of value and distribution. Some of it planted endless puzzles that taxed later writers, such as the distinction between the measure and the cause of value and between productive and unproductive labour, but much of it became 'classical' in the literal sense of the word, such as the masterful explanation of the structure of relative wages in Book I, Chapter 10 and the defence of the so-called saving-is-spending theorem in Book II, Chapter 3. But Books III to V are full of material one would not expect to find in an economic treatise, such as an account of the economic development of Europe since the fall of the Roman Empire, a criticism of the colonial policies of European nations, an analysis of the different methods of administering justice in primitive societies, a history of the growth of standing armies, a history of education in the middle ages and the growth and decline of the temporal power of the Church, all expounded in magnificent eighteenth-century prose.

However, one of the pervasive features of the book that has made it more attractive to twentieth- than to eighteenth- or nineteenth-century readers is Adam Smith's constant preoccupation with the political stance of social groups, particularly businessmen, who organise themselves to press governments to give them legal monopolies and special privileges. He also had a lively sense of the self-interested action of statesmen and politicians. He was indeed a genuine forerunner of public choice theory and the theory of economic regulation, associated in the twentieth-century with names such as James Buchanan and George Stigler.

Although he took a deeply cynical view of the behaviour of businessmen and legislators and reserved for government the provision of those social services which could not or would not be provided by private action, it was as an exponent of free trade, free enterprise, the free movement of people and goods — in short, *laissez-faire* and the untrammelled operation of the market — that he made his mark on the history of economics and on the dominant intellectual outlook of the western world. There are those who would say that this is not at all what Adam Smith intended. No doubt it was not the whole of his intentions but there is also no doubt that it was an important part of his complex message. To call him a spokesman of the industrial bourgeoisie is to belittle him, but is is not to do him a gross injustice.

*Secondary Literature*
J. Viner, 'Smith, Adam', *International Encyclopedia of the Social Sciences,* vol. 14, ed. D.L. Sills (Macmillan Free Press, 1968); S. Hollander, *The Economics of Adam Smith* (University of Toronto Press, 1973); A.S. Skinner and T. Wilson (eds.), *Essays on Adam Smith* (Clarendon Press, 1975); R.H. Campbell and A.S. Skinner, *Adam Smith* (Croom Helm, 1982).

# Sombart, Werner (1863-1941)

Werner Sombart started his career as a Marxist in the 1890s and ended it as a Nazi sympathiser in the 1930s, completing in the interim as many as seven books on the origins of capitalism, each of which presented a different explanation of how capitalism had come about. One of Sombart's first publications was an article on Marx celebrating the publication in 1894 of Volume III of *Capital*. Two years later he published *Socialism and the Social Movement* (1896). It too was very sympathetic to Marx but subsequent editions of the enlarged work became increasingly hostile to both socialism and Marxism. In 1902 he published a major two-volume work, *Der moderne Kapitalismus,* followed by a third volume in 1927, in which he attributed the emergence of industrial capitalism to the growth of the 'spirit' of rationalism and acquisitiveness within the womb of feudal society, and predicted that capitalism would inevitably give way to socialism.

In *The Jew and Modern Capitalism* (1911) he explained that the 'spirit' of capitalism was introduced into Northern Europe by the dispersion of the Jews after the Inquisition, bringing with them a new morality, a new conception of legal relations, and a genius for commercial enterprise. In *Der Bourgeois* (1913) (translated into English as *The Quintessence of Capitalism,* 1915), he combined his thesis on Judaism with an attack on Max Weber's thesis that Calvinism had played a key role in creating the spirit of modern capitalism. Sombart argued that Calvinism in particular and Puritanism in general were actually hostile to the bourgeois values of thrift, rational calculation and this-worldliness. At the same time, however, he also argued an almost unique identity of views between Jews and Puritans, concluding paradoxically that 'Puritanism is Judaism', meaning that Judaism had shaped the spirit of capitalism as early as the sixteenth century, after which Puritanism had arrived on the scene to borrow Judaism's moral justification of private enterprise.

As if all this were not confusing enough, he also published two *Studien zur Entwicklungsgeschichte des modernen Kapitalismus (Studies in the History of the Development of Modern Capitalism)* (1913), the first one of which, *Luxury and Capitalism,* traced the early growth of capitalism from the twelfth century onwards to the growth of towns, the growth of credit banking and particularly the rise of chivalry, resulting in a new type of emancipated woman who gave the former thrifty wives of merchants an appetite for extravagance and luxury goods. 'Luxury then', he concluded, 'gave birth to capitalism.' Putting all his books on capitalism together, he had clearly over-explained its origins: he had provided so many explanations of the emergence of capitalism as to make what was once an historical puzzle seem an inevitable event that would have happened anyway even if this or that element had been missing.

Sombart was born in 1863 in Ermsleben, Germany. His father was a landowner, an industrial entrepreneur, and a liberal member of the Reichstag. He studied law, economics and history at the Universities of Pisa, Rome and Berlin, receiving his doctorate from the University of Berlin in 1888 with a thesis supervised by Schmoller (q.v.) and Adolph Wagner (1835-1917), the leading members of the younger German Historical School. After two years with the Bremen Chamber of Commerce, he entered his academic career with a post at the University of Breslau, moving to the Handelshoch Schule in Berlin in 1906. When both Schmoller and Wagner died in 1917, Sombart succeeded them as professor at the University of Berlin. One of his last publications was *A New Social Philosophy* (1934) in which he attempted to analyse the social problems of the time 'from the point of view of the national socialist [i.e. Nazi] way of thinking'. The Nazis must have had some difficulty with Sombart's earlier views on the role of Jews in history, but nevertheless permitted him to retire gracefully from teaching in 1935 and even reprinted parts of *A New Social Philosophy* in 1937. Sombart died in the middle of World War II in 1941.

*Secondary Literature*
J. Kuczynski, 'Sombart, Werner', *International Encyclopedia of the Social Sciences,* vol. 15, ed. D.L. Sills (Macmillan Free Press, 1968); F.M. Baglione, 'Sombart, Werner', *Thinkers of the 20th Century,* E. Devine *et al.* (eds.) (Macmillan, 1983).

# Spiethoff, Arthur (1873-1957)

Arthur Spiethoff devoted his entire professional life to the study of a single subject, business cycles. His point of departure was the earlier work of Juglar (q.v.), the analysis of Marx, the work of a Russion Marxist, Tugan-Baranovsky (1865-1919), and the chapters on economic fluctuations in Schmoller's *Grundriss (Outline)* (1900-4) to which Spiethoff had contributed as an assistant. He was painfully aware that there was little in the way of a satisfactory theory of business cycles that could account at one and the same time for their periodicity and their origin in the very structure of the capitalist system. By this time it was common knowledge that economic fluctuations are always more marked in the capital goods industries than in consumer goods industries and Spiethoff struggled all his life to work this fact into a consistent theoretical framework. His writings show a disdain for all varieties of monetary theories of business cycles, which find the cause of cycles in banking and credit policies, and a market preference for 'real' theories which trace the boom and slump to waves of capital investment. Nevertheless, the treatment is sufficiently eclectic to include virtually all the elements found in the writings of other business-cycle theorists — such as crop failures, monetary factors, pervasive changes in psychological confidence, uncoordinated variations in saving and investment, etc.

Spiethoff published his first paper on business cycles in 1902 and this was followed by a steady stream of articles, summed up in a famous essay on 'Krisen' (Crises) in the *Handwörterbuch der Staatswissenschaften (School Dictionary of Political Science)* (1923), which has appeared in English as 'Business Cycles' (1953). He also tried to resolve the old battle between the orthodox view of the absolute truth of economic theories and the German Historical School's contention that theories are only valid for their own time and place. In two papers, 'The Historical Character of Economic Theories' (1952) and 'Pure Theory and Economic Gestalt Theory' (1953), he formulated the concept of economic styles which are said to be valid for typical historical variations in economic life. On balance, however, the argument in these two papers amounts to little more than a defence of the traditional standpoint of German historical economists expressed in new language.

*Secondary Literature*
G. Clausing, 'Spiethoff, Arthur', *International Encyclopedia of the Social Sciences,* vol. 15, ed. D.L. Sills (Macmillan Free Press, 1968).

# Steuart, James Denham (1712-1780)

Sir James Steuart was a British mercantilist, the last in a long line stretching back to the sixteenth century. He published his great treatise, *An Inquiry into the Principles of Political Economy* (1767) nine years before Adam Smith's *Wealth of Nations* made mercantilism a dirty word in intellectual circles. Moreover, Smith dealt him a mortal blow by ignoring him and, as we know from private correspondence, deliberately failing to cite him even in places where his arguments directly confronted those of Steuart. As a result, Steuart's book fell into total oblivion and was never referred to by any of the English classical economists. Marx noticed him however, and he gradually enjoyed some attention from the members of the German Historical School in the late nineteenth century who appreciated his historical bent and his belief that economic development must be consciously managed by the state. More recently, he has been hailed as a forerunner of the 'economics of control' and the concept of development planning.

He was born in Edinburgh in 1712, the son of the Solicitor-General of Scotland under Queen Anne and George I. After studying law at the

University of Edinburgh, he travelled extensively on the Continent. His involvement in the Jacobite cause to wrest Scotland free of England forced him to remain abroad until 1763. Returning to Scotland, he devoted the rest of his life to literary pursuits, dying in 1780.

As a Scotsman, he shared the same intellectual mentors as Adam Smith (q.v.), and it is interesting to see the same theory of historical stages of development in the writings of Steuart as in those of Adam Smith, namely, a hunting stage, succeeded by a pastoral stage, succeeded by a commercial stage in which the subsistence economy finally gives way to an exchange economy, the growth of towns and the emergence of a national market. The only difference is that this is a spontaneous process in Smith and a government-sponsored process in Steuart. Moreover, the degree of government intervention in Steuart becomes more critical as the process of commercialisation and industrialisation proceeds. He was particularly worried about population growth — where his views bear an uncanny resemblance to the later views of Malthus (q.v.) — the growth of foreign trade as commercialisation drives up wages and profits at home faster than abroad, and the displacement of labour by the introduction of new machines. In consequence, he advocated the entire armoury of mercantilist policies: the regulation of foreign trade to induce an inflow of gold; the promotion of industry by inducing cheap raw material imports; protective duties on imported manufactured goods; encouragement of exports, particularly finished goods because they are labour-intensive; control of the size of population by emigration and immigration to keep wages low; all capped by a denial of Hume's argument that an inflow of gold will only raise prices and thus drive gold abroad again.

If Steuart is still worth reading, he is worth reading only as a lesser Smith, sharing the same broad sociological and historical perspective but lacking not so much theory of value and distribution as a grasp of the doctrine of the unintended social consequences of individual actions.

*Secondary Literature*
W. Stark, 'Steuart, James Denham', *International Encyclopedia of the Social Sciences,* vol. 15, ed. D.L. Sills (Macmillan Free Press, 1968); A.S. Skinner, 'Introduction', J. Steuart, *Inquiry into the Principles of Political Economy* (Oliver & Boyd, 1976).

# Thornton, Henry (1760-1815)

Henry Thornton's *Inquiry into the Nature and Effects of the Paper Credit of Great Britain* (1802) is the greatest work of the nineteenth century on monetary theory: it was not equalled until Wicksell's *Interest and Prices* (1898) and Fisher's *Purchasing Power of Money* (1911). Apart from addressing himself to the outstanding monetary problem of his times — What are the effects of paper money on prices under a system which prohibits the convertibility of rates and coins into gold? — Thornton made three original contributions to monetary economics. The first was the fundamental distinction between nominal and real rates of interest, that is, between the actual market rate and the inflation-corrected rate of interest: when prices are rising at 5 per cent per annum, a market rate of interest of 10 per cent is equivalent to a 5 per cent yield on money invested; thus, inflation tends automatically to raise the market rate of interest. The second was the equally fundamental distinction between the market and the 'natural' rate of interest, that is, between the market rate at which funds may be borrowed and the expected rate of return on investment. Thornton employed this latter distinction to refute the real bills doctrine endorsed by Adam Smith, namely, the view that banks will never cause inflation as long as they confine themselves to lending only for projects that are automatically self-liquidating — say, a sale of goods on 30-days' credit — in bankers' language, they must discount only 'real' commercial bills and avoid lending for capital investment. But when the expected natural rate of interest exceeeds the market rate, there is an insatiable demand for loans, and even bank lending on good security will not prevent an inflationary rise of prices. His third contribution was the notion that inflation is capable of increasing output and employment even in situations of full employment by forced saving — what Thornton called the 'defalcation of revenue'; inflation imposes involuntary saving on fixed-income recipients, thus financing the extra investment.

Thornton was born in 1760 into a prosperous banking family and himself joined a banking firm when he was 24-years-old. Two years earlier he had been elected to a Parliamentary seat which he retained until his death. He was related by marriage to William Wilberforce, the leader of the anti-slavery agitation, around whom grew up what came to be known as the Clapham sect, an evangelical movement within the Church of England, so-named because so many of them, including Thornton, lived in the London suburb of Clapham. Thornton was an active member of the Clapham sect all his life, opening sunday schools, sending missionaries to the colonies, and reprinting the Bible in cheap editions.

This was one side of his life. The other was dealing expertly with problems of currency and banking in Parliament. He was a member of a number of Parliamentary committees reporting on the state of the currency, and had a hand in writing the famous Bullion Committee Report of 1810, which shaped the nature of monetary theory for an entire generation. In his book he had taken pains to defend the Bank of England against the charge that the suspension of cash payments had permitted an excessive issue of paper money, being therefore, responsible for inflation during the years of the Napoleonic wars. In short, he defended the Bank against a 'monetarist' attack. However, by the time of the Bullion Committee he had become more critical of the Bank and was willing to agree that some contraction of the note issue was desirable. Nevertheless, he never went as far as Ricardo in blaming the whole of wartime inflation on the irresponsible policies of the Bank of England.

Thornton's *Inquiry* was well received when it was published, —

even Ricardo (q.v.) refrained from criticising it openly; and John Stuart Mill (q.v.) lauded it in his *Principles of Political Economy* (1848). Nevertheless, the book's reputation went into a slow decline throughout the nineteenth century, possibly because much of its institutional material had become outdated. Thus, when Wicksell (q.v.) revived Thornton's distinction between the market and the natural rate of interest at the close of the century, he took the idea from Ricardo, unaware that it was more clearly expounded by Thornton. It was only in the twentieth century, largely as a result of the efforts of Jacob Viner and Friedrich Hayek, that Thornton's *Inquiry* was rediscovered as the repository of much of the best of modern monetary theory.

*Secondary Literature*
T.W. Hutchison, 'Thornton, Henry', *International Encyclopedia of the Social Sciences,* vol. 16, ed. D.L. Sills (Macmillan Free Press, 1968).

# Thünen,
# Johann
# Heinrich von
# (1783-1850)

Thünen is two and perhaps even three economists in one: to economic geographers, he is the 'father' of location theory, that branch of economics which is concerned with the role of distance and area in economic life; to theoretical economists, he is one of the independent discoverers of the so-called 'marginal productivity theory of distribution'; and to mathematical economists and econometricians, he is an important pioneer in the use of calculus to obtain solutions to maximisation problems, many of which he then checked against data he collected from his own agricultural estate.

He is also one of the prime examples in the history of economic thought of a neglected genius. There were many reasons why he was a prophet with little honour in any country and even less in his own, Germany. First of all, he was a liberal and free-trader in an era when liberalism was anathema in Germany. Secondly, he was a 'pure' theorist, who extolled Newtonian equilibrium methods in the analysis of social questions at a time when Germany was dominated by the anti-theoretical bias of the Historical School. Finally, he lacked academic status and even a university degree. To these three factors, we may add three more: his great masterpiece, *The Isolated State,* appeared in three volumes and five instalments over a 37-year period (vol.1, 1819, revised 1826 and 1842; vol.2, part I 1850; vol.2, part II, vol. III, 1863), so that its final impact was necessarily long delayed; he made constant use of algebra and differential calculus long before mathematical reasoning had become an acceptable mode of expression in the social sciences; lastly, he wrote cryptically and obscurely, constantly moving back and forth among various central questions, usually without announcement or explanation. Even in a subject as renowned for its badly written great books as economics (e.g. Ricardo's *Principles,* Marx's *Capital,* Walras's *Elements,* and Keynes's *General Theory*), *The Isolated State* stands out as a formless monster — less a book than a collection of notes, comments, arithmetical examples and mathematical formulae, in which the main lines of argument can frequently only be discerned with the benefit of hindsight.

Still, exercising that hindsight, what a book it is! Many eighteenth-century economists, including Cantillon (q.v.) and Adam Smith (q.v.), had much to say about the economic effects of space, but only Thünen had the vision to postulate an abstract spatial model that highlights the role of distance and area by its very construction. On the opening page of his *Isolated State,* Thünen tells us to consider an 'ideal' or 'isolated' or closed-off state — a featureless plain without roads or navigable rivers and restricted to the use of horse-drawn wagons as the only mode of transportation, having a single town at its centre producing manufactured articles and supplied by farmers in the surrounding plain with all its agricultural produce — and asks us to consider what, in such circumstances, will determine the prices that farmers receive for their output, the rents that are earned by various units of land, and the associated patterns of land use that accompany such prices and rents. The argument culminates in the demonstration that the pattern of land use and even the intensity with which different crops will be cultivated takes the form of a series of concentric rings spreading out from the central town to the edge of the isolated state. This concept of a closed economy in idealised space was radically new, which fully justifies Thünen's claim to the title of 'father' of spatial economics.

All this takes up the whole of the first volume of *The Isolated State.* It is only in the second volume, that Thünen introduces the question of functional income distribution in accordance with the principle of marginal productivity. Grounding the whole analysis in his own empirical estimates of production relations in agriculture, he provided an extraordinarily modern exposition of the marginal productivity theory of distribution — literally 60 years ahead of his time! Unfortunately, he became convinced that the absense of free land held down wages under normal capitalist conditions and so launched on an analysis of a profit-sharing economy made up of producer cooperatives in which the wage, he argued, would be a 'natural wage' exceeding the wage determined under a regime of private ownership of capital. His formula for that 'natural wage', $\sqrt{ap}$ — the geometric mean between the minimum subsistence wage and the average product of a working family — was endlessly misunderstood and ridiculed, thus adding still another reason for neglecting his contributions. Nevertheless, some later economists did sing his praises: both John Bates Clark (q.v.) and Wicksell (q.v.) paid tribute to his discovery of the marginal productivity principle, and Marshall (q.v.) above all praised Thünen's theory of location, interest and rent, the more remarkable in his case as he was not generally inclined to acknowledge inspiration from others. (Thünen and Cournot (q.v.) are in fact the only economists to whom Marshall expressed direct indebtedness.)

Thünen was born in 1783 on the North Sea coast of East Germany. He had a mixed school career, leaving at 16 for an apprenticeship on a farm and returning at 19 to study agronomy at an agricultural college. At this college, at the age of 20, he wrote a paper which laid down a sketch of the concept of an 'isolated state', the idea which was later to become the keystone of his *magnum opus*. He left the college before finishing the course and enrolled in a seminar run by Albrecht Thaer, whose *Introduction to a Knowledge of English Agriculture* (1798) had sparked off a movement for the reform of agriculture in Germany, advocating the principles of extensive farming and the introduction of the English crop-rotation system. Thünen became an enthusiastic disciple of Thaer, determined to try out his ideas on a farm of his own. After attending the University of Göttingen for two terms, he married, leased a farm from his brother-in-law, and began to search for a suitable property to buy. In 1810, a few days after his 27th birthday, he bought a large estate south-east of Rostock (now in the Democratic Republic of Germany).

The years 1810 to 1815 were largely taken up with working out a basic system of accounts for his estate. This initial period was followed by four more years of detailed calculation, after which the first draft of *The Isolated State* was rapidly produced in 1819 (just when Ricardo, whom Thünen had not read at this stage, was working on the second edition of his *Principles*); he revised his draft in 1824 and only published it in 1826, revising it again for a second edition in 1842. This is the first volume of *The Isolated State,* which completed his rent and location theory. His theory of the natural wage was not published until 1850 as the first part of the second volume of the work, appearing shortly after his death at the age of 67. The second part of this second volume, together with a third volume, was published posthumously in 1863; these remain to this day untranslated into English.

In the last years of his life, Thünen took a new interest in social questions. He introduced a profit-sharing scheme for his tenants on the estate and was invited to stand for election to the liberal National Assembly at Frankfurt-am-Main — the so-called 'Professors' Parliament'. He declined on grounds of ill-health, but his two sons were elected instead. He died in 1850 and was buried in the village churchyard next to his estate. Under his name on the gravestone is engraved, in accordance with his own instructions, the mystical formula for the natural wage: $A = \sqrt{ap}$.

*Secondary Literature*
P. Hall, 'Introduction', *Von Thünen's Isolated State* (Pergamon, 1966); A.H. Leigh, 'Thünen, Johann Heinrich von', *International Encyclopedia of the Social Sciences,* vol. 16, ed. D.L. Sills (Macmillan Free Press, 1968).

# Tooke,
# Thomas
# (1774-1858)

Thomas Tooke is the founder of the contra-quantity theory of money — the view that monetary policy is powerless to influence prices because the supply of money depends on the flow of money expenditure and hence is the result and not the cause of price changes. Not that he ever developed a rigorous, coherent argument against the quantity theory of money but he did supply the material for such an argument in his commentaries on the raw price data that he spent a lifetime collecting. His *History of Prices and the State of the Circulation* first appeared in two volumes in 1838, covering the period 1793-1837, and was then extended in 1857 with the assistance of William Newmarch (1820-82) into a massive 6-volume work on the half-century 1793-1856. Although the concept of index numbers had already been invented, Tooke and Newmarch in fact made no attempt to sum up their evidence in terms of index numbers; nevertheless, their book inspired Jevons (q.v.) in the early 1860s to construct the first index number of a price series.

Tooke's work on the history of prices was part and parcel of his relentless criticism of the 'currency principle', namely, that Bank of

England notes in a mixed gold paper currency should be made to vary exactly as would a metallic currency, so that they would respond automatically to an inflow or outflow of gold. He was the principal spokesman of the Banking School which denied any need for statutory control of the currency so long as notes were freely convertible into gold inasmuch as what was called 'the needs of trade' automatically controlled the volume of notes issued, not to mention the fact that bank deposits and other forms of credit were available as substitutes for bank notes. In two long pamphlets, *An Inquiry into the Currency Principle* (1844) and *On the Bank Charter Act of 1844* (1856), he attacked the famous Bank Act 1844, which had sought to enact the currency principle, the former being published just before the Act was passed and the latter after the Act had had to be twice suspended to rescue failing banks.

Tooke was born in Russia in 1774 where his father was a clergyman of an English church. He was educated privately in Russia and England and entered business in his late twenties as a partner in a firm trading with Russia; he remained active in the Russian trade until his retirement in 1836. In the 1820s, long before he became an historian of prices and a critic of prevailing banking policies, he was prominent as a lobbyist for business interests anxious to remove trade barriers. He was the author of the London Merchants' Petition presented to the House of Commons in 1820, one of the first public expressions in Britain of widespread political support for the cause of free trade. In the following year he joined Ricardo (q.v.), Malthus (q.v.), McCulloch (q.v.) and Torrens (q.v.) in founding the Political Economy Club, and was an active member of the club until his death in 1858.

*Secondary Literature*
T.E. Gregory, *An Introduction to Tooke and Newmarch's A History of Prices* (London School of Economics, 1928); F.W. Fetter, 'Tooke, Thomas', *International Encyclopedia of the Social Sciences,* vol. 16, ed. D.L. Sills (Macmillan Free Press, 1968).

# Torrens, Robert (1780-1864)

Robert Torrens was one of the many minor but occasionally highly original English economists who flourished in the quarter century between the death of Ricardo in 1823 and the publication of John Stuart Mill's magisterial *Principles of Political Economy* (1848). After an early career as a professional soldier, he became a newspaper proprietor, a Member of Parliament, a promoter of schemes for the colonisation of Australia, and a tireless publicist on economic questions, writing almost 100 books and pamphlets in a lifespan of 84 years. His *Essay on the External Corn Trade* (1815) shared the simultaneous but independent discovery of the law of diminishing returns with Ricardo, Malthus and Edward West (1782-1828); it also contained the discovery of the principle of comparative advantage in international trades, two years before Ricardo expounded it in his *Principles*. Torrens' only full-scale treatise on economics, *An Essay on the Production of Wealth* (1821), was less original, but nevertheless full of cogent comments on value, rent, profits and Say's law of markets.

One of his more notorious later contributions came in a series of letters, reprinted as *The Budget* (1841-42), in which he demonstrated that free trade is not necessarily optimal for each and every country: a particular country can alter the terms of trade in its own favour by a tariff on imports; once some countries have tariffs, it is an error to think that either domestic or global welfare is improved by the unilateral rather than the reciprocal elimination of tariffs. Torrens was violently attacked for this abrogation of the classical Ricardian doctrine on free trade but the argument stuck and survived to modern times as a genuine qualification of the theory that free trade is the best of all possible worlds for every country.

It was in the field of banking, however, that Torrens established his reputation in his own times. He was a leader of the Currency School, arguing that the primary duty of the Bank of England as the central bank was to maintain a sufficient reserve of gold bullion to safeguard the stability of the monetary system, based as it was on coins, paper notes and bank cheques. The basic thesis — the 'currency principle' — was that a mixed currency should be made to vary in the same way as a metallic currency, namely, in response to inflows and outflows of bullion from abroad. The way to ensure that this would happen was to keep the issue of paper notes strictly proportionate to the amount of gold in the banking system. The Bank Charter Act 1844, separating the issue and the banking departments of the Bank of England, was the legislative expression of the doctrines of the Currency School. Torrens wrote the classic defence of that Act, *The Principles and Practical Operation of Sir Robert Peel's Bill of 1844* (1848).

*Secondary Literature*
L. Robbins, *Robert Torrens and the Evolution of Classical Economics* (Macmillan, 1958); B. Corry, 'Torrens, Robert', *International Encyclopedia of the Social Sciences,* vol. 16, ed. D.L. Sills (Macmillan Free Press, 1968).

# Turgot, Anne Robert Jacques (1727-1781)

Jacques Turgot was a leading physiocrat, an economic theorist whose *Reflections on the Formation and Distribution of Riches* (1770) was a major influence on Adam Smith, and an early example of the economist as policy-maker. Under Louis XV he was chief administrator of the district of Limoges for 13 years (1761-74). When Louis XVI came to the throne in 1774, Turgot was appointed to the key position of Minister of Finance, Trade and Public Works. One of his first acts was to abolish all restrictions on the internal grain trade in France. Next, he commuted the famous *corvée* (building and maintaining roads by forced labour) into money payments, dissolved all the mediaeval guilds, and enforced strict economy in public expenditure. These measures soon alienated the king, who dismissed Turgot in 1776 and revoked all his edicts. When the French Revolution broke out in 1789, some saw the dismissal of Turgot 13 years earlier as the first concrete sign of the total inability of the monarchy to carry out the reforms that might have forestalled the Revolution.

The *Reflections* is a remarkable book, containing not only the skeleton of the structure of Adam Smith's *Wealth of Nations* — particularly the concept of the division of labour, the distinction between the market and the natural equilibrium price of commodities, and the stress on the volume of real savings as the prime determinant of an economy's rate of growth — but going beyond Adam Smith in the analysis of the relation between profit and interest and the clear statement of the law of diminishing returns in agriculture. Turgot was even more vehement than Smith in insisting on the notion that least government in economic matters is best government and, without invoking Smith's striking simile of 'the invisible hand', left no doubt that the forces of the market could be relied on to drive an economy automatically to an equilibrium position. But that is not to say that, had Smith never lived, Turgot might have supplied later economists with all the ingredients of the Smithian Heritage. Turgot's work lacked the architectonic design and grand historical sweep of Smith's book, the wealth of illustrations and examples, and the effective attack on existing government policies. It is fair to say that his style of reasoning was much more like that of Ricardo than that of Adam Smith, which is one reason why some modern commentators (such as Schumpeter (q.v.)) have praised him as superior to the latter.

*Secondary Literature*
W. Stark, 'Turgot, Anne Robert Jacques', *International Encyclopedia of the Social Sciences,* vol. 16, ed. D.L. Sills (Macmillan Free Press, 1968); P.D. Groenewegen, *The Economics of A.R.J. Turgot* (Martinus Nijhoff, 1977).

# Veblen, Thorstein Bunde (1857-1929)

Thorstein Veblen is to economics what Jonathan Swift is to English literature: a master of the art of satire. Is is essential to effective satire that its message be ambiguous: the reader should never be sure whether the author is absolutely serious or just pulling his or her leg. That quality is certainly present in Swift's *Gulliver's Travels* and it is also present in Veblen's *Theory of the Leisure Class* (1899), *The Instinct of Workmanship* (1914), *Imperial Germany and the Industrial Revolution* (1915), *The Higher Learning in America* (1918), *Absentee Ownership* (1923), and his many essays. In fact, it is there in everything he wrote except *The Theory of Business Enterprise* (1904), which is as near as he ever came to writing a conventional academic book.

No matter which of these books we open, we find the idea that life in a modern industrial community is the result of a polar conflict between 'pecuniary employments' and 'industrial employments', between 'business enterprise' and 'the machine process', between 'vendibility' and 'serviceability' — in short, between making money and making goods. There is a class struggle under capitalism, not

256

between the bourgeoisie and the proletariat, but between businessmen and engineers. Pecuniary habits of thought unite bankers, brokers, lawyers and managers in a defence of private acquisition; in contrast, the discipline of the machine unites workers in industry and more especially the technicians and engineers who supervise them.

It is in these terms that Veblen describes modern industrial civilisation. As we read him, we have the feeling that something is being explained. And yet in the end the ambiguity of the message remains. He appears to offer a fundamental critique of the market mechanism and a call for something like a technocratic revolution, but Veblen warns us specifically against the belief that the engineers are capable of taking over and running the system, which leaves us wondering just what he is saying. But perhaps the desire to pin him down precisely misses the point: it is, after all, satire and is designed to open your eyes, not to close your mind.

Veblen had little use for the abstract-deductive approach of neoclassical economics. Economics ought to be an evolutionary science, he argued, meaning an inquiry into the genesis and growth of economic institutions. He defined institutions, however, somewhat idiosyncratically as a complex of habits of thought and conventional rules of behaviour. Thus, 'institutional economics' would appear to be about the study of the intellectual patterns and social mores that become crystallised in economic organisations. But what Veblen actually gave his readers was sociological criticism of the prevailing culture, dressed up with instinct psychology, racist anthropology and a flight of telling adjectives: 'conspicuous consumption', 'pecuniary emulation', 'ostentatious display', 'absentee ownership', 'the instinct of workmanship', and the like. It was a mixture so unique and individual to Veblen that even his most enthusiastic disciples were unable to extend or develop it. It is true that Veblen is supposed to have founded the American School of Institutionalist Economics, which survives in a fashion to this very day. But that is only because he attracted two followers, Mitchell (q.v.) and Commons (q.v.), who fashioned institutional economics in the spirit rather than the letter of Veblen. Their work confirms the proposition that Veblen was in a class of his own: for better or for worse, his books are not about economic theory at all but rather about how to interpret the values and beliefs of those whom he ironically labelled as 'captains of industry'. Still, it must be admitted that his works make better reading and linger longer in the mind than many a great book on economic theory.

Veblen was born in Cato, Wisconsin in 1857, the sixth child in a large farming family of first-generation Norwegian immigrants. He graduated from Carleton College, Minnesota in 1880, receiving his PhD in philosophy at Yale in 1884. Failing to find a teaching post, he returned to his family in Minnesota and spent seven years reading and rusticating. In 1891 he enrolled as a graduate student in economics at Cornell University under James L. Laughlin (1850-1933); when Laughlin moved to the University of Chicago in the following year, Veblen went with him to take up his first teaching assignment. He spent 14 years on the Chicago faculty, followed by three at Stanford University (1906-9). Although *The Theory of the Leisure Class* and *The Theory of Business Enterprise* had now made him famous, his unorthodox personal life, his eccentric style of teaching, and the general notoriety of his economic opinions made it increasingly difficult for him to find a teaching post after leaving Stanford under a cloud in 1909. In 1911 he finally found a niche at the University of Missouri. Retiring in 1918 at the age of 61, he spent the rest of his life writing and teaching occasionally at the New School for Social Research, New York. He died in 1929 in relative obscurity, his earlier fame having by then largely evaporated because of his persistent failure to attach himself to any definite movement or campaign.

*Secondary Literature*
J. Dorfman, *Thorstein Veblen and His America* (Augustus M. Kelley, 1961); A.K. Davis, 'Veblen, Thorstein', *International Encyclopedia of the Social Sciences,* vol. 16, ed. D.L. Sills (Macmillan Free Press, 1968).

# Wakefield, Edward Gibbon (1796-1862)

It was part and parcel of the doctrines of Ricardian economics that capital, unlike labour, could never be in excess supply: provided the corn laws were repealed and wheat were freely imported, there would be unlimited opportunities for investing capital profitably; Say's law of markets ensured that, whatever the temporary difficulties, supply invariably creates its own demand. Malthus's attack on Say's law made no substantial dent in this belief of the ability of the economic system to create full employment of labour and full capacity-utilisation of the capital stock without the intervention of government. The weakness of this argument was at first more obvious on the side of labour than on that of capital. The Malthusian theory of population suggested that much labour was redundant, and efforts to relieve poverty and to raise wages by emigration had already gathered steam in Malthus's own lifetime. Even before Malthus's death in 1834, a powerful pamphlet by Wakefield, *A Letter from Sydney, the Principal Town of Australasia* (1829), actually written in a London prison but purporting to be penned by an English emigrant in Australia, gave a new twist to the debate by suggesting that 'systematic colonisation'

might be the answer to the over-supply of both capital and labour in Britain. Wakefield in this and other writings set off a furious colonisation debate, which persuaded such stalwarts as Torrens (q.v.) and John Stuart Mill (q.v.) that capital was indeed becoming redundant in Britain and that colonies might serve to absorb surplus capital. In his *Principles of Political Economy* (1848), Mill still defended Say's law, but with a new caution that reflected the influence of Wakefield's writings.

Wakefield's system of colonisation broke with the older view that land should be freely available to emigrants in new countries and that emigration was only suitable for unskilled workers or skilled workers displaced by technical progress. If land is freely available, Wakefield argued, the result is small-scale farming on isolated settlements and the failure of wage labour and hence manufacturing to emerge (how Marx gloated over this fatal admission by Wakefield!). To remedy this situation, Wakefield proposed that land in new territories should be sold at a 'sufficient price' to restrict access to it, and the proceeds from the land sales be used to finance the further emigration of voluntary settlers, properly distributed by sex, age and skill; once the colonial population reached a level of 50,000, the colony should be granted self-government. These proposals were expounded and defended with such verve and eloquence that they soon won over the whole of British public opinion to a more positive attitude towards the colonisation of Canada, Australia and New Zealand.

Wakefield was born in London and had a chequered school career in both London and Edinburgh. After the death of his first wife, he tricked a schoolgirl heiress into marriage; the marriage was annulled and Wakefield was sent to London's notorious Newgate Prison for three years. His enforced idleness resulted not only in the *Letter from Sydney* but also *Facts Relating to the Punishment of Death in the Metropolis* (1831), a Benthamite treatise on criminology, which laid down the now much-debated maxim that what deters criminals is not the severity of the punishment but the certainty of being apprehended; in short, there is no cheap way of deterring crime. In 1834, three years after regaining his freedom, Wakefield organised the South Australia Association and succeeded in persuading Parliament within a year to establish the colony of South Australia on his own lines. In 1838, he advised Lord Durham on his famous *Report on the Affairs of British North America,* which set Canada on the course towards self-government. In the 1840s, he played a similar role in the

260

colonisation of New Zealand and subsequently acted as an advisor to the government of the new colony. He died in 1862 after a long bout of illness.

*Secondary Literature*
D. Winch, *Classical Political Economy and Colonies* (Harvard University Press, 1965); R. Lekachman, 'Wakefield, Gibbon', *International Encyclopedia of the Social Sciences,* vol. 16, ed. D.L. Sills (Macmillan Free Press, 1968).

# Walras, Léon (1834-1910)

Jevons' *Theory of Political Economy* (1871) was not well received when it appeared, but it was read. Menger's *Principles of Economics* (1871) was both read and well received, at least in his own country. But Walras's two-part *Elements of Pure Economics* (1844-77) was monstrously neglected everywhere despite his indefatigable efforts to get the book noticed. That was in part because Walras set himself a task that went beyond Jevons and Menger, his co-discoverers of marginal utility theory, namely, to write down and solve the first multi-equational model of general equilibrium in all markets. In addition, Walras went far beyond Jevons in employing a mathematical mode of exposition, and this was enough to scare off most of his contemporary readers. But whereas Jevons and Menger are now regarded as historical landmarks, rarely read purely for their own sake, posthumous appreciation of Walras's monumental achievement has grown so markedly since the 1930s that he may now be the most widely-read nineteenth-century economist after Ricardo and Marx, particularly since the translation of the *Elements* into English in 1954.

Walras was born in 1834 in Evreux, a provincial town in Normandy, France, the son of an economist, Auguste Walras, from whom he derived not only his starting point in utility maximisation as the key to unlock all doors in economics, but also his social views, such as land nationalisation and the radical reform of the tax system. He graduated from the University of Paris, first in letters in 1851 and then in science in 1853. After some years as an unsuccessful engineering student at the École des Mines, Paris, he tried his hand at journalism, lecturing, published a romantic novel, worked as a clerk for a railway company, and directed a bank for cooperatives. In 1870, at the age of 36, he was narrowly voted into a newly-created post of professor of political economy at the University of Lausanne where he remained for over 20 years. He had already published two books on social philosophy and had earlier divided his life-work into pure economics, applied economics and social or normative economics. Once he obtained the Lausanne Chair, however, he concentrated on pure economics and taught himself calculus. In fact, he was never able to produce the systematic treatise on applied and social economics which he earlier envisaged and had to be satisfied with publishing collections of his essays on those subjects. Most of his efforts were taken up with polishing successive editions of the *Elements* (1889, 1896, 1900), each of which added huge chunks to the first edition; and with carrying on an enormous and almost daily correspondence with literally hundreds of economists throughout the world.

Walras's comprehensive analysis of general equilibrium is built up step-by-step in a process of ever-decreasing abstractions, starting from the case of two-party, two-commodity barter to multi-party, multi-commodity exchange of given stocks of goods, to production and the markets for productive services, to saving and capital formation, and, lastly, the use of money and credit. In his analysis of two-commodity barter he employed the same consumer allocation formula as Jevons — in equilibrium the ratio of the marginal utilities from each of the two goods must for each party be equal to the ratio of their prices — but unlike Jevons he then employed it rigorously to deduce declining demand functions for goods. His procedure in all cases of multi-commodity exchange was to write down the abstract demand and supply equations on the assumption of perfect competition, perfect mobility of the factors of production and perfect price flexibility and then to 'prove' the existence of a general equilibrium solution for this set of simultaneous equations by

263

counting the number of equations and unknowns; if they were equal, he concluded that general equilibrium solution was at least possible. This strictly static picture of the determination of equilibrium was then followed up by a quasi-realistic explanation of how the competitive mechanism might actually establish such an equilibrium. He called the automatic adjustments of price in response to excess demand or supply one of *tâtonnement,* that is, of groping by trial and error without central direction. Unfortunately, he continuously amended his account of *tâtonnement* in successive editions of the *Elements* — or rather gave one account of it in his theory of exchange and another in his theory of production, so that to this day it has been argued that he never provided any convincing exposition of how competition actually yields a multi-market general equilibrium solution for all prices of both goods and productive services.

In the first edition of the *Elements,* his theory of production assumed that production is characterised by fixed technical coefficients, ruling out factor substitution. It was only in the third edition in 1896 — apparently as a result of the prompting of Barone (q.v.), his Italian disciple — that he provided an analysis of how these coefficients are themselves determined, now adopting a fully-fledged marginal productivity theory of distribution. Similarly, in the fourth edition (1900) of the *Elements,* he introduced a utility theory of saving, and a treatment of the pricing of capital goods. Also in *Théorie de la monnaie* (1886), he elaborated a theory of the value of money by carrying over the formal analysis of utility maximisation previously applied to consumption.

Walras's contributions have continued to attract controversy down to the present. Some have accused him of sterile formalism, being more concerned with the elegant form of economic theory than with its substantive content. Others have argued that whatever the value of his work for his own time, the influence of his writings have encouraged the empty mathematisation of economics at the expense of relevance to practical problems. But others have expressed boundless admiration both for his vision and for his accomplishments. As Schumpeter once said: 'As far as pure theory is concerned, Walras is in my opinion the greatest of all economists. His system of economic equilibrium, uniting as it does the quality of 'revolutionary' creativeness with the quality of classical synthesis, is the only work by an economist that will stand comparison with the achievements of theoretical physics'.

*Secondary Literature*
W. Jaffé, 'Walras, Leon', *International Encyclopedia of the Social Sciences,* vol. 16, ed. D.L. Sills (Macmillan Free Press, 1968); *Jaffé's Essays on Walras,* ed. A.D. Walker (Cambridge University Press, 1983).

# Weber, Alfred (1868-1958)

Alfred Weber, the brother of the more famous sociologist Max Weber, made a single contribution to economics in his book, *Theory of the Location of Industries* (1909), but it is a contribution which has had a lasting influence on the literature dealing with plant location. Long before Weber, Thünen (q.v.) and Launhardt (q.v.) had put location theory on the map. Nevertheless, Weber's book must be regarded as the first successful treatise on location theory in the sense of inspiring continuous interest and ongoing inquiry in location theory as a specialised branch of economics. Weber's speculations on plant location had been anticipated in many respects by Launhardt, but he went well beyond Launhardt in adding differential labour costs and differential transport costs and in introducing 'agglomeration economies' — those reductions in unit costs due solely to the clustering or agglomeration of plants in nearby locations. Even in his handling of the classical 'three-points problem' in location theory (the optimal location of an industrial plant using raw materials located in two different places and serving a market located in a third place), Weber developed a simpler and more general graphic technique for analysing such problems than anything achieved by Launhardt.

In the true fashion originated by Thünen, Weber conceived of his analysis as a pure theory of location, which is independent of topography, climate, the technology of transportation, the quality of management etc., focusing almost entirely on the influence of transport costs as linear functions of distance and the weight of products transported. Industrial plants are taken to produce single, given commodities by means of fixed input–output coefficients, and the problem is to determine their optimum geographical location, the solution of which turns out to be almost solely a matter of minimising the total transport costs of inputs and outputs. Weber emphasises the question of whether raw materials enter into the finished product to the full extent of their weights or whether, as in the case of iron ore in the smelting of steel, they lose all or part of their weight through combustion or other means of refinement. When the productive process is weight-gaining, the location of the plant is pulled towards the point of consumption; on the other hand, when it is weight-losing, the plant is oriented towards the locations at which raw materials are deposited. He does allow, however, for cases where plant locations deviate from their transport orientations because labour cost differences outweigh variations in transport costs. In addition to variable labour costs, there are offsetting agglomeration economies in the form of improved marketing outlets, greater proximity to auxiliary industries, and access to existing pools of labour, which create a tendency towards the clustering of plants in city centres. All these elements are expressed by means of a number of numerical ratios and graphed in terms of 'isodapanes' (contours of equal increments in the total transfer costs of inputs and outputs).

Criticisms of Weber have become the stock-in-trade of commentaries on the history of spatial economics. He is constantly accused of neglecting demand; of concentrating on the uninteresting case of producers and consumers bunched at single-point locations instead of being continuously dispersed over economic space; of operating with transport functions that vary only linearly with weight and distance as if by straight airline routes; and, in general, of casting the question of plant location in an engineering rather than an economic context — that is, in terms of the physical characteristics of raw materials and production processes rather than prices and substitution ratios. Weber never replied to any of the criticisms levelled against him but for almost 20 years a long list of his pupils continued to apply his ideas to studies of the location of specific German industries. Weber himself turned towards a totally different style of location theory, only touched upon in the closing chapter of the *Theory of Location of Industries,* and more in keeping with the historical and evolutionary preoccupations of the German Historical School. By the First World War, however, he had abandoned location theory altogether for sociology and political science. He retired from his professorship at the University of Heidelberg in 1933, and published his last book in 1953 at the age of 85, five years before his death. He never wrote on location theory again, however.

*Secondary Literature*
E. Salin, 'Weber, Alfred', *International Encyclopedia of the Social Sciences,* vol. 16, ed. D.L. Sills (Macmillan Free Press, 1968).

# Weber, Max (1864-1920)

No one needs to be told that Max Weber was a famous sociologist: endless are the books on Marx, Durkheim and Weber as the founding fathers of modern sociology. But Max Weber was also an economist and economic historian, equally famous for his methodological pronouncements on the use of ideal types and the possibility of a value-free social science as for his studies of the Protestant origins of capitalism.

Max Weber was born in Erfurt, Germany in 1864, attended the local high school and the Universities of Heidelberg, Göttingen and Berlin studying law. After the obligatory law degree in 1886 he published a dissertation in 1889 on mediaeval trading companies in Italy and Spain, followed by a post-doctoral *habilitation* on Roman agrarian history (1891). Serving his first academic post in law at the University of Berlin in 1892, he supervised an elaborate empirical study of agrarian workers in Prussia, which led to an appointment as professor of economics, first at the University of Freiburg in 1894 and then at Heidelberg in 1896. In 1898 he suffered a nervous breakdown and was granted more or less permanent leave without pay. It was eight years before he resumed his scholarly work.

His characteristic methodological views were announced in an influential essay, 'On the Objectivity of the Sociological and Social-Political Knowledge' (1904), and his famous historical thesis in a book, *The Protestant Ethic and the Spirit of Capitalism* (1904-5). From this time on he lived as a private scholar, mostly in Heidelberg, extending his work on the sociology of religion into a study of Judaism, Hinduism, Confucianism, Buddhism and Islam, analysing the role of bureaucracy and political authority in industrial societies, and elaborating his views on the nature and scope of social science. Owing to chronic ill-health, much of his later writings consist of unfinished fragments which were edited and published posthumously. Even his finished writings, however, are tortuously written — the worst examples of what is implied by a 'Germanic style' — and have created endless controversies.

Weber's *Protestant Ethic and the Spirit of Capitalism*, better known through Tawney's glosses in his *Religion and the Rise of Capitalism* (1926), was intended to resolve the paradox of the evident economic success of members of Protestant sects in spite of the condemnation of the acquisitive spirit in Protestant theology. It is frequently understood as standing Marx on his head, attributing the rise of capitalism not to technology or the changing relations between social classes but to purely ideological elements, such as the ethical code of conduct instilled by the spread of Protestantism in the sixteenth and seventeenth centuries. But Weber did not actually deny the Marxist philosophy of history. His argument was that it was too simple and that Protestantism played an important positive role in fostering the spirit of capitalism. No doubt, even the rise of Protestantism itself might be explained by economic forces but Weber apparently regarded that question as premature. His later studies of eastern religions were designed to provide additional evidence about the cultural context in which capitalism is either encouraged or discouraged. He never lived to complete his research programme so as to resolve the fundamental question which his book had posed: Is something like Protestantism a necessary or merely a sufficient condition for the emergence of industrial capitalism? The book initiated a great debate that began in Weber's own lifetime and still shows no sign of abating. Whatever Weber may have meant to say, it is difficult to think of a better example than *The Protestant Ethic and the Rise of Capitalism* of the almost impossible problem of pinning down a genuinely casual explanation in history.

Weber's methodological belief in the possibility — note that word — of value-free social science was a reaction against the use of academic chairs by Schmoller (q.v.) and the other founders of the *Verein für Sozialpolitik (Union for Social Policy)* to preach particular social and political views. Essentially, Weber said little more than what Hume (q.v.) had said over a century ago, namely, that no definite conclusions of how the world should be run can be derived from even an exhaustive study of how the world is. Economists have had no difficulty with Weber's argument, accustomed as they are to the old Senior–Mill–Keynes distinction between normative and positive economics. But the Weber thesis of value-neutrality has been endlessly attacked by sociologists and political scientists; even economists misunderstood the full import of Weber's argument, believing that it somehow rules out normative analysis as unscientific. But Weber was in fact keen to promote a rational discussion of the norms of economic policy. His point, however, was to insist that such a discussion had to be clearly distinguished from a purely positive study of economic problems.

Weber's other main contribution to methodology lay in his concept of ideal types married to *Verstehen* (understanding) doctrine. Insisting that explanation in the social sciences is conceptually different from explanation in the natural sciences because it involves human motivations, he concluded that adequate explanation in the social sciences involves abstractions, hence ideal types, which embody the inside understanding of how human agents behave, as distinct from the outside understanding of atoms and genes by physicists and biologists. Here, as elsewhere, later generations spent almost as much time disputing exactly what he meant as in arguing over whether he was correct.

*Secondary Literature*
R. Bendix, 'Weber, Max', *International Encyclopedia of the Social Sciences,* vol. 16, ed. D.L. Sills (Macmillan Free Press, 1968); A. Sica, 'Weber, Max', *Thinkers of the 20th Century,* E. Devine *et al.* (eds.) (Macmillan, 1983).

# Wicksell, Knut (1851-1926)

There never was a more divided, almost schizoid economist than Knut Wicksell. His writings are addressed to his colleagues and have an austere flavour of economic theorising for the sake of economic theorising. In his private life, however, he was a free thinker, a socialist with a very small s, a feminist, a passionate believer in birth control and family limitation, and a man so disdainful of social conventions that he served a two-month prison sentence for uttering blasphemous remarks in a lecture, and refused to sign an application for a professorship to the King of Sweden with the standard words 'Your Majesty's most obedient servant', thus depriving himself of a Chair until the advanced age of 52.

Wicksell had four heroes in economics: Ricardo, Thünen, Walras and Böhm-Bawerk; and his life-work was dedicated to integrating general equilibrium theory, the Austrian theory of capital and interest and the marginal productivity theory of distribution. His first work, *Value, Capital and Rent* (1893), was only a foretaste of his larger *Lectures on Political Economy* (1901-6), interrupted by a study of public finance, *Finanztheoretische Untersuchungen (Investigations in the Theory of Finance)* (1896), which remains, astonishingly, untranslated into English to this day, and a work on monetary economics, *Interest and Prices* (1898), which contained his most original contribution to economics.

Born in Stockholm in 1851 into a middle-class family, Wicksell took his first degree in mathematics at the University of Uppsåla in 1876. His interest in social problems led him to the literature on neo-Malthusianism, as the population control movement was then called, and from there to the study of economics. From 1885, a small inheritance allowed him to travel to England, France, Germany and Austria to study theoretical economics, which also gave him the opportunity to meet all the leading radical reformers of the day. Throughout the 1880s and early 1890s he earned a meagre living by pouring out hundreds of newspaper articles on such wide ranging subjects as alcoholism, prostitution, freedom of speech, the rights of women and the constitutional role of the monarchy; always returning, however, to his favourite theme, the dangers of over-population and need to combat it by the spread of birth control devices. In 1895 he obtained a doctorate from the University of Uppsåla with a thesis on the incidence of taxation, but it took yet another degree in law before he was offered his first teaching appointment at the University of Lund in 1899 at the age of 48. He taught at Lund until his retirement in 1916, adding the *Lectures on Political Economy* to his three previously published books in economics. He remained a radical even in old age, publishing a plea for atheism in an anarchist paper in 1923. He died in 1926 (a year which also saw the death of Marshall, Edgeworth and Wieser) at the age of 74.

Wicksell's books contained numerous corrections and refinements of the new economics, made up as it was at the time he was writing of three separate schools of thought, the Cambridge School, the Austrian School and the Lausanne School. His treatment of utility theory improved on Jevons (q.v.), Menger (q.v.) and even Walras (q.v.) and his exposition of marginal productivity theory was superior to that of Wicksteed (q.v.) Barone (q.v.) and John Bates Clark (q.v.). He considerably modified even as he defended Böhm-Bawerk's theory of capital, and did much to stimulate Walras to elaborate the role of capital formation in the third edition of the latter's *Elements* (1900). In particular, he was virtually the only economist of note around the turn of the century to emphasise that what Marshall called 'the doctrine of maximum satisfactions' and even Pareto's modest definition of a social optimum in terms of unanimous consent depends critically on the prevailing distribution of income (or rather factor endowments) that generates the competitive price solution; in short, he was the first economist fully to realise that all the proofs that perfect competition achieves an efficient allocation of resources tell us nothing about the 'justice' of income distribution. He developed the implications of this insight for the pricing of public utilities and the construction of both tax and expenditure systems. In *Finanztheoretische Untersuchungen* he came close to the modern doctrine of public goods and the problem of getting people to reveal their preference for non-marketable public goods.

In *Interest and Prices,* his most enduring contribution, he more or less founded modern macroeconomics by going back to Tooke's contra-quantity theory of money, according to which the price level is determined not by the quantity of money but by the national income in the form of the total flow of expenditures on goods and services. While rejecting Tooke's argument, he restated the old quantity of money so as to emphasise expenditure flows, carefully distinguishing the direct effect of an increase in the quantity of money on prices via the cash balances individuals are willing to hold and the indirect effect on prices that operate through variations in the rate of interest. The idea that this indirect effect arises when the money rate of interest deviates from the real rate of return on new capital projects had appeared earlier in the writings of Thornton and Ricardo. Wicksell seems to have been inspired by a single passage in Ricardo's *Principles* (1817), a book which he was in the habit of reading again and again. He called this real rate of return the 'natural rate of interest', arguing that if it exceeded the loan rate of interest for any reason whatsoever, a 'cumulative process' of price inflation would result, coming to a halt only if the banking system runs up against a legal or conventional reserve requirement. This led him to analyse the criteria of monetary equilibrium in the sense of a monetary and banking system that would maintain a stable level of prices. In the ensuing debate with his colleague, David Davidson (1854-1942), Wicksell went far down the road of converting the old quantity theory of money into a fully-fledged macroeconomic theory of determination of prices. It was still a far cry from the later Keynesian theory of income determination, but it contained all the seeds of that later development and a whole host of Swedish economists, who were once Wicksell's pupils, such as Bertil Ohlin (1899-1979) and Gunnar

Myrdal (1898-), managed subsequently to reap the harvest that Wicksell had sown.

*Secondary Literature*
T. Gårdlund, *The Life of Knut Wicksell* (Almqvist & Wicksell, 1958); C.G. Uhr, *Economic Doctrines of Knut Wicksell* (University of California Press, 1960); T. Gårdlund, 'Wicksell, Knut', *International Encyclopedia of the Social Sciences,* vol. 16, ed. D.L. Sills (Macmillan Free Press, 1968).

# Wicksteed, Philip Henry (1844-1927)

If Jevons can be said to have had any personal followers at all, Philip Wicksteed must count as the first of them. Born in Leeds in 1844 and educated in classics and theology at University College, London and Manchester New College, Wicksteed followed his father as a Unitarian minister. A scholar of literature and philosophy, he translated Aristotle's *Physics* and Dante's *Divine Comedy,* coming to economics relatively late as a result of the Henry George campaign of 1879. By the time he read Jevons' *Theory of Political Economy* (1871) in 1882, Jevons was already dead. Two years later he was the first English economist to attack Marxist economics from the standpoint of marginal utility theory; George Bernard Shaw replied to him and, after a counter-reply from Wicksteed, was converted and announced himself a 'convinced Jevonsian'. Despite the attack on Marxism, however, Wicksteed remained all his life sympathetic to socialist ideals although sceptical of socialist theory; also, like so many nineteenth-century economists, he never abandoned his belief in land nationalisation.

His first publication was *The Alphabet of Economic Science* (1888), a brief textbook of the new economics which did much to popularise the adjective 'marginal', and the term 'marginal analysis'. But it was *An Essay on the Coordination of the Laws of Distribution* (1894) which first established his reputation among professional economists. The laws of distribution in classical economics had consisted of quite separate and rather different explanations for the incomes of each of the three main classes — landlords, capitalists and workers — based on the special characteristics of the factors of production each of them owned. The new economics struggled to find a coordinated explanation of all factor payments in terms of the increment to output that the marginal unit of any factor produces. This marginal productivity theory of distribution had already emerged in the writings of a large number of economists in the late 1880s and early 1890s, in particular those of Edgeworth (q.v.), J.B. Clark (q..v.) and Marshall (q.v.), but nevertheless remained full of puzzles. Ricardo's theory of differential rent appeared to be a type of marginal productivity theory in which variable units of composite doses of capital and labour are applied to a fixed quantity of land, leaving rent as a residual that accrues to intramarginal landowners. But if we now apply variable units of land to a fixed quantity of capital and labour, will rent as the marginal product of land come out the same as intramarginal rent in Ricardo, leaving interest and wages as the residual?

Wicksteed's answer to that question was, of course, yes: the Ricardian theory is simply a special case of the more general marginal productivity theory. At the same time he posed another question which was to haunt marginal productivity theory for a decade or more: if each of the factors of production is paid the value of its marginal product, will the sum of these marginal productivity payments add up to or exactly exhaust the market value of output, leaving no residual whatsoever? Wicksteed again answered yes to that question and tried to show that it is perfect competition which guarantees the adding-up or exhaustion of the product theorem. What he was getting at was the idea that perfect competition is only compatible with constant costs or constant returns to scale, such that a change in the quantity of all the inputs employed always results in an identical change in the volume of output, in which case it is indeed true that the total product will be exactly exhausted by factor payments in accordance with marginal productivity. But he never succeeded in expressing this idea precisely and did not even notice that constant returns to scale implies that the underlying production function is, as mathematicians say, 'homogeneous of the first degree'. A well-known mathematical theorem, namely Euler's theorem of homogeneous functions, can be employed to give a simple but elegant proof of the adding-up theorem. It was not Wicksteed but a reviewer of his book, A.W. Flux (1867-1942), who first noticed this connection and provided the proof. Wicksteed himself actually withdrew the adding-up theorem in later writings in response to criticism which was as confused as his own demonstration of the theorem. It took years, in fact, to sort out all the misunderstandings which had now been generated.

Wicksteed's most lasting contribution was his charming and eloquently written *Common Sense of Political Economy* (1910), another attempt at a textbook, but this time on a large scale. The book was in part an attempt to show that economics was more than just a subject: it was a theory of rational choice in all department of life or what modern Austrian economists called 'praxeology'. *Common Sense of Political Economy* also contained a number of unique features, such as the extensive use of the concept of opportunity costs in which the cost of anything is the value of what is given up to obtain it, which is why, Wicksteed insisted, it is misleading to treat cost of production as a separate element in price-determination in addition to demand: supply curves are really 'reverse demand curves'. For these and other reasons, Wicksteed's book was closer in spirit to Menger and the other members of the Austrian School than to Marshall and the Cambridge School.

*Secondary Literature*
W.D. Grampp, 'Wicksteed, Philip Henry', *International Encyclopedia of the Social Sciences,* vol. 16, ed. D.L. Sills (Macmillan Free Press, 1968).

# Wieser, Friedrich von (1851-1926)

Friedrich von Wieser was, after Böhm-Bawerk (q.v.), Menger's (q.v.) second most important disciple. Fellow students and friends, later brothers-in-law, the two came under Menger's intellectual influence in their twenties when they both read Menger's *Principles* (1871). Because of Menger's early retirement, all the later prominent Austrian economists, such as Mises, Schumpeter and Hayek were not students of Menger but rather of Wieser and Böhm-Bawerk at the University of Vienna where Wieser spent many years (1883, 1903-17, 1918-23), some of which overlapped with those of Böhm-Bawerk (1904-14).

Born in Vienna in 1851, Wieser studied law at the University of Vienna and entered government service immediately after he graduated in 1872. He remained a civil servant for over 10 years but took leave for two years to study at the Universities of Heidelberg, Jena and Leipzig with Roscher (q.v.), Knies and other members of the 'older' Historical School. This led to the writing of his first book *Über der Uhrsprung und die Hauptgesetze des wirtschaftlichen Werthes (On the Origin and the Principal Laws of Economic Value)* (1884), which showed how the value of the factors of production is determined by utility via a process of 'imputation' even though they are never purchased by consumers; this book was also the first to coin the term *Grenznutzen* (marginal utility). The book gained him a lectureship at the University of Vienna, followed by a professorship at Charles University, Prague. He spent 19 years in Prague from 1884-1903 and it was there that he wrote *Natural Value* (1889), his best-known work. The title expressed his belief that value or price is a 'natural' category, in the sense that it makes its appearance in any rationally-ordered society, whatever the institutions of property. Large parts of the book were concerned to show how such natural values would be determined in a centrally-planned economy, and it was thus Wieser that Ludwig von Mises (1881-1973) sought to refute when he developed the argument that rational economic calculations are impossible under socialism.

When Menger resigned his Chair at the University of Vienna in 1903, Wieser succeeded him. His next great work and crowning achievement was *Social Economics* (1914), an attempt at a systematic treatise on political economy, which continually contrasted the determination of value in an ideal competitive economy with that in the modern social economy, characterised by imperfections of competition and the presence of business and labour power blocs. He offered a wide agenda for state action to regulate this social economy based on what would nowadays be called cost-benefit analysis. On balance, this forgotten work will surprise anyone who believes that Austrian economics was always concerned to justify the market mechanism and to reject any and all forms of government intervention. Wieser showed in this book that Austrian utility theory coupled with a sociological power theory is capable of yielding a programme of economic policy that assigns even greater significance to the state than the welfare economics of Marshall (q.v.) and Pigou (q.v.).

Towards the end of the First World War, Wieser served first as a member of the Austrian Parliament and then as Minister of Commerce. Following the collapse of the Austro-Hungarian Empire, he returned to the University of Vienna, publishing his last work *Das Gesetz der Macht (The Law of Power)* (1926) shortly before his death.

Wieser never had the influence of Böhm-Bawerk, partly no doubt because his startling originality of approach, and in particular his interest in the relationship between economics and sociology, did not strike a responsive chord among contemporary economists. Unlike

Böhm-Bawerk, whose debates with colleagues brought him into contact with all the leading economists of the day, Wieser never engaged in controversy, cited few contemporary writers, and generally gave the air of thinking things out for himself. Nevertheless, in Austria itself he attracted more followers than Böhm-Bawerk, including a number who carried on the seeds he had sown in *Social Economics* to produce what briefly became a distinctive Austrian School of public finance.

*Secondary Literature*
F.A. von Hayek, 'Wieser, Friedrich von', *International Encylopedia of the Social Sciences,* vol. 16, ed. D.L. Sills (Macmillan Free Press, 1968); R.B. Ekelund, Jr, 'Power and Utility: The Normative Economics of Friedrich von Wieser', *Review of Social Economy,* 28 September 1970.

# Index of Names
# (other than main entries)

# Index of Subjects

Acceleration principle, 1, 54

Business cycles, 1-2, 5-6, 99,
  104-5, 169, 172-3, 239-40

Capital theory, 25-7, 51-2, 197-8
Classical economics, 6, 233

Entrepreneurship, 212, 215-16

General equilibrium theory, 11,
  41, 78
Growth theory, 120-1, 138, 157

Laissez-faire, 14, 119

Marginal cost pricing, 124
Marginal productivity theory, 11-12, 4
  50-1, 94, 136, 148, 172, 185, 248,
  264, 277
Marginal revolution, 160-1
Marginal utility of income, 20-1
Marxism, 22, 28-9, 138-9, 276
Mercantilism, 174-5, 196

Pareto-optimality, 184-5
Perfect competition, concept of
  54, 55, 70
Physiocracy, 194-6
Purchasing-power parity theory,
  42-3

Quantity theory of money, 2, 36,
  79, 97, 132, 134, 178, 250, 274

Rent theory, 103
Roundabout production, 1, 24, 26

Socialism, economic theory of,
  12, 116-17
Specie-flow mechanism, 175

Time – preference, 10, 25-6, 75, 197

Utalitarianism, 16
Utility theory of value,
  18, 83, 88, 125-26, 136, 162, 230

Wages-fund doctrine, 26, 35
Welfare economics, 189-90